ALABAMA JUSTICE

ALABAMA JUSTICE

THE CASES AND FACES THAT CHANGED A NATION

STEVEN P. BROWN

The University of Alabama Press Tuscaloosa

The University of Alabama Press
Tuscaloosa, Alabama 35487-0380
uapress.ua.edu

Typeface: Scala Pro

Cover image: Autherine Lucy, left, accompanied by Thurgood Marshall of the NAACP, walking past the federal courthouse in Birmingham, Alabama, on the day a federal judge ordered her readmission to the University of Alabama; courtesy of the Alabama Department of Archives and History, donated by Alabama Media Group; detail of photo by Norman Dean, *Birmingham News*

Cover design: David Nees

200 ALABAMA BICENTENNIAL

Cataloging-in-Publication data is available from the Library of Congress.

ISBN: 978-0-8173-2070-6
E-ISBN: 978-0-8173-9323-6

CONTENTS

FIGURES

ACKNOWLEDGMENTS

After five years of graduate work in constitutional law under the supervision of University of Virginia professors David M. O'Brien and Henry J. Abraham, I believed that I had a good understanding of many of the Supreme Court's landmark rulings as well as the history behind and parties involved in those decisions. It was not until I took a position at Auburn University in 1998, however, that I noticed how many significant cases that the Court had taken from my adopted state. In my constitutional law classes that first year, I was struck by how many times I seemed to preface my comments with, "Here's another great case from Alabama." Presuming that others were as little acquainted as I was with Alabama's connection to the Supreme Court, I considered writing a book about those decisions, but life and other research projects intervened.

Almost twenty years later, I had lunch with Thomas Bryant after hearing a presentation he made on behalf of the Alabama Humanities Foundation. I mentioned some of these landmark cases to him, and as we discussed the upcoming bicentennial of Alabama statehood, Thomas saw the potential for a project that could satisfy my desire to do something with those rulings as well as educate others about them. He put me in touch with Phillip Ratliff and Backstory Educational Media. Together, Phil and I envisioned and, with the help of Jay Lamar and Steve Murray, created a traveling exhibit about significant Supreme Court cases from Alabama that began its two-year tour throughout the state in January 2019. The tremendous interest in and enthusiasm for that exhibition suggested a need for a more detailed treatment of the cases it considered, and this book is the result.

From the beginning, it was a considerably different project from any of my other published research. Although I have incorporated selections of the Court's actual rulings, I have tried to present the information in this book in a way that would make the general principles that it discusses accessible to anyone who has an interest in the Supreme Court. In addition, as my sole motivation in writing was to acquaint others with the cases and faces that have made such a difference in American constitutional law, I have purposely avoided scrutinizing every detail of these cases, the parties that brought the disputes, and the judges who ruled on them. That exercise properly belongs to lengthier treatments about each individual case or justice, many of which are included in the bibliography.

This book would not have been possible without the financial support for the traveling exhibit (for which the initial research that led to this volume was conducted) provided by the Alabama Bicentennial Commission; the Alabama Humanities Foundation; and Auburn University's Office of the Vice President for Research, Office of Outreach, College of Liberal Arts, and Department of Political Science. The Alabama Department of Archives and History provided summer research funding that was critical to the completion of this book. The archives also devoted other important resources to the exhibit, as did the Alabama Bicentennial Commission and the Alabama Bench and Bar Historical Society. I am especially grateful to Jay Lamar, executive director of Alabama200, and Steve Murray, director of the Alabama Department of Archives and History, for their support, motivating influence, and friendship.

I gratefully acknowledge the following for their help with my specialized research requests: Nancy Dupree, reference archivist, and the staff at the Alabama Department of Archives and History, Montgomery; LaFrederick Thirkill, principal, Orchard Knob Elementary School, Chattanooga, Tennessee; Matthew Hofstedt, associate curator, Supreme Court of the United States, Washington, DC; Fred Schilling, court photographer, Supreme Court of the United States, Washington, DC; and Sheila Washington, director, Scottsboro Boys Museum and Cultural Center, Scottsboro.

The University of Alabama Press has once again been a wonderful partner. Dan Waterman's support never waned even when my own focus and desire to write sometimes did. Much of the material on Justice John McKinley in the last chapter of this book is drawn from my *John McKinley and the Antebellum Supreme Court: Circuit Riding in the Old Southwest* (2012), and I want to thank the press for granting permission to use it. The anonymous reviewers of the original manuscript were incredibly helpful, and I am grateful for their thoughtful and specific recommendations for improvement. I also want to thank Danyel Peters, who both assisted with the preliminary research and reviewed early versions of the chapters, and Rachel Brown, who read virtually every word of the entire manuscript. Dawn Hall deserves a special mention for her copyediting talents, which were so critical to this finished book.

Finally, I want to note the passing of my mentor and friend, Professor David M. O'Brien, in December 2018. He was an extraordinary person who possessed a prodigious intellect and work ethic, a wonderfully accessible writing style, and a genuine gift for teaching. I, along with all those who were influenced by his example, will miss him greatly. This book is for him, for the thousands of constitutional law students I have taught at Auburn during the last twenty years, and, as always, for Melanie.

ALABAMA JUSTICE

INTRODUCTION

Alabama is known for many things. First-time visitors are astonished at the spectacular natural beauty that stretches from the Appalachian Mountains in the northern portions of the state to the sugar-white sand beaches that frame the clear blue waters of the Gulf of Mexico to the south. Within this environment, one can find more than just beauty. Due to the unique combination of its geography, climate, soil, and water resources, Alabama has a greater array of plant and animal life than forty-five other states and is the most biodiverse of any state east of the Mississippi River.

Those who have yet to experience Alabama for themselves have nevertheless felt its influence through the musical legacies of Hank Williams, the King of Country Music; W. C. Handy, the Father of the Blues; and the many popular and Grammy-award-winning songs across all genres that were recorded at or produced by the FAME and Muscle Shoals sound studios. For decades, high school teachers across the country have assigned their students the writings of Truman Capote, Harper Lee, and other authors with connections to the state. Elementary schoolchildren know the courage of Helen Keller, Rosa Parks, and Coretta Scott King—all from Alabama. It is the birthplace of Jesse Owens, Joe Louis, Hank Aaron, and many other athletes who left an indelible imprint on their respective sports.

The state has made its own mark on American history beginning with the Creek War and Andrew Jackson's rise to national prominence. The twenty-two million acres he forced the Creek Nation to surrender led to the Alabama Fever land rush, which saw tens of thousands of people from across the country and even overseas flock to Alabama to make their fortune in its fertile soil. So massive was this migration that in 1819, just five years after the Creeks ceded their land, Alabama entered the union as the twenty-second state.

Better known to most Americans is Alabama's role in the Civil War. Montgomery was the first capital of the Confederacy, and Jefferson Davis took the oath of office as president of the Confederate States of America on the steps of the Alabama state capitol building. Nearly a century later, the state would become the birthplace of the civil rights movement. Rosa Parks's bus ride, the organizational meetings at Martin Luther King's Dexter Avenue Baptist Church, the 16th Street Baptist Church bombings, and the Selma March along with several other important events—both inspiring and horrific—associated with the movement took place in Alabama. These, in turn, would be the motivating influences behind two of the federal government's most important domestic achievements in the twentieth century: the Civil Rights Act of 1964 and the Voting Rights Act of 1965. Finally, in one of the most significant technological achievements in the history of the world, Huntsville's Marshall Space Flight Center envisioned and designed the Saturn V rockets that launched man to the moon.

It is certainly true that every state has its own natural beauty and can claim its own celebrities, sports figures, historical events, and significant people whose impact has spread far beyond its boundaries. Alabama, however, has an additional legacy that few can match. Americans who have no interest in Alabama's natural environment, people, sports, literature, or history, or who could not care less about the state—and who might even deliberately attempt to avoid anything associated with it—are still influenced by Alabama because of the law.

The state has played a major part in a remarkable set of landmark United States Supreme Court rulings that continue to touch the life of every American. Some of these historic cases came about because of laws and policies that reflected the state's unassailably negative treatment of its black citizens. It should come as no surprise that the racist cultural and social norms of the early and mid-twentieth century were reflected in government action during that era that was eventually challenged in court. Other significant Alabama cases, however, arose out of disputes involving religious expression, gender discrimination, and the struggle for political power between rural and urban voters. Perhaps unexpectedly, few of the challenged laws or policies that led to these momentous decisions were unique to Alabama. In the early years of the civil rights movement, for example, there was little to distinguish Alabama from other southern states that discriminated against their African American citizens. Similarly, the strict libel laws of Alabama that the Supreme Court reviewed were no different from those that existed in many other parts of the country, and its badly malapportioned legislature, the subject of another historic case, mirrored one or both chambers in virtually every statehouse in the nation. These facts thus beg the question: why was Alabama at the center of all of these cases?

There is, of course, no way to know the answer, but factors related to timing and culture were at least partially responsible. Many of these cases were decided in the 1950s and 1960s during a time of increased social awareness that was fueled, in part, by the national news media, particularly the growing power of television. During this same period, the federal judiciary, led by the Supreme Court, transformed itself into an agent of social and political change. While Chief Justice Earl Warren oversaw the judicial revolution that took place during his tenure (1953–69), his colleagues, including Associate Justice Hugo Black of Alabama, had no qualms about abandoning the Court's tradition of judicial restraint when the legislative and executive branches at both the national and state level failed to protect the rights of their citizens. Into this setting came well-trained lawyers, civil rights organizations, and other groups that correctly anticipated that the judiciary would be more receptive to their concerns than legislative and executive officials had been previously.

None of these factors provide the definitive answer to "Why Alabama?" However, that may be the wrong question. Perhaps "Why Alabamians?" is the more appropriate inquiry. In 1939, the state adopted as its motto the words *Audemus jura nostra defendere*, Latin for "We Dare Defend Our Rights." During the mid-twentieth century, Alabamians who may have never considered those words before began to take them seriously and turned to litigation to bring them to life. The result was a series of Supreme Court decisions that affected far more than just the citizens of their state.

These rulings permanently transformed the Court itself. Alabama-based cases saw the Court assume new powers unto itself, such as overseeing the apportionment of legislative districts, adopting new standards like the actual malice test for libel, and even creating new rights with the freedom of association. In so doing, these cases and the Alabamians who brought them not only changed the Court, they changed the nation.

There are many Supreme Court decisions involving Alabama, but the cases in this book were selected, in part, for their particular constitutional significance. That importance stems not just from their inclusion within the accepted canon of "great" Supreme Court decisions or the way they expanded fundamental rights but also from, as described throughout this book, their continuing impact on every American. Encompassing religion, criminal law, and racial and gender discrimination, among other things, the selected cases represent the breadth of constitutional issues that the Court has considered from Alabama. The chapters that follow begin their consideration of each case by examining the circumstances that created the dispute. They then provide the historical and constitutional background to the cases they discuss followed by a review of the path of litigation. Excerpts from the Court's actual rulings are then presented along with a brief account of the aftermath and significance of those decisions.

Chapter 1 examines *Wallace v. Jaffree* (1985) and an Alabama law authorizing a moment of silence or prayer in public schools. The Court reaffirmed its previous decisions regarding teacher-led prayer and struck down the law as unconstitutional. Nevertheless, in this important First Amendment case, it also gave its blessing to moments of silence policies that were not motivated by religion, a guiding influence on state laws pertaining to a moment of silence in public schools ever since.

An attempt by Alabama authorities to force the NAACP to disclose its membership roster forms the background to chapter 2. When the organization refused, a state judge fined it $100,000 and forbade it from further operating within the state. In striking down the attorney general's effort to compel disclosure in *NAACP v. Alabama* (1958), the Supreme Court formally announced First Amendment protection for the freedom of association. The Court's decision subsequently served as a foundation on which many other groups erected their own claims to be free of governmental regulation. In recent years, however, that foundation has become less sure, as the War on Terror has increased governmental interest in the individuals and organizations with whom Americans associate.

Chapter 3 covers *New York Times v. Sullivan* (1964), a case that arose from a newspaper advertisement. Believing that the ad defamed him, the police commissioner of Montgomery brought legal action. In its decision, the Court set forth the actual malice test, which sets a high standard for public officials and public figures to meet in order to recover damages for critical comments that they think are defamatory. With regard to politicians, the freedom to criticize government leaders has always been the hallmark of a free society, but Donald Trump's 2016 election and the widespread condemnation and protests he has faced ever since has made this case and the freedom it protects uniquely relevant today.

Alabama received worldwide scrutiny with the criminal trials of the Scottsboro Boys, which are the subject of chapter 4. The Court used the tragic circumstances of their case to proclaim a due process right to effective counsel in *Powell v. Alabama* (1932). Although the Court's recognition of that right actually did relatively little to help the young men in this case, it has benefited every American facing criminal charges ever since.

Chapter 5 reviews one of the best-known cases from Alabama, *Gomillion v. Lightfoot* (1960). In an attempt to neutralize the political power of a growing number of African American voters, the state legislature altered the boundaries of the city of Tuskegee from a virtual square to a twenty-eight-sided figure. The result was that nearly all of the city's four hundred black voters, as well as the well-known Tuskegee Institute, were placed outside of the city limits. The Court struck down racial redistricting in *Gomillion*, and, at the same time, opened the door for the justices to consider other non-race-based actions that dilute the voting power of American citizens.

The equal protection clause of the Fourteenth Amendment and *Frontiero v. Richardson* (1973) are the focus of chapter 6. Lieutenant Sharron Frontiero's request to obtain increased housing and living allowances from the US Air Force after her spouse became a full-time student was denied, even though such applications were routinely approved when submitted by male officers. The justices ruled for Frontiero and in the process invoked gender discrimination for the first time in American history to strike down a federal policy.

One of the difficulties of any representative democracy is safeguarding the right of its citizens to have a voice in its governance. As chapter 7 discusses, this is achieved by allocating seats in the legislature in a manner that reflects the population as a whole. The Supreme Court took the case of *Reynolds v. Sims* (1964) because reapportionment had not occurred in the Alabama legislature (or that of several other states at that time) for sixty years. The result was that legislators from rural areas containing a fraction of the state's population controlled the legislative process, effectively denying substantive political participation to those living in more densely populated urban places. Chief Justice Earl Warren oversaw many Court decisions that brought about sweeping changes in American society, but he always considered the reapportionment cases like *Reynolds v. Sims* to be the most important of his tenure because they gave citizens an equal voice in their government.

The final case is *Katzenbach v. McClung* (1964) in chapter 8. This dispute pitted an iconic Birmingham restaurant, Ollie's Barbecue, against the United States Congress. Ollie's represented the concerns of many small business owners throughout the South who believed that Congress lacked the authority to subject them to the requirements of the Civil Rights Act of 1964. The Supreme Court upheld the law and, in the process, vastly expanded Congress's regulatory authority under the Constitution's commerce clause.

Chapter 9 focuses on the three Alabamians who have served on the United States Supreme Court. Their cumulative influence on the institution of the Court, constitutional interpretation, and the day-to-day rights and liberties every American enjoys is impossible to measure. This chapter describes the backgrounds and Supreme Court careers and contributions of Associate Justices John McKinley, John Archibald Campbell, and Hugo Black.

McKinley sat on the Supreme Court from 1837 to 1852, a period when the Court's annual term in Washington, DC, lasted only a few months. When the Court was not in session, the justices were required to travel to an assigned grouping of states called a circuit and hear disputes throughout that area. McKinley was the first and only justice to preside over the original Ninth Circuit, which consisted of Alabama, Arkansas, Louisiana, and Mississippi. Traveling some 10,000 miles annually, his circuit responsibilities seriously affected his health, but he persevered in his duties even after becoming partially paralyzed.

Beginning with George Washington's first appointments to the Court, practically every justice had complained about the rigors of circuit duty, but to no avail. McKinley's massive 206,000-square-mile circuit and his difficulty in reaching all of the court sites within it finally forced Congress to confront the problem. Congress split his circuit, reduced the number of times the justices needed to attend circuit, and, eventually, removed the justices' circuit-riding duties altogether.

John Archibald Campbell had been a child prodigy. He was one of the most prominent and successful attorneys in antebellum America and was handpicked by the justices in 1853 to serve with them after disputes between the president and the Senate left a vacancy on the Court unfilled for eight months. Campbell was generally viewed as the most brilliant man on the bench during his tenure on the Supreme Court. His impact was severely curtailed, however, when he resigned after just eight years of service when Alabama seceded from the union.

His most important contribution came in 1873 when, as an attorney in private practice, he argued the *Slaughterhouse Cases* before his former colleagues on the Court. There he contended that the protections of the Fourteenth Amendment applied to more than just newly freed slaves. Although not expressly stated in that amendment, he believed that Americans had other basic fundamental rights beyond those already spelled out in the Bill of Rights. His argument continues to this day. The notion that there are constitutionally protected, albeit unenumerated, rights, has been at the heart of some of America's most divisive constitutional controversies over the past fifty years. These include the right of privacy, abortion, the right to die, gay marriage, and parental rights.

Hugo Black was Franklin Roosevelt's first appointee to the Supreme Court, and he played a key role in the sweeping changes in American society that resulted from the Court's decisions during his service from 1937 to 1971. A member of the Ku Klux Klan as a young man, Black became one of the Supreme Court's foremost champions of racial equality. In addition, his opinions in cases dealing with religion, speech, obscenity, criminal justice, and civil rights challenged the accepted religious, moral, and social standards of his day in the name of individual freedom.

Black personally engineered a judicial revolution of his own by his absolute conviction that the Bill of Rights restrained government at all levels, and not just the national government as was generally believed at the time. Any American who has ever wondered if he or she could claim constitutional protection against a state or local government law, policy, or official can thank Hugo Black for insisting that the Bill of Rights did just that.

As noted earlier, every state has its own outstanding scenery, historic sites, and famous people. Each has undoubtedly found its way into the casebooks as well when its laws and policies were challenged. No state, however, can match the constitutional, legal, political, and social results wrought by the cases, across a wide variety of issues, and the faces, the parties, attorneys, and justices, from Alabama. It may have been individual Alabamians who "dared to defend their rights," but every American now and in the future is a beneficiary.

1

A MOMENT OF SILENCE

Public School Prayers and *Wallace v. Jaffree* (1985)

"CONGRESS SHALL MAKE NO LAW respecting an establishment of religion." The founders surely could not have predicted the controversy that would repeatedly erupt because of these simple ten words that open the First Amendment to the United States Constitution. How does the establishment clause apply, for example, against government-imposed restrictions on immigrants from majority-Muslim nations? Do state governments violate the establishment clause when they exempt those with religious concerns but not others from mandatory childhood vaccination laws? Does the establishment clause require municipalities to excise any reference to religion from their city flags, seals, and mottos as well as from their public buildings and parks? Recent questions such as these have few direct precedents to guide them and yield no easy answers.

Yet, even when legal precedents are available, church and state issues can scarcely avoid controversy. This should not be surprising given the Supreme Court's struggle to embrace a single historical narrative regarding the purpose and reach of the establishment clause. The justices themselves have added to the confusion by creating, expanding, or, at times, ignoring various legal tests for determining establishment clause violations. Add into this mix a metaphorical "wall of separation" that was never fully explained by either Roger Williams or Thomas Jefferson (or by any of the Supreme Court justices who borrowed the figure of speech from them), and the Court's problems with religion become clear.

In 1985, the Court had the opportunity to directly confront the mess it had made of religion. In so doing, the justices responded with several rival interpretations of the establishment clause. What began as a short classroom

Figure 1. Ishmael Jaffree. Courtesy of *Lagniappe Mobile*. Photograph by Dan Anderson, 2014.

prayer before meals thus became one of the most significant religion cases of the 1980s as American educators, legislators, historians, and lawyers turned their attention to Mobile, Alabama.

THE STORY

Shortly after the beginning of the 1981–82 school year, Ishmael Jaffree sat down with his five-year-old son and asked him about all of the new and exciting things he was learning in kindergarten. He was astonished when his little boy responded with a prayer that the class said before eating their lunch. Jaffree subsequently discovered that all three of his elementary-school-aged children were participating in lunchtime prayer activities led by their Mobile County public schoolteachers. Each day the children and their classmates would sing, "God is great, God is good, Let us thank Him for our food; Bow our heads, we all are fed, Give us Lord our daily bread. Amen." Or they would recite "For health and strength and daily food, We praise Thy name, O Lord." One teacher also regularly led her class in the Lord's Prayer.[1]

The teachers' actions troubled Jaffree for both philosophical and constitutional reasons. He believed that the daily prayers and recitations established and reinforced a religious viewpoint that he neither supported nor wanted for his children. Jaffree had been raised a Baptist while growing up in Ohio and as a child had even stood with his devout mother on the street corners of Cleveland proclaiming Christianity to any passersby who would listen.[2] He began to question both his religious beliefs and religion in general during college, and by the time he married his wife, Mozelle (a committed member of the Baha'i faith), he had pronounced himself agnostic.

The Jaffrees agreed early in their marriage that they would not attempt to steer their children toward either faith or doubt. Instead, they would encourage them to consider a variety of perspectives. "I want my children not to accept everything that is told to them," Jaffree would later explain, "and be free to examine, to explore, to ponder, to think about, to be exposed to different philosophies."[3] For Ishmael Jaffree, the daily expressions of lunchtime grace and the Lord's Prayer were offensive not only because of their religious content, but also because they represented a far more narrow worldview than what he wanted for his children.

Jaffree was concerned about the classroom religious activities for another reason. After graduating from Cleveland-Marshall College of Law, he and Mozelle moved to Mobile where he went to work with the local office of the Legal Services Corporation, a federally funded organization that provides civil litigation services for low-income Americans. As a law school graduate and practicing attorney, he was well acquainted with Supreme Court precedent regarding prayer in public schools.

Throughout the school year, Jaffree shared his personal and constitutional concerns about the prayers with Mobile County school authorities. The teachers refused to cease the practice, but they did offer to let his children opt out of the daily religious exercises. However, Jaffree believed that this would only draw further attention to his three children and increase already simmering resentment against his family over the issue. At the end of the school year and having been unable to resolve the dispute to his satisfaction, he filed a federal lawsuit against the three teachers and their principals, the superintendent, and each member of the Board of School Commissioners of Mobile County. The lawsuit argued that the prayers and religious songs in the classroom violated the establishment clause of the First Amendment.

He also expanded the lawsuit to include then-governor Fob James Jr.

and several other government officials, hoping to hold them responsible for previously enacted statutes that he believed also violated the establishment clause. One of these was a moment of silence law passed in Alabama in 1978, which was virtually indistinguishable from similar laws in many other states. It instructed first- through sixth-grade teachers to oversee a one-minute period of silence for meditation at the beginning of each school day.[4] Three years later, the Alabama legislature amended and expanded the law to permit all public school teachers in all grades to announce to their classes that the moment of silence could now "be observed for meditation or voluntary prayer."[5] Jaffree believed that religious purposes were behind the passage of both of these laws and that they countenanced and even encouraged religion in the public schools.

Most legal observers at the time saw no problem with the 1978 moment of silence law, but the 1981 amendment was an entirely different matter. Its passage clearly reflected Alabama lawmakers' belief that they could authorize prayer in schools despite Supreme Court decisions to the contrary. On its face, permitting teachers to suggest options for students to exercise during their moment of silence would seem to be of little constitutional significance. However, on the legislature's nearly unanimous approval of the amendment, Donald G. Holmes, the state senator who introduced the measure, revealed that its purpose was not so much about alternatives as it was about, as he put it, specifically "return[ing] voluntary prayer to the public schools."[6] "Hundreds of Alabamians," he added, "have urged my continued support for permitting school prayer since coming to the Alabama Senate. . . . [B]y passage of this bill in the Alabama legislature, our children in this state will have the opportunity of sharing in their spiritual heritage of this state and country."[7]

Jaffree's concerns began to attract statewide media attention shortly after he filed his lawsuit, but national and even international coverage of the case exploded after Governor James convened a special session of the legislature in June 1982. The governor had been expected to introduce an anticrime package but tasked the legislators instead with creating a law "to provide for a prayer that may be given in public schools."[8] They responded with a statute that read, in part, "From henceforth, any teacher or professor in any public educational institution within the state of Alabama, recognizing that the Lord God is one, at the beginning of any homeroom or any class, may pray, [and] may lead willing students in prayer."[9]

The law went on to offer specific wording that teachers and students could use, even recommending a prayer written by the governor's son, Fob James III, who, like Ishmael Jaffree, was also an attorney in Mobile. The younger James's prayer read as follows: "Almighty God, You alone are our God. We acknowledge You as the Creator and Supreme Judge of the world. May Your justice, Your truth, and Your peace abound this day in the hearts of our countrymen, in the counsels of our government, in the sanctity of our homes, and in the classrooms of our schools in the name of our Lord. Amen."[10] On July 12, 1982, Governor James signed the new school prayer bill into law, declaring, "It's time to address the [Supreme Court's *Engel v. Vitale*] decision, not by trying to find a loophole but by contesting the grounds" on which it was founded.[11]

Jaffree immediately challenged the new law in US District Court in Mobile where Judge W. Brevard Hand presided. In a curious exchange during the two-day hearing on the matter in August, Fob James III, on behalf of the state, argued that the district court lacked authority to hear the case "because prayer flows from the Almighty and neither this Court nor any court has jurisdiction over the requirements of the Lord or the prayers of his people."[12] Judge Hand rejected that claim outright, dryly adding, "I do not perceive of this as a suit against the Almighty. The Lord is not a defendant—the state is."[13] A week later, while finding no constitutional fault with the original 1978 statute that provided a moment of silence for meditation alone, Hand issued a preliminary injunction against both of its successor laws pending a trial on the merits.

Coming just three weeks before the start of the 1982–83 school year, the injunction spurred Governor James into taking two very unusual and public actions relative to the case. The first was his attempt to file a petition in person with the US Supreme Court asking the justices to "return all authority over religion, including school prayer, to the states" because their 1962 *Engel* decision was a "dangerous usurpation of power."[14] The clerk of the Court refused to accept his petition because the Alabama laws in question had yet to be adjudicated in the lower courts. Then, at a later press conference to discuss his failed petition, James dramatically announced a second course of action. "I am today encouraging all Alabama school officials," he declared, "as well as the people of Alabama to stand on their constitutional rights, to ignore this federal court injunction and to proceed with prayer in the classrooms, with blessings at mealtime and with any other heart-felt prayer."[15] James's petition and public call for Alabamians to disregard the federal court order only attracted further attention to the school prayer statutes and heightened anticipation of the trial.

The religious activities in Mobile's public schools and the Alabama laws were expected to be the focus of the arguments in Judge Hand's courtroom, but the Supreme Court surprisingly found itself on trial as well. Its fifty-year-old doctrine of "incorporation" was called into question along with its entire establishment clause jurisprudence. Through the efforts of both parties, Jaffree's claim was thus transformed from a disagreement over a lunchtime prayer into a major First Amendment case about religion in the public schools, the authority of the Supreme Court, and the force of precedent.

THE CONSTITUTIONAL BACKGROUND

Although the Court reviewed claims involving religion as early as 1815, they were relatively few in number until the modern era.[16] This is largely because for its first 150 years, the Court believed that the Bill of Rights did not protect individuals against state or local government intrusion on their rights. That meant that the Court would consider disputes where national government action had infringed on a person's rights, but those who brought claims against state governments were required to look to their state courts for relief. Those courts, in turn, relied on their own state constitutions and state bills of rights for guidance. In other words, the Constitution's Bill of Rights protected Americans against national government action only. This interpretation of the Bill of Rights might seem unusual today, but it was set forth early on by the Court and enjoyed majority support among the justices for well over a century.

John Marshall was a delegate to the 1788 Virginia state convention that ratified the Constitution and was a member of the state committee that forwarded around twenty proposed amendments limiting national government power to Congress for its consideration in drafting what would become the Bill of Rights.[17] That personal experience and perspective guided him forty-five years later when, as chief justice of the United States Supreme Court, he declared that the Fifth Amendment's eminent domain clause did not protect a Maryland man's property against actions taken by the city of Baltimore.[18]

Writing for a unanimous Court in *Barron v. Baltimore* (1833), Marshall recalled the tremendous distrust of the proposed new government that emerged from the Constitutional Convention of 1787. Fearing that the new national government would overwhelm them all, the various state ratifying conventions submitted constitutional amendments to constrain its powers. Congress adopted several of these, which became the first ten amendments to the Constitution (or what is now known as the Bill of Rights).[19] The founding generation clearly recognized, as Marshall put it in *Barron*, that "these amendments demanded security against the apprehended encroachments of the general [or national] government."[20] In other words, as he stressed, the Bill of Rights is "intended solely as a limitation on the exercise of power by the government of the United States, and [are] not applicable to the legislation of the states."[21]

Marshall's conviction that the protections of the Bill of Rights were meant to limit only the powers of the national government went largely unchallenged by most of those who followed him to the Supreme Court.[22] With the 1868 passage of the Fourteenth Amendment, however, some justices began to question why states were specifically forbidden by that amendment from "depriv[ing] any person of life, liberty, or property, without due process of law . . . [or denying to an individual] the equal protection of the laws" and yet could still infringe on the rights protected by the first ten amendments. For the next seventy years, the justices wrestled with the question of whether the Fourteenth Amendment's due process clause actually "incorporated" (or made applicable against state and local government action) the specific guarantees of the Bill of Rights.

By the 1930s, majorities on the Court developed that were prepared to acknowledge incorporation and hold that certain rights were indeed "safeguarded by the due process clause of the Fourteenth Amendment from invasion by state action."[23] In their 1947 decision in *Everson v. Board of Education*, a narrow majority of the Court formally incorporated the establishment clause, thus making state and local government action relative to religion subject to the protections of the First Amendment.[24] In his opinion for the Court, Justice Hugo Black explained that this meant that "neither a state nor the Federal Government can set up a church. Neither can pass laws which aid one religion, aid all religions, or prefer one religion over another. . . . No tax in any amount, large or small, can be levied to support any religious activities or institutions, whatever they may be called, or whatever form they may adopt to teach or practice religion."[25] Incorporation, however, was not *Everson*'s only legacy. Justice Black also used the case to assert that the establishment clause "was intended to erect 'a wall of separation' between church and State."[26] That metaphor has been fused to issues of religion ever since, but because Black failed to clarify what it actually required, the "wall of separation" continues to perplex both the Court and the country.

In the early 1960s, the Court relied on both incorporation and the wall metaphor in cases that held similarities to *Jaffree*. In *Engel v. Vitale* (1962), the Court struck down a requirement by a local New York school board that students begin their day with a prayer written by the New York State Board of Regents.[27] Writing again for the majority, Justice Black declared, "It is neither sacrilegious nor antireligious to say that . . . [the] government in this country should stay out of the business of writing or sanctioning official prayers."[28]

A year later, the Court considered state laws in Pennsylvania and Maryland requiring schools to begin each instructional day with readings from the Bible and/or leading students in reciting the Lord's Prayer.[29] The Court struck down both practices and, in turn, fashioned a two-part test for determining establishment clause violations. The first part or prong of what became known as the *Schempp* test asked whether there was a secular purpose to the governmental action being challenged. The second prong questioned whether the primary effect of that action either advanced or inhibited religion. A violation of either part of the *Schempp* test invalidated the government law, policy, or regulation.[30]

In its 1971 decision in *Lemon v. Kurtzman,* the Court added a third prong and reconstituted the whole as the *Lemon* test.[31] That final point is concerned about whether the action in question "foster[s] an excessive entanglement between government and religion."[32] Although the Court has since developed other criteria independent of *Lemon* for assessing violations of the establishment clause, the *Lemon* test remains valid. It was the primary precedent in Jaffree's case and was expected to guide the district court's consideration of his claim.[33]

THE LITIGATION

The Supreme Court's incorporation doctrine and establishment clause precedents figured prominently in Judge Hand's August 1982 decision to impose an injunction on the recently passed Alabama prayer bill and the earlier law that permitted voluntary prayer during the moment of silence. "The clear import of these controlling decisions," he wrote, "appears . . . to be that the state should not involve itself in either prescribing or proscribing religious activity."[34] He issued the injunction because he could find no secular purpose to either of the two Alabama statutes as required by the first prong of the *Lemon* test, and also because he believed that there was a "substantial likelihood [that Jaffree would] prevail on the merits" once the case formally came before him again at trial in November.[35] These, along with similar sentiments expressed by Hand in August, left observers wholly unprepared for his ruling on the matter a few months later.

In his January 1983 decision, Judge Hand adopted a history of the drafting and ratification of the First and Fourteenth Amendments that had been presented during the November trial and which was supported by several noted historians. However, that version differed dramatically from accounts of the same events maintained by other historians and previously articulated by the Supreme Court. Of course, judicial opinions that consider and interpret historical facts and circumstances differently from those rendered by other judges are not uncommon. What is unusual, however, is for a lower federal court judge to use his or her historical interpretation as the basis for rejecting long-established Supreme Court precedent. In doing precisely that, Hand spared neither the Court, its landmark decisions on religion, nor his fellow Alabamian, Justice Hugo Black, in his extraordinary ruling.

Hand began by insisting that Black's opinion in *Everson* had entirely "misread the congressional debate surrounding the passage of the [F]ourteenth [A]mendment when he concluded that Congress intended to incorporate the Bill of Rights against the states."[36] The "wall of separation" metaphor that Black had invoked in *Everson* was similarly misguided, according to Hand's historical review, because the wall between church and state was not nearly "as high and impregnable as Justice Black's revisionist literary flourish would lead one to believe."[37] In short, as Hand put it, "the United States Supreme Court has erred in its reading of history."[38] Since the historical record he consulted justified neither the Court's incorporation doctrine nor its establishment clause jurisprudence, he could only reach one conclusion: "Because the Establishment Clause of the First Amendment to the United States Constitution does not prohibit the state from establishing a religion, the prayers offered by the teachers in this case are not unconstitutional."[39] Based on this reasoning, Judge Hand dissolved his earlier injunction against the two Alabama prayer statutes, permitting them to stand.[40] One month later, however, Justice Lewis Powell of the Supreme Court acting in his role as circuit justice issued an order preventing Hand from lifting the injunction until the issue could be heard by the United States Court of Appeals for the Eleventh Circuit.[41]

On appeal, the Eleventh Circuit quickly dispensed with both Judge Hand's rationale and ruling. While acknowledging Hand's point that there were indeed a variety of historical interpretations of the First and Fourteenth Amendments, the appellate court argued that none of that really mattered because the Supreme Court had already decided which version to accept. From there, the appellate decision went on to school Hand in the doctrine of precedent. "[T]he Supreme Court is the ultimate authority on the interpretation of our Constitution and laws"; the ruling declared, "its interpretations may not be disregarded."[42] It recognized that lower court judges like Hand might well believe the Supreme Court to be mistaken in its rulings, but they were nevertheless "bound to adhere to th[ose] controlling decisions."[43] The Eleventh Circuit minced no words in proclaiming to Judge Hand and the world, "If the Supreme Court errs, no other court may correct it."[44]

The appellate judges then addressed the religious activities in Mobile's public schools as well as the Alabama prayer statutes against the background of Supreme Court precedent because Hand had failed to do so in his ruling. They concluded that the teacher's classroom religious activities lacked the secular purpose required by the first prong of the *Lemon* test. Similarly, the lower court found religious motivation behind the legislature's passage of the meditation or prayer statute (given the comments of State Senator Holmes during its consideration in the legislature) and the James prayer law, both of which again violated the first prong of *Lemon*. The court also held that both school prayer statutes had the primary effect of advancing religion, a violation of *Lemon*'s second prong.

The Eleventh Circuit emphasized that its ruling was not intended to eliminate all moment of silence statutes: "We do not imply that simply meditation or silence is barred from the public schools" it said, "we hold [only] that the state cannot participate in the advancement of religious activities through any guise, including teacher-led meditation. It is not the activity itself that concerns us; it is the purpose of the activity that we . . . scrutinize."[45]

The state of Alabama and its newly elected governor, George Wallace (in his fourth and final term), appealed the Eleventh Circuit's decision to the Supreme Court. The Court granted certiorari to the case, limited its consideration only to the constitutionality of the meditation and voluntary prayer law, and scheduled oral arguments for December 4, 1984. At that time, Paul M. Bator, deputy solicitor general of the United States, joined John S. Baker, who represented the state of Alabama. The Court granted Bator permission to participate because the Reagan administration had taken an interest in the case and sought a reversal of the lower court's ruling.

Almost immediately after Baker began his presentation at oral arguments, the justices challenged him to explain why it was necessary to add prayer to the previous state law authorizing a moment of silence. He responded that students may not have known what options they had during that quiet period. "[T]he statute," he argued, "merely informs students that [they] . . . can pray silently during that minute."[46] Justice John Paul Stevens was particularly aggressive in questioning why the statute needed to inform the students of anything. If prayer was a permitted implicit option under the previous law, why did Alabama find it necessary to make it explicit? Neither Baker nor Bator answered the question satisfactorily, but the latter attempted to use the same question to his advantage. "How can it be unconstitutional," Bator asked rhetorically, "for Alabama simply to say what was already the fact?"[47]

Jaffree's attorney, Ronnie L. Williams, concentrated his remarks on the *Lemon* test. There was clearly no secular legislative purpose to the law, he argued, since the Alabama lawmaker who introduced the legislation admitted that its purpose was "to bring prayer back to the public schools."[48] The law also could not claim to be neutral, he maintained, because it promoted religion every time a teacher announced that prayer was a possibility. For Williams, the teacher's role was the critical difference between the earlier moment of silence law and the more recent versions passed by the legislature.

Under the earlier law, the teacher gave students no prompts regarding permissible activities during the moment of silence. Williams even acknowledged that the previous law permitted teachers to answer student questions about whether or not they could pray during the silent period in the affirmative. The subsequent law, however, entirely changed the constitutionality of a teacher's actions. Under the challenged statute, the teacher would remind his or her students every morning that they could pray during the moment of silence. That was unconstitutional, Williams said, not only because the students were an impressionable captive audience, but also because of all of the possible uses of the moment of silence time, "that teacher will be suggesting or implying that prayer is the preferred activity."[49]

Having heard from the lawyers representing both parties at oral argument, the justices took up the matter themselves in conference. The following June, they announced their 6–3 ruling.

THE DECISION

Wallace v. Jaffree (6–3)
472 U.S. 38 (1985)

JUSTICE STEVENS delivered the opinion of the Court.

At an early stage of this litigation, the constitutionality of three Alabama statutes was questioned: (1) § 16-1-20, enacted in 1978, which authorized a 1-minute period of silence in all public schools "for meditation"; (2) § 16-1-20.1, enacted in 1981, which authorized a period of silence "for meditation or voluntary prayer"; and (3) § 16-1-20.2, enacted in 1982, which authorized teachers to lead "willing students" in a prescribed prayer to "Almighty God . . . the Creator and Supreme Judge of the world."

At the preliminary-injunction stage of this case, the District Court distinguished § 16-1-20 from the other two statutes. It then held that there was "nothing wrong" with § 16-1-20, but that §§ 16-1-20.1 and 16-1-20.2 were both invalid because the sole purpose of both was "an effort on the part of the State of Alabama to encourage a religious activity." After the trial on the merits, the District Court did not change its interpretation of these two statutes, but held that they were constitutional because, in its opinion, Alabama has the power to establish a state religion if it chooses to do so.

The Court of Appeals agreed with the District Court's initial interpretation of the purpose of both § 16-1-20.1 and § 16-1-20.2, and held them both unconstitutional. We have already affirmed the Court of Appeals' holding with respect to § 16-1-20.2. Moreover, appellees have not questioned the holding that § 16-1-20 is valid. Thus, the narrow question for decision is whether § 16-1-20.1, which authorizes a period of silence for "meditation or voluntary prayer," is a law respecting the establishment of religion within the meaning of the First Amendment.

Appellee Ishmael Jaffree is a resident of Mobile County, Alabama. On May 28, 1982, he filed a complaint on behalf of three of his minor children; two of them were second-grade students and the third was then in kindergarten. The complaint named members of the Mobile County School Board, various school officials, and the minor plaintiffs' three teachers as defendants. The complaint alleged . . . that two of the children had been subjected to various acts of religious indoctrination "from the beginning of the school year in September, 1981"; that the defendant teachers had "on a daily basis" led their classes in saying certain prayers in unison; that the minor children were exposed to ostracism from their peer group class members if they did not participate; and that Ishmael Jaffree had repeatedly but unsuccessfully requested that the devotional services be stopped. . . .

In its lengthy conclusions of law, the District Court reviewed a number of opinions of this Court interpreting the Establishment Clause of the First Amendment, and then embarked on a fresh examination of the question whether the First Amendment imposes any barrier to the establishment of an official religion by the State of Alabama. After reviewing at length what it perceived to be newly discovered historical evidence, the District Court concluded that "the establishment clause of the first amendment to the United States Constitution does not prohibit the state from establishing a religion." In a separate opinion, the District Court dismissed appellees' challenge to the three Alabama statutes because of a failure to state any claim for which relief could be granted. The court's dismissal of this challenge was also based on its conclusion that the Establishment Clause did not bar the States from establishing a religion. . . .

The Court of Appeals . . . , not surprisingly, reversed. . . . [It] noted that this Court had considered and had rejected the historical arguments that the District Court found persuasive and that the District Court had misapplied the doctrine of *stare decisis*. . . .

Our unanimous affirmance of the Court of Appeals' judgment . . . makes it unnecessary to comment at length on the District Court's remarkable conclusion that the Federal Constitution imposes no obstacle to Alabama's establishment of a state religion. Before analyzing the precise issue that is presented to us, it is nevertheless appropriate to recall how firmly embedded in our constitutional jurisprudence is the proposition that the several States have no greater power to restrain the individual freedoms protected by the First Amendment than does the Congress of the United States.

As is plain from its text, the First Amendment was adopted to curtail the power of Congress to interfere with the individual's freedom to believe, to worship, and to express himself in accordance with the dictates of his own conscience. Until the Fourteenth Amendment was added to the Constitution, the First Amendment's restraints on the exercise of federal power simply did not apply to the States. But when the Constitution was amended to prohibit any State from depriving any person of liberty without due process of law, that Amendment imposed the same substantive limitations on the States' power to legislate that the First Amendment had always imposed on the Congress' power. This Court has confirmed and endorsed this elementary proposition of law time and time again. . . .

Just as the right to speak and the right to refrain from speaking are complementary components of a broader concept of individual freedom of mind, so also the individual's freedom to choose his own creed is the counterpart of his right to refrain from accepting the creed established by the majority. At one time it was thought that this right merely proscribed the preference of one Christian sect over another, but would not require equal respect for the conscience of the infidel, the atheist, or the adherent of a non-Christian faith such as Islam or Judaism. But when the underlying principle has been examined in the crucible of litigation, the Court has unambiguously concluded that the individual freedom of conscience protected by the First Amendment embraces the right to select any religious faith or none at all. This conclusion derives support not only from the interest in respecting the individual's freedom of conscience, but also from the conviction that religious beliefs worthy of respect are the product of free and voluntary choice by the faithful, and from recognition of the fact that the political interest in forestalling intolerance extends beyond intolerance among Christian sects—or even intolerance among "religions"—to encompass intolerance of the disbeliever and the uncertain. As Justice Jackson eloquently stated in *West Virginia Board of Education v. Barnette* (1943): "If there is any fixed star in our constitutional constellation, it is that no official, high or petty, can prescribe what shall be orthodox in politics, nationalism, religion, or other matters of opinion or force citizens to confess by word or act their faith therein."

The State of Alabama, no less than the Congress of the United States, must respect that basic truth.

When the Court has been called upon to construe the breadth of the Establishment Clause, it has examined the criteria developed over a period of many years. Thus, in *Lemon v. Kurtzman* (1971), we wrote: "First, the statute must have a secular legislative purpose; second, its principal or primary effect must be one that neither advances nor inhibits religion, finally, the statute must not foster 'an excessive government entanglement with religion." It is the first of these criteria that is most plainly implicated in this case. . . .

In applying the [first prong of the *Lemon*] test, it is appropriate to ask "whether government's actual purpose is to endorse or disapprove of religion." In this case, the answer to that question is dispositive. For the record not only provides us with an unambiguous affirmative answer, but it also reveals that the enactment of [the statute] was not motivated by any clearly secular purpose—indeed, the statute had *no* secular purpose.

The sponsor of the bill that became [law], Senator Donald Holmes, inserted into the legislative record—apparently without dissent—a statement indicating that the legislation was an "effort to return voluntary prayer" to the public schools. Later Senator Holmes confirmed this purpose before the District Court. In response to the question whether he had any purpose for the legislation other than returning voluntary prayer to public schools, he stated: "No, I did not have no other purpose in mind." The State did not present evidence of *any* secular purpose. . . .

We must, therefore, conclude that the Alabama Legislature intended to change existing law . . . for the sole purpose of expressing the State's endorsement of prayer activities for one minute at the beginning of each school day. The addition of "or voluntary prayer" indicates that the State intended to characterize prayer as a favored practice. Such an endorsement is not consistent with the established principle that the government must pursue a course of complete neutrality toward religion.

The importance of that principle does not permit us to treat this as an inconsequential case involving nothing more than a few words of symbolic speech on behalf of the political majority. . . .

We conclude that [the law] violates the First Amendment.

The judgment of the Court of Appeals is affirmed.

Justice Powell, concurring.

I concur in the Court's opinion and judgment that [the Alabama law] violates the Establishment Clause of the First Amendment. . . .

I would vote to uphold the Alabama statute if it . . . had a clear secular purpose. Nothing in the record before us, however, identifies a clear secular purpose, and the State also has failed to identify any nonreligious reason for the statute's enactment. Under these circumstances, the Court is required by our precedents to hold that the statute fails the first prong of the *Lemon* test, and therefore violates the Establishment Clause.

Justice O'Connor concurring in the judgment.

Nothing in the United States Constitution as interpreted by this Court or in the laws of the State of Alabama prohibits public school students from voluntarily praying at any time before, during, or after the schoolday. Alabama has facilitated voluntary silent prayers of students who are so inclined by [its law] which provides a moment of silence in [the public] schools each day. The parties to these proceedings concede the validity of this enactment. At issue in these appeals is the constitutional validity of an additional and subsequent Alabama statute which both the District Court and the Court of Appeals concluded was enacted solely to officially encourage prayer during the moment of silence. I agree with the judgment of the Court that . . . [this law] violates the Establishment Clause of the First Amendment. . . .

I am not ready to abandon all aspects of the *Lemon* test. I do believe, however, that the standards announced in *Lemon* should be reexamined and refined in order to make them more useful in achieving the underlying purpose of the First Amendment. . . . Last Term, I proposed a refinement of the *Lemon* test with this goal in mind [in *Lynch v. Donnelly* (1984)].

The *Lynch* concurrence suggested that the religious liberty protected by the Establishment Clause is infringed when the government makes adherence to religion relevant to a person's standing in the political community. Direct government action endorsing religion or a particular religious practice is invalid under this approach because it "sends a message to nonadherents that they are outsiders, not full members of the political community, and an accompanying message to adherents that they are insiders, favored members of the political community." Under this view, *Lemon*'s inquiry as to the purpose and effect of a statute requires courts to examine whether government's purpose is to endorse religion and whether the statute actually conveys a message of endorsement.

The endorsement test is useful because of the analytic content it gives to the *Lemon*-mandated inquiry into legislative purpose and effect. In this country, church and state must necessarily operate within the same community. Because of this coexistence, it is inevitable that the secular interests of government and the religious interests of various sects and their adherents will frequently intersect, conflict, and combine. A statute that ostensibly promotes a secular interest often has an incidental or even a primary effect of helping or hindering a sectarian belief. Chaos would ensue if every such statute were invalid under the Establishment Clause. For example, the State could not criminalize murder for fear that it would thereby promote the Biblical command against killing. The task for the Court is to sort out those statutes and government practices whose purpose and effect go against the grain of religious liberty protected by the First Amendment.

The endorsement test does not preclude government from acknowledging religion or from taking religion into account in making law and policy. It does preclude government from conveying or attempting to convey a message that religion or a particular religious belief is favored or preferred. . . .

A moment of silence law that is clearly drafted and implemented so as to permit prayer, meditation, and reflection within the prescribed period, without endorsing one alternative over the others, should pass this test. . . .

The Court does not hold that the Establishment Clause is so hostile to religion that it precludes the States from affording schoolchildren an opportunity for voluntary silent prayer. To the contrary, the moment of silence statutes of many States should satisfy the Establishment Clause standard we have here applied. The Court holds only that Alabama has intentionally crossed the line between creating a quiet moment during which those so inclined may pray, and affirmatively endorsing the particular religious practice of prayer. This line may be a fine one, but our precedents and the principles of religious liberty require that we draw it. In my view, the judgment of the Court of Appeals must be affirmed.

Justice Rehnquist, dissenting.

Thirty-eight years ago this Court, in *Everson v. Board of Education* [1947], summarized its exegesis of Establishment Clause doctrine thus: "In the words of Jefferson, the clause against establishment of religion by law was intended to erect 'a wall of separation between church and State.'"

This language from *Reynolds* [*v. United States* (1879)], a case involving the Free Exercise Clause of the First Amendment rather than the Establishment Clause, quoted from Thomas Jefferson's letter to the Danbury Baptist Association the phrase "I contemplate with sovereign reverence that act of the whole American people which declared that their legislature should 'make no law respecting an establishment of religion, or prohibiting the free exercise thereof,' thus building a wall of separation between church and State."

It is impossible to build sound constitutional doctrine upon a mistaken understanding of constitutional history, but unfortunately the Establishment Clause has been expressly freighted with Jefferson's misleading metaphor for nearly 40 years. Thomas Jefferson was of course in France at the time the constitutional Amendments known as the Bill of Rights were passed by Congress and ratified by the States. His letter to the Danbury Baptist Association was a short note of courtesy, written 14 years after the Amendments were passed by Congress. He would seem to any detached observer as a less than ideal source of contemporary history as to the meaning of the Religion Clauses of the First Amendment.

Jefferson's fellow Virginian, James Madison, with whom he was joined in the battle for the enactment of the Virginia Statute of Religious Liberty of 1786, did play as large a part as anyone in the drafting of the Bill of Rights. He had two advantages over Jefferson in this regard: he was present in the United States, and he was a leading Member of the First Congress. But when we turn to the record of the proceedings in the First Congress leading up to the adoption of the Establishment Clause of the Constitution, including Madison's significant contributions thereto, we see a far different picture of its purpose than the highly simplified "wall of separation between church and State." . . .

On the basis of the record of these proceedings in the House of Representatives, James Madison was undoubtedly the most important architect among the Members of the House of the Amendments which became the Bill of Rights, but it was James Madison speaking as an advocate of sensible legislative compromise, not as an advocate of incorporating the Virginia Statute of Religious Liberty into the United States Constitution. . . .

It seems indisputable from these glimpses of Madison's thinking, as reflected by actions on the floor of the House in 1789, that he saw the Amendment as designed to prohibit the establishment of a national religion, and perhaps to prevent discrimination among sects. He did not see it as requiring neutrality on the part of government between religion and irreligion. Thus the Court's opinion in *Everson*—while correct in bracketing Madison and Jefferson together in their exertions in their home State leading to the enactment of the Virginia Statute of Religious Liberty—is totally incorrect in suggesting that Madison carried these views onto the floor of the United States House of Representatives when he proposed the language which would ultimately become the Bill of Rights.

The repetition of this error in the Court's opinion in *McCollum v. Board of*

Education (1948) and *Engel v. Vitale* (1962) does not make it any sounder historically. Finally, in *Abington School District v. Schempp* (1963), the Court made the truly remarkable statement that "the views of Madison and Jefferson, preceded by Roger Williams, came to be incorporated not only in the Federal Constitution but likewise in those of most of our States." On the basis of what evidence we have, this statement is demonstrably incorrect as a matter of history. And its repetition in varying forms in succeeding opinions of the Court can give it no more authority than it possesses as a matter of fact; *stare decisis* may bind courts as to matters of law, but it cannot bind them as to matters of history. . . .

Notwithstanding the absence of a historical basis for [its] theory of rigid separation, the wall idea might well have served as a useful albeit misguided analytical concept, had it led this Court to unified and principled results in Establishment Clause cases. The opposite, unfortunately, has been true; in the 38 years since *Everson* our Establishment Clause cases have been neither principled nor unified. Our recent opinions, many of them hopelessly divided pluralities, have with embarrassing candor conceded that the "wall of separation" is merely a "blurred, indistinct, and variable barrier," which "is not wholly accurate" and can only be "dimly perceived." . . .

Whether due to its lack of historical support or its practical unworkability, the *Everson* "wall" has proved all but useless as a guide to sound constitutional adjudication. . . .

But the greatest injury of the "wall" notion is its mischievous diversion of judges from the actual intentions of the drafters of the Bill of Rights. The "crucible of litigation," is well adapted to adjudicating factual disputes on the basis of testimony presented in court, but no amount of repetition of historical errors in judicial opinions can make the errors true. The "wall of separation between church and State" is a metaphor based on bad history, a metaphor which has proved useless as a guide to judging. It should be frankly and explicitly abandoned.

The Court has more recently attempted to add some mortar to *Everson*'s wall through the three-part test of *Lemon v. Kurtzman* which served at first to offer a more useful test for purposes of the Establishment Clause than did the "wall" metaphor. Generally stated, the *Lemon* test proscribes state action that has a sectarian purpose or effect, or causes an impermissible governmental entanglement with religion.

Lemon cited *Board of Education v. Allen* (1968) as the source of the "purpose" and "effect" prongs of the three-part test. The *Allen* opinion explains, however, how it inherited the purpose and effect elements from *Schempp* and *Everson*, both of which contain the historical errors described previously.

Thus the purpose and effect prongs have the same historical deficiencies as the wall concept itself: they are in no way based on either the language or intent of the drafters.

The secular purpose prong has proved mercurial in application because it has never been fully defined, and we have never fully stated how the test is to operate. If the purpose prong is intended to void those aids to sectarian institutions accompanied by a stated legislative purpose to aid religion, the prong will condemn nothing so long as the legislature utters a secular purpose and says nothing about aiding religion. Thus the constitutionality of a statute may depend upon what the legislators put into the legislative history and, more importantly, what they leave out. . . .

These difficulties arise because the *Lemon* test has no more grounding in the history of the First Amendment than does the wall theory upon which it rests. The three-part test represents a determined effort to craft a workable rule from a historically faulty doctrine; but the rule can only be as sound as the doctrine it attempts to service. The three-part test has simply not provided adequate standards for deciding Establishment Clause cases, as this Court has slowly come to realize. . . .

If a constitutional theory has no basis in the history of the amendment it seeks to interpret, is difficult to apply and yields unprincipled results, I see little use in it.

THE AFTERMATH AND SIGNIFICANCE OF *WALLACE V. JAFFREE*

Jaffree's significance is threefold: First, and on the broadest level, it revealed the establishment clause fissures on the Court at that time in perhaps their greatest detail. While *Lemon* controlled the majority's opinion in this case, Justice Sandra Day O'Connor clearly believed that *Lemon* was insufficient to guide other establishment clause claims that might arise. In her concurring opinion, she recommended that her colleagues reconsider the "endorsement test" that she had developed the previous year in *Lynch v. Donnelly*.[50] That test required the justices to review government laws and policies challenged under the establishment clause against the perception that such laws and policies conveyed to the public. As O'Connor argued in *Lynch*, "Endorsement sends a message to non-adherents that they are outsiders, not full members of the political community, and an accompanying message to adherents that they are insiders, favored members of the political community."[51] It was crucial, she continued, that "government practices not have the effect of communicating a message of government endorsement or disapproval of religion."[52]

While the Court still has not broadly embraced O'Connor's endorsement test, it has accepted her challenge to step away from the rigidity of *Lemon*. In a 1992 case dealing with clergy prayers before graduation ceremonies, the Court ignored *Lemon* entirely in holding that practice unconstitutional.[53] Writing for the majority in *Lee v. Weisman*, Justice Kennedy announced an establishment clause "coercion standard" that essentially declared that the government could not force anyone to participate in religious exercises such as occurred in this case when a short invocation was offered at the beginning of a public school graduation. Since the mid-1990s, the Court has also recognized the role of the free speech clause in protecting some elements of religious expression in the public square.[54] This approach, by definition, abandons not only the *Lemon*, endorsement, and coercion tests but also the establishment clause itself.

A second significant contribution of *Jaffree* was Justice William Rehnquist's dissenting opinion. He was elevated to chief justice the following year, and though much loved by his colleagues, he was never able to win their support for the views he expressed in that case. Conservatives consider his dissent to be one of his finest opinions for calling the Court to task for what Rehnquist believed was a badly mistaken reading of American history where church and state was concerned. Earlier justices disagreed with the Court's establishment clause jurisprudence, but none had marshalled their opposition with the level of historical detail that Rehnquist included in his lengthy dissent.[55]

A young attorney working in the Reagan White House at the time made an interesting observation about Rehnquist. In a memo to White House counsel Fred Fielding, thirty-year-old John Roberts speculated that Rehnquist's dissent was written more like a majority opinion and that the Alabama law actually had five votes to uphold at some point. He argued that Rehnquist lost the support of Justices Powell and O'Connor when he overreached in seeking to jettison the *Lemon* test and undo forty years of establishment clause jurisprudence.[56] Twenty years later, Roberts succeeded Rehnquist as chief justice of the United States.

Third, in striking down Alabama's 1981 "meditation or voluntary prayer" statute, the Court effectively gave its blessing to moment of silence laws around the country. Justice Stevens's opinion in *Jaffree* flatly stated that "the legislative intent to return prayer to the public schools is, of course, quite different from merely protecting every student's right to engage in voluntary prayer during an appropriate moment of silence during the schoolday."[57] That acknowledgment coupled with the separate statements of Justices Powell and O'Connor that they would have voted to uphold the

Alabama law as written had its purpose truly been secular in nature did not go unnoticed. Indeed, Justice O'Connor's concurrence basically provided states with instructions on how to create a constitutional moment of silence law.

At the time *Jaffree* was decided, twenty-five states had moment of silence laws; now some thirty-five do. More important than the numerical increase has been the jurisprudential shift relative to moment of silence laws. According to a report from the Pew Research Center's Religion and Public Life Project, the "lower courts have responded to the high court's signals. Before the [*Jaffree*] ruling, almost all courts that heard challenges to moment-of-silence statutes found such laws to be unconstitutional; since 1985, however, almost all court decisions have upheld moment-of-silence laws."[58]

Despite the apparently settled law on moments of silence, other religious issues continue to roil the public schools. This is a result of, among other things, expanding religious diversity, a greater awareness of First Amendment religion and speech rights, and the increasing presence of interest groups and well-funded public interest law firms that advocate, as the case may be, for stronger or weaker connections between church and state. The Court itself is also responsible for the seemingly never-ending conflict over the role of religion in the public square.

As mentioned earlier, the Court's landmark 1947 decision in *Everson* invoked the wall of separation between church and state but failed to articulate exactly what that phrase meant. Consequently, as one critic observed, "The wall has done what walls usually do: it has obscured the view. It has lent a simplistic air to the discussion of a very complicated matter. Hence it has caused confusion whenever it has been invoked. Far from helping to decide cases, it has made opinions and decisions unintelligible. The wall is offered as a reason. It is not a reason; it is a figure of speech."[59]

There is, perhaps, no better indication of the confusion caused by the wall metaphor than a lower federal court decision in a later case that was remarkably similar to *Jaffree*. In early 2000, the Virginia General Assembly amended an existing moment of silence statute to require each school in the state to recognize one minute of silence during which schoolchildren were to, "in the exercise of his or her individual choice, meditate, pray, or engage in any other silent activity which does not interfere with, distract, or impede other pupils."[60] The sponsor of the legislation, Warren Barry, was quoted as saying that he introduced the bill in response to school violence and the recent shootings at Columbine High School in Colorado that left fifteen children and teachers dead and twenty-four wounded. He hoped that an introspective moment each morning, to include silent prayer, would soften the feelings and attitudes that led to student violence. When asked by the press if his intent was to return prayer to the public schools, Barry responded, "This country was based on belief in God, and maybe we need to look at that again."[61]

The law was challenged as a violation of the establishment clause by several families in Virginia who raised the same concerns as Ishmael Jaffree had and who relied heavily on *Wallace v. Jaffree* for support. However, declaring that a statute can have "dual legitimate purposes—one clearly secular and one the accommodation of religion," a divided panel of judges on the US Court of Appeals for the Fourth Circuit ruled that the law did not violate the *Lemon* test. The wall of separation had not been breached, it concluded, and the law was constitutional.[62] In October 2001, the United States Supreme Court refused to hear the case, leaving the lower court ruling in place.

2

COMPELLED DISCLOSURE

Freedom of Association and *NAACP v. Alabama* (1958)

In 1831, a twenty-five-year-old aristocrat named Alexis de Tocqueville came to the United States on assignment from the French government to study this country's prison systems. In nine short months, he crisscrossed his way from New York City to Green Bay, Wisconsin, and from New Orleans to Washington, DC, meeting the people who lived in the young nation and observing American life. He then returned to France and filed his report. He also began to compile his notes and observations about his journey, which he later published in two volumes titled *Democracy in America*. Tocqueville's work was immediately greeted with extraordinary international acclaim and was acknowledged in Europe and the United States as the single best source for understanding American life and politics at the time. It was also hailed as the best book ever written about democracy generally—a reputation, incidentally, that it continues to enjoy in many circles today.

Among his observations, Tocqueville noted that Americans of the Jacksonian era understood the consequences of associating with others better than anyone else in the world. They understood that their ability to create social and political change increased as the number of their like-minded supporters expanded. Thus, he wrote, "The most natural right of man, after that of acting on his own, is that of combining his efforts with those of his fellows and acting together. Therefore the right of association . . . [is] almost as inalienable as individual liberty."[1] Yet, as fundamental as this right appeared to be, Americans' ability to unite their efforts with others free of government infringement would not receive constitutional protection for more than a century after Tocqueville's journey. The Supreme Court

Figure 2. Autherine Lucy, *left*, accompanied by Thurgood Marshall of the NAACP and Birmingham lawyer Arthur Shores, 1956. Courtesy of the Alabama Department of Archives and History.

finally pronounced a "freedom to engage in association" in the 1958 case of *NAACP v. Alabama*, and, in so doing, created a modern civil liberty.

THE STORY

Although few are acquainted with the Court's landmark ruling on the freedom of association, nearly every American, including young schoolchildren, are familiar with what prompted it. On December 1, 1955, Rosa Parks boarded a Montgomery city bus and took her place in the first row behind the section of seats reserved for white passengers. As the bus proceeded on its route, that section filled up completely and a white man was left standing in the aisle. The bus driver instructed Parks and the other African Americans on her row to vacate their seats so that the man and subsequent white passengers would have a place to sit. The other African Americans complied with the directive, but Rosa Parks ignored it. When she refused to obey the bus driver's second order to move, he notified local police who boarded the bus and arrested Parks for disorderly conduct.

Four days later, a judge found her guilty and fined her ten dollars. Not coincidentally, that same day, December 5, 1955, the Montgomery Bus Boycott began. City bus companies lost thousands of dollars as an estimated 90 percent of their African American ridership refused to use the segregated buses for over a year. The boycott also provided unity, energy, and leadership to the fledgling civil rights movement, which the national media helped to introduce to an increasing number of Americans outside of the South.

Two months later, Autherine Lucy began classes as the first African American student at the University of Alabama. University officials originally accepted Lucy in 1952, but when they learned she was black, they rescinded their offer of admission. Thurgood Marshall and other prominent attorneys with the National Association for the Advancement of Colored People (NAACP) fought a three-year legal battle that resulted in a federal court order requiring the university to enroll Lucy. On the evening of the first day of classes, Friday, February 3, 1956, people began to gather for what became a weekend long demonstration.

The *Montgomery Advertiser* reported that protestors burned crosses in front of the football stadium and elsewhere on University Boulevard. They also sang "Dixie" and chanted "Keep Bama white" and "To hell with Autherine" during rallies held at the Denny Chimes.[2] The protesting crowd swelled to more than three thousand by Monday morning. Campus and city officials who tried to calm the situation, including the university president's wife and Tuscaloosa police officers, were pelted with eggs, small rocks, and mud balls as the crowd shouted racial epithets.

Lucy herself was struck by eggs just after her last Monday class while being escorted by the dean of women, Sarah Healey. As they tried to leave campus, some demonstrators threw rocks, cracking all of the windows of Dean Healey's car, while others rushed the vehicle trying to open its locked doors. One protestor hurled a large rock that completely shattered the vehicle's rear window, barely missing the occupants inside.[3] That night the University of Alabama Board of Trustees suspended Lucy for her own safety as well as that of others on campus.

Alabama newspapers condemned the violence but insisted that those responsible included not only the individuals who had thrown rocks and eggs but also the NAACP and the United States Supreme Court. It was the Court's 1954 decision in *Brown v. Board of Education*, the *Anniston Star* argued, that "force[d] on the South a way of life that is repugnant to our people as a whole."[4] The NAACP had exacerbated the problem, the newspaper continued, by forcing "a member of their race into a company where it was plainly written that she would not be welcomed."[5]

Political leaders in Alabama saw the Montgomery Bus Boycott and the University of Alabama demonstrations as both distressing and profoundly embarrassing to the state, particularly as national media coverage of the civil rights movement increased. However, the concerns of these politicians were rooted in more than just anxiety about the state's reputation in the eyes of the rest of the country. Many political leaders throughout the South, regardless of their personal views on the matter, sensed that their own electoral survival turned on their efforts to maintain segregation in the aftermath of the Supreme Court's ruling in *Brown*.[6] Politicians who had previously staked out moderate positions on the topic, using muted rhetoric and issuing calls for compromise, were either defeated at the polls or came to embrace pro-segregationist views coupled with strident language in order to retain their positions. They also began to use the power and authority of their political offices to reinforce the pillars of their segregated society that had begun to totter after the *Brown* decision.

Politicians from across the South met to share resistance policies, map out tactics, and, where possible, create strategies that could work across several states. With politicians committed to segregation at the state and local level, increasingly vocal white constituents encouraging them on, and few concerns about either President Eisenhower or Congress taking any significant action at the national level that might affect the states, the path to maintaining segregation in the South seemed clear—with one exception: the federal courts. Yet, even the courts had (and still have) their own inherent check on their power. Since they are reactive institutions, the judiciary must wait for "a case or controversy" to come before it.[7] No matter how much they might wish to do so, judges simply cannot reach out to address even grave injustices within their jurisdiction unless a case is brought before them. Lawyers and litigants are therefore a necessary part of any effort to use the judicial process to create legal and social change.

Where racial matters were concerned, no organization was more active in recruiting people to file suit, had more resources to draw on, or had more experienced attorneys than the NAACP. Much to the consternation of southern segregationists, the NAACP, by way of its litigating arm, the Legal Defense and Education Fund, was not only active but also increasingly successful in its courtroom efforts on behalf of African Americans in the South. The NAACP's strategy was, as Fred Gray (attorney for Rosa Parks and the organizers of the Montgomery Bus Boycott) subtitled his autobiography, "changing the system by the system."[8] Segregationists thus realized that the outcome of almost any effort they expended to preserve the status quo in their society would be short-lived so long as NAACP lawyers were capable of recruiting litigants and assisting them to bring cases to court. NAACP officials realized this too, but they were still surprised by the action taken by Alabama attorney general John Patterson during the summer of 1956.

On June 1 of that year, Patterson sought an injunction from Circuit Judge Walter B. Jones that would force the NAACP to cease operations within the state. Jones was the son of former Alabama governor and federal district judge Thomas Goode Jones. He was a respected jurist and legal scholar in his own right who was then serving as the president of the Alabama State Bar Association. Two years earlier, as a circuit judge sitting in Montgomery, Jones received a special appointment from the Alabama Supreme Court to Phenix City, where he and others were tasked with dismantling the corrupt political system that had allowed organized crime to thrive there for decades and that was responsible for the 1954 assassination of Albert Patterson, the attorney general's father. The Phenix City trials forged a bond between Jones and John Patterson such that a biographer of the latter later noted, "Jones was one of Patterson's allies and a definite advantage in any legal battle."[9] Judge Jones was also an ardent segregationist.

Less than a year after Patterson requested the injunction against the NAACP, Judge Jones summarized his racial views in an article written for the *Montgomery Advertiser*. For more than three decades, he provided a weekly "Off the Bench" feature for the newspaper that contained his personal reflections and insights. In his March 4, 1957, column, "I Speak for the White Race," Jones declared, "[A] massive campaign . . . of propaganda is now being directed against the white race, particularly by those who envy its glory and greatness. Because our people have pride of race, we are denounced as bigoted . . . by those who wish an impure mixed breed."[10] He went on to mock the "[p]seudo-scientists [who] tell us there is no such thing as a superior race," responding with a long list of notable explorers, artists, writers, inventors, statesmen, and others as evidence of white supremacy. He concluded by encouraging his readers to "stand up in honor and glory with a just pride in the [white] race's achievements" and to join him in "maintain[ing] at any and all sacrifice the purity of our blood strain and race."[11]

Against the backdrop of Jones's white supremacist views and his personal friendship with Patterson, the attorney general's petition for a temporary injunction against the NAACP was grounded in three charges. The first was that the group was responsible for the Montgomery Bus Boycott, which was going into its seventh month. Second, the attorney general asserted that the NAACP had encouraged and even paid African Americans like Autherine Lucy to test the University of Alabama's whites-only admission policy. These actions and the NAACP's role in them, Patterson contended, "resulted in violations of our laws and tend[ed] in many instances to create a breach of the peace."[12]

The NAACP was certainly aware of plans for the bus boycott (Rosa Parks was a member of a local NAACP chapter, after all, as were other Montgomery area activists) and had provided legal representation to Autherine Lucy when the University of Alabama rescinded her admission in 1952. Yet, Patterson knew that it would be difficult to demonstrate his claim that the organization had actually instigated the contentious events of the previous several months. The validity of his third charge against the NAACP, however, was not in dispute at all: that it had failed to properly register to do business in the state.

Alabama required all out-of-state corporations to file a copy of their charter with state officials, establish a formal place of business, and designate an agent to act on their behalf prior to engaging in any business. The NAACP was incorporated in New York in 1911, and had a presence in Alabama as early as 1918, opening a regional office in Birmingham in 1951. However, during its entire time in Alabama the NAACP had never filed the proper documentation or paid the registration fees because it did not believe it was required to do so as a nonprofit organization.

Judge Jones considered the attorney general's charges and granted the temporary injunction. This essentially prohibited the NAACP and any of its affiliates or members in Alabama from conducting any further activities within the state until a trial could be held on the merits of Patterson's claims. The NAACP asked the judge to remove the restraining order, and he responded by scheduling a formal hearing on that request for mid-July. Just prior to that hearing, however, and at the behest of state officials who said they needed more information from the NAACP in order to prepare their case, Jones imposed additional requirements on the organization. He gave NAACP officials two weeks to provide state officials with the following materials: information on all field offices within Alabama, a year's worth of bank statements and canceled checks, letters and other correspondence dealing with the Montgomery Bus Boycott and the integration of the University of Alabama, names of contributors, property records, and a list of the names and addresses of all NAACP members in the state.

The NAACP scrambled to put together much of the requested information, but it steadfastly refused to turn over its membership list, believing that its supporters would face public ridicule, loss of employment, harassment, and even physical danger if their identity became known. In failing to fully comply with the judge's order, however, the organization found itself in contempt of court, which earned it a $10,000 fine. Judge Jones gave NAACP leaders five additional days to produce the membership list, at which time he promised to rescind the fine; he also threatened to increase it substantially if they did not. True to his word, when the NAACP again refused to make public the names of its members, Jones held the organization in further contempt and increased the fine to $100,000, a potentially crippling amount for a group whose primary funding came from two-dollar annual membership dues. The NAACP turned to the Alabama Supreme Court for relief.

THE CONSTITUTIONAL BACKGROUND

The Constitution says nothing about a freedom of association. However, the ability to create social and political change as individuals combine their efforts with like-minded people is closely related to the rights to assemble and petition. These rights receive far less attention than their more well-known First Amendment cousins of religion, speech, and press, but they are just as critical to a free society. Modern Americans take for granted that if they are upset with laws, governmental policies, or public officials, they can voice that displeasure directly to policy makers in hopes of creating change. They can also share their views with others whose cumulative voice is so much louder and whose numbers are so much greater that it is impossible for policy makers to ignore. The First Amendment rights to "petition the Government for a redress of grievances" (or to tell the government that it needs to correct or change something) and "the right of the people peaceably to assemble" (in both physical and—in the modern era—online settings) to discuss and debate are both fundamental ways of producing change between elections. Not surprisingly, they are also the most feared by totalitarian regimes.

It was Tocqueville who declared, "Despotism, by its very nature suspicious, sees the isolation of men as the best guarantee of its own permanence. So it usually does all it can to isolate them."[13] Oppressive governments have few worries about the single protestor who calls for political or social reform. Their countries may be governed by charters that profess respect for fundamental rights, and their leaders may even give audience to that protestor citing respect for free speech or the right to petition. The dedication of such governments to fundamental liberties, however, cannot be determined solely by what their constitution says or by how they treat isolated individuals. The truest test of their commitment is in how they respond to expanding numbers of citizens who hold views similar to the lone protestor.

Since 1977, the United States Department of State has published an annual review of human rights practices in other nations.[14] The report details how in many countries, public meetings are forbidden, antigovernment organizations are prohibited, and opposition party members are persecuted. Those with views deemed subversive to the government are harassed, imprisoned, or executed. Government agencies monitor the telecommunications and internet usage of their citizens to further control the information they may access and share with others and strictly regulate nongovernmental groups and associations. For the little appreciation they receive from most Americans, the interconnected nature of assembly, petition, and association provides the bedrock of liberty that allows other rights to flourish.

Yet, even in this country, these freedoms have not always been respected. Well-known examples of government restrictions on associational rights can be seen during the founding era itself with the 1798 Sedition Act as well as in various Civil War–era laws, in the Espionage and Sedition Acts of the early 1900s, and during the Red Scare period of the 1940s and 1950s.

The Supreme Court's early view of the freedom of association was generally negative. In 1915, for example, the Supreme Court upheld a Mississippi statute that abolished fraternities and sororities and withheld university honors and diplomas from students who were already members of such organizations unless they agreed in writing to disassociate with those groups. While not unsympathetic to the students' freedom of association claims, the Court conceded that the purpose of higher education in Mississippi and the tax dollars that supported it gave the state the authority to remove those influences "that divided the attention of the students" and distracted them from their studies.[15]

In 1928, the Court upheld a New York law requiring any organization of more than twenty people that demanded an oath as a condition of membership to submit a listing of its officers and members to state officials. Because it exempted labor unions, Civil War veterans' associations, and "benevolent" societies, the law was accused of targeting the Ku Klux Klan. Given the history and motives of the KKK, the Court held that a state could require such information of any organization involved in "acts and conduct inimical to personal rights and public welfare."[16] Although the Court's decision specifically noted the KKK's past history as a reason for treating it differently from other groups, attorneys for Alabama would later claim that there was little practical difference in the membership listing requested by New York in this case and what they sought from the NAACP.

A decade later, the justices considered the case of an Oregon man who attended a public meeting and spoke to the assembled crowd about the poor conditions in the local jail.[17] Because the meeting was sponsored by the Communist Party, the speaker, Dirk DeJonge, was convicted of violating Oregon's criminal syndication law and sentenced to seven years imprisonment. The justices unanimously reversed his conviction in *DeJonge v. Oregon* (1937). In striking down the law, they also set forth bold principles of speech, assembly, and association that were especially applicable to ideas and groups that fell outside the mainstream. "The greater the importance of safeguarding the community from incitements to the overthrow of our institutions by force and violence," the Court declared, "the more imperative is the need to preserve inviolate the constitutional rights of free speech, free press and free assembly in order to maintain the opportunity for free political discussion."[18] The Court went on to underscore: "Therein lies the security of the Republic, the very foundation of constitutional government."[19] Subsequent Court rulings, however, failed to live up to this lofty challenge in large measure because of the fears of Communism resonating throughout America immediately after World War II.

The 1950s saw the Court warm to the associational claims of organizations like the NAACP, while rejecting the same arguments when made by the Communist Party. For example, the Court upheld a Maryland law forbidding candidates for public office from being placed on the ballot unless they took an oath that they were not affiliated with anyone who sought to "overthrow the government by force or violence."[20] Schools received the Court's blessing to refuse to hire teachers who were members of "subversive groups," as did cities, which were allowed to fire public employees who refused to disclose current or past membership in Communist organizations.[21]

However, as the makeup of the Court shifted, the justices began to acknowledge that association with or even membership in a subversive group could be a protected right, particularly if the stated purpose of that organization—to overthrow the government—remained in the realm of ideas, advocacy, and discussion. Against the withering influence of McCarthyism, for example, the Court rebuked Congress in 1957 for summoning private individuals to testify publicly about their lives and associational relationships and thereby engage "in a program of exposure for the sake of exposure."[22] Chief Justice Earl Warren declared, "the mere summoning of a witness and compelling him to testify, against his will, about his beliefs, expressions or associations is a measure of governmental interference. And when those forced revelations concern matters that are unorthodox, unpopular, or even hateful to the general public, the reaction in the life of the witness may be disastrous."[23]

In a conclusion that could have obviously applied to the fourteen thousand Alabamians on the NAACP's membership listing sought by Alabama officials, Warren added, "Nor does the witness alone suffer the consequences. Those who are identified by witnesses, and thereby placed in the same glare of publicity, are equally subject to public stigma, scorn and obloquy."[24]

THE LITIGATION

The NAACP immediately appealed the huge fine and contempt order to the Alabama Supreme Court, commencing a decade of litigation to be able to operate again within the state. When NAACP attorneys initially appealed to the Alabama Supreme Court, the judges rebuffed them for not filing for a writ of certiorari, which would permit that court to review the matter in its entirety. Yet, when the organization subsequently petitioned for certiorari, the court chastised it for not seeking a writ of mandamus. Certiorari, the court held, would be appropriate if the entire case was before it to review, but it was not. Only the contempt order and fine were currently before the court, and since the NAACP was opposed to those, the judges noted, it should have sought mandamus review of those actions. That the NAACP's own experienced attorneys had committed these procedural irregularities caused the state court to add, rather condescendingly, "Where a party to a cause elects not to avail of such remedies [such as the writ of mandamus], . . . he necessarily assumes the consequences."[25]

In its brief opinion on the merits, the state court went on to utterly reject the NAACP's concerns about making public its membership list and characterized the NAACP's failure to produce the listing instead as a "brazen defiance of the [lower court's] order."[26] The Alabama Supreme Court also refused to second-guess the high fine levied by Judge Jones, holding that, under the circumstances, $100,000 was not excessive. Indeed, as the NAACP had refused Jones's offer to rescind the original $10,000 fine by failing to produce the membership list and had yet to abide by his order even after the penalty increased tenfold, apparently "neither fine," the Alabama Supreme Court mused, "was severe enough."[27]

In short, in the opinion of the Alabama Supreme Court, the NAACP had no one to blame for the denial of its appeal except itself for not complying with Judge Jones's order and for not following the proper filing procedure. The real consequence of the state court's decision, however, was not just the upholding of the fine or the requirement that the NAACP must still produce its membership list. So long as the organization was still in contempt, Jones refused to schedule a hearing on his original restraining order. That meant the NAACP was still forbidden from conducting any activities within the state. By the time the Alabama Supreme Court rejected the NAACP's second appeal, the "temporary" injunction against the organization was more than six months old.

Attorneys for the NAACP then appealed to the United States Supreme Court, which scheduled oral arguments on the matter for January 1958. Robert Carter, general counsel for the NAACP, argued on behalf of the organization, while Assistant Attorney General Edmon L. Rinehart represented the state. Amid aggressive questioning from the justices, Carter stressed three points: First, as a procedural matter, he argued that the Alabama Supreme Court could have reviewed the contempt charge and fine regardless of whether brought by certiorari or mandamus, as it had previously considered cases that had been brought up under the wrong proceeding.

Second, the order demanding the NAACP's membership list was not required by the Alabama law regulating out-of-state corporations. That law asked for a copy of an organization's charter, an address for operations within the state, and a listing of officers. In addition, between 1918 and 1956, Alabama officials had never once requested any of that information from the NAACP. It was clear to Carter that it was only the burgeoning civil rights movement and the events of the previous several months that had spurred the state to take the action that it did. He contended further that in an increasingly tense racial environment, the state's demand for the names of the fourteen thousand members of the NAACP in Alabama was a violation of the First Amendment that could do real harm to the people on that list if they were publicly identified.

Third, Carter argued that the state's actions had placed the NAACP in an impossible position: either reveal its membership as a condition for conducting further business in Alabama with all of the anticipated consequences of public exposure or continue to disobey the production order, be held in contempt, and be denied the ability to operate within the state. Either choice would essentially end support for the organization inside Alabama. The state's actions, as Justice Felix Frankfurter observed at oral arguments, had essentially given the NAACP "a death sentence *pro tem*."[28]

For the state, Edmon Rinehart strenuously objected to that characterization, arguing that the NAACP had put itself into that position by failing to follow the proper procedure necessary to have the contempt order reviewed. Under repeated questioning from the justices, however, Rinehart acknowledged that the Alabama Supreme Court had, in fact, previously taken up cases for full consideration brought up under the wrong proceeding.

With just a few minutes left of his allotted time, Rinehart began to argue that Alabama possessed the authority to prevent out-of-state businesses from conducting any activities if they had not properly registered. When Justice Hugo Black asked him if Alabama had ever before ousted any group that had not fully complied with the law's registration and filing requirements, Rinehart reluctantly admitted that it had not.

Justice Frankfurter then asked if organizations like the NAACP had standing to sue on behalf of their members whose constitutional rights had been violated. Rinehart responded by saying a corporation lacked standing in such instances. Frankfurter pressed, even when its members "don't step forward . . . because they are potentially in a damageable condition if they do make disclosure?"[29] "Damageable by who," Rinehart responded, "is an important question."[30]

He assured the Court that the state would do nothing to pressure individuals. The pressure, Frankfurter replied, was the state's ability to compel disclosure. Might that not affect individuals in a negative way, he wondered. Rinehart airily responded, "I don't believe that there's anything in the law that says that the mere fact that a person may become unpopular as a result of a disclosure gives him a constitutional right to secrecy."[31] "That isn't the implication of my question," Frankfurter retorted. "Is it conceivable that an individual might . . . say 'If I make a disclosure that I am a member of the NAACP, I'll lose my business.' Is that an inconceivable hypothesis?"[32] Rinehart could only respond that the entire matter was speculation before it was time to conclude his argument.

The following June, the Court issued its unanimous ruling in the matter.

THE DECISION

NAACP v. Alabama (9–0)
357 U.S. 449 (1958)

JUSTICE HARLAN delivered the opinion of the Court.

We review from the standpoint of its validity under the Federal Constitution a judgment of civil contempt entered against petitioner, the National

Association for the Advancement of Colored People, in the courts of Alabama. The question presented is whether Alabama, consistently with the Due Process Clause of the Fourteenth Amendment, can compel petitioner to reveal to the State's Attorney General the names and addresses of all its Alabama members and agents, without regard to their positions or functions in the Association. The judgment of contempt was based upon petitioner's refusal to comply fully with a court order requiring in part the production of membership lists. Petitioner's claim is that the order, in the circumstances shown by this record, violated rights assured to petitioner and its members under the Constitution.

Alabama has a statute similar to those of many other States which requires a foreign corporation, except as exempted, to qualify before doing business by filing its corporate charter with the Secretary of State and designating a place of business and an agent to receive service of process. The statute imposes a fine on a corporation transacting intrastate business before qualifying and provides for criminal prosecution of officers of such a corporation. The [NAACP] is a nonprofit membership corporation organized under the laws of New York. Its purposes, fostered on a nationwide basis, are those indicated by its name, and it operates through chartered affiliates which are independent unincorporated associations. . . . [It] has never complied with [Alabama's] qualification statute, from which it considered itself exempt.

In 1956 the Attorney General of Alabama brought an equity suit in the State Circuit Court, Montgomery County, to enjoin the Association from conducting further activities within, and to oust it from, the State. . . .

Petitioner demurred to the allegations of the bill and moved to dissolve the restraining order. It contended that its activities did not subject it to the qualification requirements of the statute and that in any event what the State sought to accomplish by its suit would violate rights to freedom of speech and assembly guaranteed under the Fourteenth Amendment to the Constitution of the United States. Before the date set for a hearing on this motion, the State moved for the production of a large number of the Association's records and papers, including bank statements, leases, deeds, and records containing the names and addresses of all Alabama "members" and "agents" of the Association. It alleged that all such documents were necessary for adequate preparation for the hearing, in view of petitioner's denial of the conduct of intrastate business within the meaning of the qualification statute. Over petitioner's objections, the court ordered the production of a substantial part of the requested records, including the membership lists. . . .

Thereafter petitioner . . . produced substantially all the data called for by the production order except its membership lists, as to which it contended that Alabama could not constitutionally compel disclosure. . . . [T]he Circuit Court made a further order adjudging petitioner in continuing contempt and increas[ed] the fine already imposed to $100,000. . . .

We thus reach petitioner's claim that the production order in the state litigation trespasses upon fundamental freedoms protected by the Due Process Clause of the Fourteenth Amendment. Petitioner argues that in view of the facts and circumstances shown in the record, the effect of compelled disclosure of the membership lists will be to abridge the rights of its rank-and-file members to engage in lawful association in support of their common beliefs. It contends that governmental action which, although not directly suppressing association, nevertheless carries this consequence, can be justified only upon some overriding valid interest of the State.

Effective advocacy of both public and private points of view, particularly controversial ones, is undeniably enhanced by group association, as this Court has more than once recognized by remarking upon the close nexus between the freedoms of speech and assembly. It is beyond debate that freedom to engage in association for the advancement of beliefs and ideas is an inseparable aspect of the "liberty" assured by the Due Process Clause of the Fourteenth Amendment, which embraces freedom of speech. Of course, it is immaterial whether the beliefs sought to be advanced by association pertain to political, economic, religious or cultural matters, and state action which may have the effect of curtailing the freedom to associate is subject to the closest scrutiny.

The fact that Alabama, so far as is relevant to the validity of the contempt judgment presently under review, has taken no direct action, to restrict the right of petitioner's members to associate freely, does not end inquiry into the effect of the production order. In the domain of these indispensable liberties, whether of speech, press, or association, the decisions of this Court recognize that abridgement of such rights, even though unintended, may inevitably follow from varied forms of governmental action. . . .

It is hardly a novel perception that compelled disclosure of affiliation with groups engaged in advocacy may constitute as effective a restraint on freedom of association as the forms of governmental action in [previous cases] were thought likely to produce upon the particular constitutional rights there involved. This Court has recognized the vital relationship between freedom to associate and privacy in one's associations. . . . Inviolability of privacy in group association may in many circumstances be indispensable to preservation of freedom of association, particularly where a group espouses dissident beliefs.

We think that the production order, in the respects here drawn in question, must be regarded as entailing the likelihood of a substantial restraint upon the exercise by petitioner's members of their right to freedom of association. Petitioner has made an uncontroverted showing that on past occasions revelation of the identity of its rank-and-file members has exposed these members to economic reprisal, loss of employment, threat of physical coercion, and other manifestations of public hostility. Under these circumstances, we think it apparent that compelled disclosure of petitioner's Alabama membership is likely to affect adversely the ability of petitioner and its members to pursue their collective effort to foster beliefs which they admittedly have the right to advocate, in that it may induce members to withdraw from the Association and dissuade others from joining it because of fear of exposure of their beliefs shown through their associations and of the consequences of this exposure.

It is not sufficient to answer, as the State does here, that whatever repressive effect compulsory disclosure of names of petitioner's members may have upon participation by Alabama citizens in petitioner's activities follows not from state action but from private community pressures. The crucial factor is the interplay of governmental and private action, for it is only after the initial exertion of state power represented by the production order that private action takes hold.

We turn to the final question whether Alabama has demonstrated an interest in obtaining the disclosures it seeks from petitioner which is sufficient to justify the deterrent effect which we have concluded these disclosures may well have on the free exercise by petitioner's members of their constitutionally protected right of association. . . .

It is important to bear in mind that petitioner asserts no right to absolute immunity from state investigation, and no right to disregard Alabama's laws. As shown by its substantial compliance with the production order, petitioner does not deny Alabama's right to obtain from it such information as the State desires concerning the purposes of the Association and its activities within the State. Petitioner has not objected to divulging the identity of its members who are employed by or hold official positions with it. It has urged the rights solely of its ordinary rank-and-file members. . . .

Whether there was "justification" in this instance turns solely on the substantiality of Alabama's interest in obtaining the membership lists. During the course of a hearing before the Alabama Circuit Court on a motion of petitioner to set aside the production order, the State Attorney General presented at length, under examination by petitioner, the State's reason for requesting the membership lists. The exclusive purpose was to determine whether petitioner was conducting intrastate business in violation of the Alabama foreign corporation registration statute, and the membership lists were expected to help resolve this question. The issues in the litigation commenced by Alabama by its bill in equity were whether the character of petitioner and its activities in Alabama had been such as to make petitioner subject to the registration statute, and whether the extent of petitioner's activities without qualifying suggested its permanent ouster from the State. Without intimating the slightest view upon the merits of these issues, we are unable to perceive that the disclosure of the names of petitioner's rank-and-file members has a substantial bearing on either of them. As matters stand in the state court, petitioner (1) has admitted its presence and conduct of activities in Alabama since 1918; (2) has offered to comply in all respects with the state qualification statute, although preserving its contention that the statute does not apply to it; and (3) has apparently complied satisfactorily with the production order, except for the membership lists, by furnishing the Attorney General with varied business records, its charter and statement of purposes, the names of all of its directors and officers, and with the total number of its Alabama members and the amount of their dues. These last items would not on this record appear subject to constitutional challenge and have been furnished, but whatever interest the State may have in obtaining names of ordinary members has not been shown to be sufficient to overcome petitioner's constitutional objections to the production order.

From what has already been said, we think it apparent that *People of State of New York ex rel. Bryant v. Zimmerman* [1928], cannot be relied on in support of the State's position, for that case involved markedly different considerations in terms of the interest of the State in obtaining disclosure. There, this Court upheld as applied to a member of a local chapter of the Ku Klux Klan, a New York statute requiring any unincorporated association which demanded an oath as a condition to membership to file with state officials copies of its "constitution, by-laws, rules, regulations and oath of membership, together with a roster of its membership and a list of its officers for the current year." In its opinion, the Court took care to emphasize the nature of the organization which New York sought to regulate. The decision was based on the particular character of the Klan's activities, involving acts of unlawful intimidation and violence, which the Court assumed was before the state legislature when it enacted the statute, and of which the Court itself took judicial notice. Furthermore, the situation before us is significantly different from that in *Bryant*, because the organization there had made no effort to comply with any of the requirements of New York's statute but rather had refused to furnish the State with any information as to its local activities.

> We hold that the immunity from state scrutiny of membership lists which the Association claims on behalf of its members is here so related to the right of the members to pursue their lawful private interests privately and to associate freely with others in so doing as to come within the protection of the Fourteenth Amendment. And we conclude that Alabama has fallen short of showing a controlling justification for the deterrent effect on the free enjoyment of the right to associate which disclosure of membership lists is likely to have. Accordingly, the judgment of civil contempt and the $100,000 fine which resulted from petitioner's refusal to comply with the production order in this respect must fall. . . .
>
> For the reasons stated, the judgment of the Supreme Court of Alabama must be reversed and the case remanded for proceedings not inconsistent with this opinion.

THE AFTERMATH AND SIGNIFICANCE OF *NAACP V. ALABAMA*

The Court's decision in favor of the NAACP did not end the dispute. Indeed, the ruling only dealt with Judge Jones's order requiring the NAACP's membership records and the subsequent fine he imposed on the organization. His earlier injunction forbidding the NAACP from operating in Alabama had not come before the Supreme Court and thus remained in place until a trial on the merits was scheduled.

Upon receiving the case on remand, the Alabama Supreme Court took the unusual step of mocking its brethren in Washington for presuming "that the interpretation by this Court of its own procedural rules [relative to the petitions for certiorari and mandamus] was erroneous."[33] It went on to assert that the US Supreme Court's opinion rested on the "mistaken premise" that the NAACP had produced all of the documentation required by the state with the exception of the membership listing.[34] Because the organization had yet to provide Judge Jones with all of the other material he requested, the Alabama Supreme Court held that the NAACP was still in contempt and refused to order Jones to hold a hearing on his initial restraining order.

Four months later, in June 1959, the Supreme Court responded by reminding the lower court that the only issue raised by either the NAACP or the state of Alabama in the briefs and oral arguments for *NAACP v. Alabama* was the membership listing. For Attorney General Patterson and the Alabama Supreme Court, the justices wrote, the argument that material other than the membership listings was needed "comes too late. The State is bound by its previously taken position, namely, that decision of the sole question regarding the membership lists is dispositive of the whole case."[35]

The Court went on to suggest that this time the Alabama Supreme Court "not fail to proceed promptly with the disposition of the matters left open under" its previous *NAACP v. Alabama* ruling.[36]

Despite that directive, the state court took more than a year to respond, again noting its "disagree[ment] with the conclusions reached by the Federal Supreme Court," but reluctantly agreed to send the case back to the circuit court.[37] However, its refusal to attend to the formalities needed to actually remand the case back to Judge Jones caused the NAACP to question the state court about the delay. To the organization's inquiries about the status of its case, the clerk of the Alabama Supreme Court simply replied that the "case will receive attention as soon as practicable, commensurate with the rest of the important business of the court."[38]

Frustrated with its attempts to make any progress to gain a hearing on Judge Jones's original order, the NAACP turned to the federal courts in June 1960. However, both the US District Court and the US Court of Appeals for the Fifth Circuit ruled that it was inappropriate for the federal courts to intervene until the state had properly adjudicated the matter. For a third time, the NAACP took the matter to the US. Supreme Court, which handed down a sternly worded one-paragraph decision in October 1961. It directed the US District Court in Montgomery to proceed to trial on the restraining order against the NAACP by January 2, 1962, if the state courts had not held a hearing on the matter by that time.

In December 1961, Judge Jones finally held a hearing on the temporary injunction requested by the state of Alabama in the summer of 1956. He concluded that the NAACP had violated state law by operating within the state without the proper permits and registration fees and that its activities were harmful to the state. He thereby lifted the temporary restraining order and imposed a permanent ban on the NAACP from ever again operating within the state. The Alabama Supreme Court affirmed his decision in February 1963 and, once again, the NAACP appealed to the United States Supreme Court.

On June 1, 1964, exactly eight years from the day Attorney General Patterson requested the injunction against the organization, the Supreme Court upheld the right of the NAACP to operate within the state of Alabama. Writing for a unanimous Court, Justice John Marshall Harlan II was clearly perturbed at the state's repeated delay in implementing the Court's previous rulings on the matter. In this fourth and final review of the NAACP's right to function in Alabama, Harlan reiterated what the case was really all about, just as he had in his original *NAACP v. Alabama* decision for the Court: "This case, in truth, involves not the privilege of a corporation to do business in a State, but rather the freedom of individuals to associate for the collective advocacy of ideas."[39] He went on to specify that the Alabama Supreme Court should vacate the permanent restraining order and do all that was necessary to permit the NAACP to fully function in the state. "Should we be mistaken in our belief that the Supreme Court of Alabama will promptly implement this [decision]," he added, "leave is given the [NAACP] to apply to this Court for further appropriate relief."[40] With that commission to Alabama and the promise of preferred assistance to the NAACP should the state again neglect its duty, the Supreme Court finally ended the dispute.

The eight-year battle between the attorney general and the NAACP had a tremendous impact in Alabama and elsewhere. Several other states copied Patterson's strategy, and the group saw its membership and donations drop significantly as people grew fearful that their support for the NAACP would be made public. Just a year after Judge Jones granted the temporary injunction and ordered them to produce the membership list, NAACP officials in New York admitted that Alabama "had been more successful than any other Southern state in fighting" the organization.[41] With the Supreme Court's final ruling on the matter in 1964, the NAACP was able to resume its efforts to win full recognition of the civil rights and liberties of African Americans.

Since the Court's broad pronouncement in *NAACP v. Alabama*, however, two developments, in particular, have contributed to the scaling back of both the protection for the freedom of association and public perceptions about its importance. The first of these was the Court's 1984 ruling in *Roberts v. United States Jaycees*, in which the justices unanimously upheld a Minnesota antidiscrimination law against the US Jaycees, whose organization did not admit women as regular members.[42] To the Jaycees' claim that the freedom of association protected its right to an all-male membership, the Court responded by recognizing a distinction among three types of associations. It declared "intimate" associations (such as those involving family relationships) to be the most protected against government regulation. "Commercial or business" associations, on the other hand, lacked such protection, which permitted the government to scrutinize their associational relationships to ensure that they did not discriminate in the hiring, firing, and overall treatment of their employees.

Between these two extremes, the Court saw the Jaycees as an example of the third type: an "expressive" association or a group of individuals combined to engage in speech or other First Amendment protected activities.A compelling government interest, the Court ruled, may justify regulation of an expressive association like the Jaycees, but such factors as an organization's size, purpose, policies, selectivity, and congeniality (or the lack thereof) may protect it against government encroachment. In *Roberts*, the Court was unable to understand how the Jaycees' expression would be unduly infringed on by the addition of female members. Furthermore, the Court could find no factors in favor of protecting the Jaycees' male membership that would sufficiently outweigh Minnesota's interest in ending discrimination against women.

Prioritizing gender neutrality over associational rights was likewise stressed at Harvard University. In March 2018 and after nearly two years of deliberation, Harvard banned its students from participating in all single-gender fraternities, sororities, and clubs. Those who choose to join such organizations (which had been moved off campus since the mid-1980s) are prohibited from serving in leadership posts for on-campus organizations or as captains of varsity athletic teams, and from applying for certain prestigious scholarships.[43] Because Harvard is a private institution, its students have no First Amendment protection against university policies. Given its prestige, however, it is likely that some public colleges and universities will follow Harvard's example. Such policies, however, naturally raise the same question dealt with in *NAACP v. Alabama*: presuming that students will not volunteer their association with a single-gender organization, will Harvard or other universities seek the membership lists of fraternities and sororities in order to identify those against whom these sanctions shall be brought?

The War on Terror has also caused Americans to question the value of the freedom of association. Four months after the attacks of September 11, 2001, a Gallup poll reported that 47 percent of Americans agreed that the government should take all steps necessary to prevent additional acts of terrorism even if such actions violated their own basic rights and liberties.[44] Since that time, the Patriot Act and other federal legislation coupled with government monitoring of organizations' and citizens' communications to identify and track terrorist activity has increased Americans' appreciation for the First Amendment's protections of speech and association. Yet, a 2016 Gallup poll revealed that nearly a third of Americans would still give up their civil rights and liberties in order to be safe.[45]

Fears of terrorism in the twenty-first century are reminiscent of the Red Scare era of the 1950s, but with one major difference. In the earlier period, governmental institutions and officials worked to publicly expose those with suspected ties to Communism as well as their fellow sympathizers. In the modern era, the vast expansion of governmental surveillance programs authorized by Congress or under the authority of executive branch officials is far less public. Significant technological advances make it nearly impossible for average Americans to know whether they and their associational relationships are under governmental scrutiny. Thus, unlike the McCarthy era, efforts to identify and track terrorists, including government excesses that affect fundamental rights, will rarely become public knowledge. Yet, as the 2016 Gallup poll noted, for many Americans the trade-off of civil liberties for security may be worth it. Surprisingly, even the Supreme Court has said as much.

Just five months after announcing its decision in *NAACP v. Alabama*, a bare majority of the Court upheld Professor Lloyd Barenblatt's contempt of Congress conviction for refusing to answer questions put to him by the House Un-American Activities Committee about his and others' affiliation with the Communist Party.[46] The Court explained that individual rights, including freedom of speech and freedom of association, are not absolute, and that sometimes "the balance between the individual and the governmental interests . . . at stake must be struck in favor of the latter."[47]

Justice Hugo Black issued a powerful dissent, well known for both the principles it affirmed as well as for, it has been argued, its hint of autobiography. The majority opinion, he declared, "balances the right of the Government to preserve itself, against Barenblatt's right to refrain from revealing Communist affiliations. Such a balance, however, mistakes the factors to be weighed."[48] The real interest at stake, he argued, was the right "of the people as a whole in being able to join organizations, advocate causes and make political 'mistakes' without later being subjected to governmental penalties for having dared to think for themselves. It is this right, the right to err politically, which keeps us strong as a Nation."[49]

Justice Black knew something about "mistakes," having joined the Ku Klux Klan in Birmingham in 1923. He resigned from the group just before running for the United States Senate in 1926, but he acknowledged its support to his victory. His association with the KKK threatened to derail his nomination to the Supreme Court, but his subsequent rulings and well-deserved title as the great civil libertarian of the Supreme Court clearly demonstrated that he had personally experienced the conversion that he characterized in *Barenblatt v. United States*. "[N]o number of laws against communism," Black declared (and he might have said the KKK in his own case), "can have as much effect as the personal conviction which comes from having heard its arguments and rejected them, or from having once accepted its tenets and later recognized their worthlessness."[50]

Black's dissent in *Barenblatt* emphasizes the freedom that people enjoy in exercising their right to associate as well as when they disassociate from a group on realizing that they made a mistake. It then contrasts that freedom with the restrictions that accompany government decisions about the organizations with which its citizens may be allowed to associate and the punishments that are inflicted on those who choose otherwise.

Disfavored groups and the issues surrounding them have changed significantly since Alabama first sought the NAACP's membership list more than six decades ago. The central issue of association as a fundamental liberty, however, has not. In words that Tocqueville might have written, constitutional scholar David Fellman declared shortly after the Court's decision in *NAACP v. Alabama* that "the right of association is central to any serious conception of constitutional democracy. . . . The individual cannot function politically with any measure of effectiveness unless he is free to associate with others without hindrance."[51] He concluded, "[T]he right of association is the rule, and at best restraints upon it are only exceptions, each of which requires specific and convincing justification."[52]

3

HEED THEIR RISING VOICES

The Actual Malice Test and *New York Times v. Sullivan* (1964)

On May 17, 1954, the Supreme Court handed down its decision in *Brown v. Board of Education of Topeka.*[1] While it focused specifically on segregated public schools, that landmark ruling also provided important momentum to the civil rights movement. Over the next six years, the *New York Times* published thousands of articles and editorials about civil rights.[2] In a March 19, 1960, editorial, one that was scarcely different from its previous statements on civil rights, the *Times* called on Congress to give meaning to the Fifteenth Amendment by adopting legislation that would protect the voting rights of African Americans. This brief, five-paragraph editorial concluded by declaring, "The growing movement of peaceful mass demonstrations by Negroes is something new in the South, something understandable and also something ominous. Let Congress heed their rising voices, for they will be heard."[3] The *New York Times* editorial board could not have imagined the lasting significance of that final sentence.

Ten days later, "Heed Their Rising Voices" appeared in large bold letters at the top of a *New York Times* full-page ad that highlighted the ongoing challenges facing civil rights protestors in the South. The ad only ran for one day but would result in several lawsuits, a huge libel award in Alabama against the newspaper, and, eventually, a landmark First Amendment ruling by the Supreme Court. The justices' decision in *New York Times v. Sullivan,* however, was not only a victory for the newspaper but also for all Americans. It constitutionalized the ability to engage in open and robust public debate, protecting Americans' right to criticize their government leaders without fear of reprisals. That right has been rarely recognized throughout world history and is not even present in all countries today, but it is the hallmark of a truly free society.

THE STORY

On Tuesday, March 29, 1960, the *New York Times* ran a full-page ad titled "Heed Their Rising Voices." Placed by a New York advertising firm on behalf of a group that called itself the "Committee to Defend Martin Luther

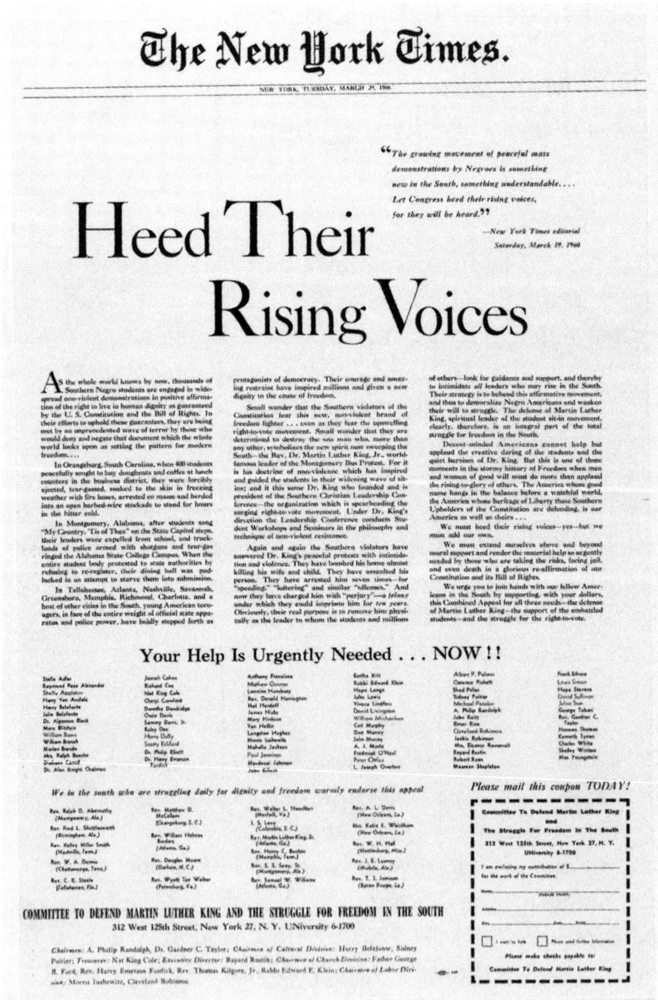

The New York Times.

"*The growing movement of peaceful mass demonstrations by Negroes is something new in the South, something understandable.... Let Congress heed their rising voices, for they will be heard.*"

—*New York Times editorial Saturday, March 19, 1960*

Heed Their Rising Voices

Your Help Is Urgently Needed . . . NOW!!

Please mail this coupon TODAY!

COMMITTEE TO DEFEND MARTIN LUTHER KING AND THE STRUGGLE FOR FREEDOM IN THE SOUTH

312 West 125th Street, New York 27, N. Y. UNiversity 6-1700

Figure 3. The "Heed Their Rising Voices" advertisement, printed in the *New York Times* on March 29, 1960.

King and the Struggle for Freedom in the South," the purpose of the ad was to raise funds for the legal defense of Martin Luther King Jr., who had been charged with perjury and tax evasion in Alabama.

The ad spoke of young African Americans throughout the South who repeatedly met segregation policies and police power with courage and peaceful restraint. It described how black students seeking service at whites-only lunch counters in Orangeburg, South Carolina, had been subjected to tear gas, fire hoses, and arrest. The ad also informed readers of a tense situation in Montgomery in which Alabama State students were expelled from school after singing "My Country, 'Tis of Thee" on the steps of the state capitol. Police were subsequently summoned and, armed with guns and tear gas, they surrounded the entire Alabama State campus. Other state authorities authorized padlocking the dining hall to further pressure the students to stand down.

The ad coupled these events with brief references to the bombing of King's home, which nearly killed his wife and children, his seven arrests, and the perjury charge he then faced that could earn him a ten year prison sentence. Readers were encouraged to commit more than just their hearts and voices to the cause of civil rights. The ad pled for donations, and if the powerful imagery of the advertisement alone was not enough to get people to contribute, the names of more than sixty celebrities were added as signatories. These included such famous African Americans as Nat King Cole, Dorothy Dandridge, Sammy Davis Jr., Sidney Poitier, and Jackie Robinson, as well as white notables like Marlon Brando, Harry Emerson Fosdick, Eleanor Roosevelt, and Frank Sinatra. Finally, twenty African American clergymen who were active in the civil rights movement in the South added their names in support.

The problem with this powerful ad (perhaps the most well-known advertisement in the history of constitutional law), was that it was not accurate. Not only was its description of some events wrong, but the ad was also not authorized to include most of the eighty names listed therein. It was basically political advertising designed to influence public opinion and secure donations, and cost the ad's organizers $4,500 to place in the *New York Times*. Despite its compelling message, a one-day run of a single advertisement (buried deep on page 25) in even a powerful newspaper like the *Times* could hardly have been expected to generate much attention. The newspaper's weekday circulation was approximately 650,000 copies, with most distributed in the Northeast. Fewer than four hundred copies of the paper's weekday issue came to Alabama, and only thirty-five to Montgomery County.[4] One of those copies, however, almost a week after its original issue, found its way into the hands of Merton Roland "Rod" Nachman Jr.

An Alabama native who received both his undergraduate and law degrees from Harvard, Nachman was just thirty-seven years old in 1960 and had already served as assistant state attorney general for five years, winning his first case before the United States Supreme Court during that time. He was also the best libel lawyer in the state.[5] Perusing the "Heed Their Rising Voices" ad, he immediately recognized that several of the statements, as he put it later, "were absolutely false and some of the [other] charges were grossly exaggerated."[6] For example, the ad claimed that the Alabama State students were expelled from school for singing "My Country, 'Tis of Thee" on the steps of the state capitol. In truth, the students had actually sung the national anthem, and while nine students were subsequently expelled, it had nothing to do with the rally at the capitol. Those students faced expulsion because they had previously conducted a lunch counter protest at the Montgomery County Courthouse grill.

The ad went on to claim that "the entire student body protested [the expulsions] to state authorities by refusing to re-register." Again, that was not true. While many students had protested the dismissal of their peers by boycotting classes for a single day, all had re-registered. The ad further claimed that the "dining hall was padlocked in an attempt to starve [the students] into submission." That simply did not happen.[7] While some young people had apparently been turned away from the dining hall, it was because they lacked the required meal ticket for entrance per university policy. There were other exaggerations and inaccuracies that Nachman believed reflected poorly on local officials. Fully aware of Alabama libel law, Nachman contacted L. B. (Lester Bruce) Sullivan, the police commissioner for Montgomery.

At the time, in Alabama and most other states, libel was still subject to the English common law standard of strict liability. This meant simply that those who published something deemed hurtful to another's reputation were liable for civil damages unless they could demonstrate the truthfulness of every word in dispute. The one initiating the action only had to demonstrate that the libel had brought him or her into public disregard or contempt. Because the ad's description of events was not accurate and because its contents reflected poorly on Montgomery Police and, by extension, the official who supervised them, Nachman had every reason to believe that Sullivan would prevail in a libel suit.

Sullivan was upset by the ad and certain that it had blemished his name and character. During Governor Gordon Persons's administration (1951–55), Sullivan had served as Alabama director of public safety, which oversaw the Alabama State Police. In 1954, and in his capacity as the state's chief law enforcement officer, he worked closely with then attorney general John Patterson and circuit judge Walter B. Jones to investigate, charge, and prosecute those responsible for the public corruption in Phenix City that had led to the assassination of Patterson's father there. The successful effort to clean up criminal activity in Phenix City brought Sullivan national attention, including invitations to consult and lecture on police and public safety initiatives throughout the country. He believed that his reputation, in Alabama and elsewhere, was threatened by the way the ad described actions of the police under his supervision.

For example, after the singing that took place on the steps of the state capitol, the ad declared, "truckloads of police armed with shotguns and tear-gas ringed the Alabama State College Campus." That was completely false. Large numbers of Montgomery City Police had previously been deployed to the school, but never in such numbers as to ring the campus and not at all in the wake of the singing demonstration at the capitol. With regard to Martin Luther King, his home had indeed been bombed, but contrary to what the ad stated, his family was not present at the time. And, unlike the Alabama State student demonstrations, the bombing had occurred before Sullivan even became police commissioner. Similarly, while the ad decried King's seven arrests for speeding, loitering, and other things, he had actually only been arrested four times, only one of which had occurred while Sullivan was in office.

Although not named anywhere in the ad, L. B. Sullivan believed he had been libeled. As commissioner, he was responsible for the Montgomery Police officers whose actions on the Alabama State campus were falsely described. When the ad denounced "the Southern violators [who] answered Dr. King's peaceful protests with intimidation and violence," to whom else could it be referring, Sullivan questioned, than to him and the police he supervised? As Sullivan's lawyers later put it to the Supreme Court, "The ordinary reader of this ad was bound to draw the plain meaning that such shocking conditions were the responsibility of the person charged with the administration of the Montgomery Police Department."[8]

On April 8, Sullivan contacted the *New York Times* demanding a retraction. Newspaper personnel attempted to accommodate him, even acknowledging that there were some discrepancies and inaccuracies in the ad. However, the paper refused to publish a retraction when Sullivan was unable to explain exactly how the ad reflected on him since he was not named anywhere.[9] On April 19, Sullivan filed a libel suit against the newspaper in Montgomery County Circuit Court, where his friend Judge Walter B. Jones presided. He also filed suit against Alabama clergymen and civil rights leaders Ralph Abernathy, Joseph Lowery, Solomon Seay Sr., and Fred Shuttlesworth, whose names were affixed to the ad. Joining them to the suit against the *Times* was a strategic move by Sullivan's attorneys to help keep the case in Alabama courts where state libel law would prevail.

Sullivan sought $500,000 from the *Times* and the same amount from each of the individual defendants. Believing the ad and other *Times* stories had libeled them as well, other city commissioners in Montgomery and Birmingham subsequently filed similar suits, such that when the trial in Judge Jones's courtroom began in November, the *New York Times* faced seven separate lawsuits and the prospect of paying Alabama politicians nearly $7 million in damages. "The lawsuits represented a threat to the paper's balance sheet," legal historian Kermit Hall later recounted, but "even more important, a chilling of its coverage of the civil rights movement."[10]

Indeed, the strict liability standard enshrined in the libel law of Alabama and many other states at the time essentially required publishers to do one of two things: either vouch for the truthfulness of every single word of everything they published and be prepared to pay significant damages for any errors, or shy away from reporting on controversial topics in order to not cause offense and attract libel action against them. The first would put publishers out of business and the second would undermine the historic role of the press to inform its readers on matters of public concern. Neither are satisfactory outcomes for those who value the role of the press in a free society.

THE CONSTITUTIONAL BACKGROUND

Generations of parents have responded to the hurt feelings of their children by teaching, "Sticks and stones may break your bones, but words can never hurt you." Little boys and girls may have believed that adage, but the history of defamation law demonstrates that adults throughout the ages almost certainly have not. In its broadest sense, defamation is the communication of a false idea that, when shared with a third party, damages another's character. Protecting one's good name, seeking redress against those who would injure it, and punishing those who make false and derogatory statements about others are features of some of the world's earliest laws.

The Code of Ur-Nammu, a series of Mesopotamian laws from 2100 BC and the oldest known legal code in existence today, for example, stipulated that a man who falsely accused a woman of adultery would pay 20 shekels of silver. Four hundred years later, Hammurabi's Code required a man to forfeit his life if he falsely accused another of a capital crime. Mosaic law expressly forbade "bear[ing] false witness against thy neighbor," "curs[ing] the ruler of thy people," and "rais[ing] a false report."[11] Under Solon's laws in early sixth-century Athens, fines were levied against those who defamed others. The Twelve Tables, the foundation of Roman law after 450 BC, dictated that a person found guilty of defaming another should be clubbed to death. The early Anglo-Saxon king Alfred the Great (AD 849–899) affixed punishments proportionate to the offense. Thus, depending on the nature of their defamatory statements, those found guilty might pay for it with their lives, or by having their tongues removed, paying fines, or standing in public with their nose between their fingers while loudly confessing themselves a liar.[12]

These legal codes illustrate that from a very early period defamation had both civil and criminal penalties. Just as it does today, the civil law historically remedied wrongs between individuals by providing for compensation for damages, including those suffered for the loss of one's reputation. In some instances, however, defaming another could also bring about criminal penalties. Criminal law punished (as it still does today) wrongs committed against society, and throughout history, those wrongs included statements deemed injurious to the living or the memory of the dead (because of its tendency to incite friends and family of the departed) or that were considered blasphemous or obscene. Not surprisingly, the harshest punishments were reserved for those who spoke poorly of or criticized their rulers and other public officials.

The law of defamation in England had important consequences for the development of the common law and for its subsequent impact on American courts. English ecclesiastical courts initially oversaw most private defamation claims after the Norman Conquest of 1066. A person found guilty of a false accusation was required to don a white shroud, hold a lighted candle, and then, kneeling before the priest and others, publicly profess his or her lie to God and the assembled body. The injured party, however, only received an apology.

The subsequent development of common law courts removed defamation from religious authorities and increasingly provided for civil remedies. The use of these courts was encouraged as an alternative for resolving disputes between individuals over insulting words and damaged reputations who might otherwise have resorted to violence to settle their differences. The civil courts dealt primarily with verbal defamation and awarded monetary damages provided that the words in question were shared with a third party and that the words were not true. If they were true, even if a person's reputation was harmed, there was no libel, and thus truth became a complete defense in English common law against civil libel claims.

In 1275, Edward I promulgated the *Scandalis Magnatum*, a series of laws in England that punished "devisers of tales . . . whereby discord or occasion of discord or slander may grow between the king and his people or the great men of the realm."[13] Subsequent laws forbade English subjects from spreading "false news and . . . horrible and false lies [about] prelates, dukes, earls, barons, and other noble and great men of the realm."[14] While giving special protection to officeholders and other notable people who could not or would not use the civil law for redress, the larger purpose of these laws was not so much about protecting an officeholder's personal reputation as to criminalize negative comments about his or her official actions. The law categorized such criticism as seditious libel because defaming a government official was seen as an attack on his or her authority, the undermining of which reflected on the integrity of the government and constituted a threat to the peace and welfare of the entire kingdom.

Earlier laws made no distinction between written or spoken defamation, but English authorities established that verbal defamation, which became known as slander, was less serious than defamation in print (what is now known as libel) because slander, while certainly damaging, was also fleeting. Spoken words simply did not have the same lasting impact as something in print. The advent of the printing press in the mid-1400s only underscored this point.

As previously mentioned, criminal libel law in England was less concerned about the reputations of private individuals than preserving social order, respect for authority, and the security of the state. As authorities came to appreciate the consequences of mass-produced and widely distributed written material, they reserved particularly harsh punishments for those convicted of seditious libel for their defamatory statements against and even general criticism about the government and its officers.

The Court of the Star Chamber assumed responsibility for most seditious libel claims in England, sentencing those found guilty to such punishments as branding of the face, loss of one or both ears, removal of the tongue, or cutting off the right hand to prevent further writing—punishments for which the court earned its notorious reputation. It was no wonder that it was reportedly said in the Star Chamber, "Let all men take heed how they complain in words against any Magistrate, for they are Gods."[15] Unlike in the civil courts, truth was no defense in criminal libel cases. If a publication printed something negative about a government official, even if the statements were true, the publisher would be punished. Certain statements could be forbidden outright if they tended to create a breach of the peace, even without naming a particular individual. Criminal libel law thereby came to encompass not only criticism of the government but also blasphemous statements against religion and obscene publications that undermined morality.[16] Early British Americans generally adopted these common law approaches to civil and criminal libel but later modified them with some protections for the freedom of speech and press.[17]

The most notable example of this during the colonial era was the trial of New York newspaper publisher John Peter Zenger in 1735. After his *New York Weekly Journal* published highly critical comments about Governor William Cosby, Zenger was charged with seditious libel. Zenger's attorneys argued that the newspaper statements, as harsh as they might have been, were true and, despite English common law to the contrary, should not be considered libelous. In a major shift in Anglo-American libel law, and in what some historians believe was the first blow for independence from Great Britain, the colonial jury that considered the case agreed. The 1791 ratification of the Bill of Rights and, particularly, the First Amendment's free speech and free press clauses, gave further protection to both the spoken and printed word against the national government. With few exceptions, however, defamation law was generally left to the states, which continued to punish individuals when their statements caused harm to others.

One of the few examples of a national defamation law was the 1798 Sedition Act, which authorized fines of up to $2,000 and two years in prison for anyone convicted of defaming the United States government, either house of Congress, or the president. Passed by an overwhelmingly Federalist Party in Congress and signed by President John Adams, also a Federalist, the Sedition Act forbade anything that a "person shall write, print, utter, or publish" that might bring government leaders into contempt or disrepute, or to excite against them . . . the hatred of the good people of the United States."[18] Nearly two dozen newspaper editors, all supporters of Thomas Jefferson's rival Democratic-Republican Party, were prosecuted under the law.

Not surprisingly, the law proved to be highly controversial and ended up playing a large role in the election of 1800 in which Adams lost his bid for a second term to Jefferson. Most members of the Federalist Party in Congress were defeated as well. The Sedition Act expired the following year (Jefferson pardoned those convicted, and Congress repaid all fines levied under the statute), but it had a lasting impact on American libel law.

Many states followed the national precedent and adopted criminal libel laws of their own. The first libel case to come before the US Supreme Court, for example, involved two newspaper editors in Connecticut who were indicted for criminal libel under a state law after alleging that President

Thomas Jefferson and Congress had bribed Napoleon with $2 million to make a treaty with Spain for Florida. The justices concluded that the federal judiciary lacked jurisdiction because common law matters such as criminal libel were an issue for the states.[19]

Two other lasting influences of the Sedition Act were that it authorized juries, as opposed to judges alone, to determine whether publications were libelous, and it permitted those prosecuted under its authority to use the truth as a defense. These too became features of subsequent state defamation laws. Such laws, incidentally, were hardly uniform. For example, while some states generally embraced the common law notion that truth was a defense in civil defamation claims, others added a requirement that any evidence of the truth be presented along with some indication that good motives and justifiable ends were behind the statements in dispute.

Motives naturally led to questions about malice, a term associated with libel law for generations. State civil libel laws varied tremendously with regard to what malice actually entailed, particularly with regard to public officials. For example, was a publication libelous simply because it got some facts wrong or because the publisher knowingly and purposely disseminated such falsehoods? Could a public official win a libel claim if he could prove that a publisher harbored a deep hatred for him? Was malice evident in sensationalized language or the use of bolder print and larger typeface in newspaper stories dealing with a particular officeholder?

In one of its rare decisions involving libel, the US Supreme Court in 1841 addressed malice in a case involving a series of letters sent to President John Tyler and members of Congress about Robert White, who held a congressional appointment as the collector of customs for Georgetown.[20] The letters complained that White had engaged in a number of inappropriate political activities and demanded that he be removed from office. White was mortified that his good name had been sullied before the president and congressional leaders, and he immediately sued those who had sent the letters. For their part, the letter writers cited British precedent that generally exempted petitions to the government, as the letters technically were, from libel action.

The Court acknowledged that "when any man shall consent to be a candidate for public office . . . , he must be considered as putting his character in issue, so far as it may respect his fitness and qualifications for office."[21] It was thus perfectly understandable that when questions arose about a person's fitness for a government position, people would make their concerns known publicly. However, such questions conferred no right to libel. As the Court observed, "The publication of falsehood and calumny against public officers . . . is an offense dangerous to the people, and deserves punishment, because people may be deceived, and reject their best citizens, to their great injury."[22] In short, the Court recognized that by virtue of their office, public officials will likely be closely scrutinized and heavily criticized. However, that did not mean that those in public office had no recourse against malicious publications. The Court ruled that White's case should have gone before a jury to determine if the contents of the letters at issue could be construed as malice.

Generally adhering to its belief that speech and press were issues for state regulation, the Court took no action against antebellum laws in the South that forbade criticism of slavery and of the state governments that supported it. And even when the national government was involved, the Court did little. For example, when the Lincoln administration was challenged for authorizing the arrest and prosecution of those suspected of "disloyal" speech in areas under martial law, the Court stated that without a specific grant of authority from Congress it was unable to hear such cases.[23]

Fifty years later, during another wartime action, Congress passed the Espionage Act of 1917 to impose fines of up to $10,000 and imprisonment for up to twenty years or both on anyone who dared to "utter, print, write, or publish any disloyal, profane, scurrilous, or abusive language about the form of government of the United States." That law was repealed just three years after its passage and before the Court had a chance to review the legislation, but it is unlikely that the justices would have strayed too far from their historic reluctance to interfere with such laws.

In 1931, however, the Court signaled a change in its approach to libel. In *Near v. Minnesota ex rel. Olson*, the justices confronted Minnesota's "Public Nuisance Abatement Law," which authorized state judges to shut down publications that were considered "malicious, scandalous, or defamatory."[24] A Minnesota judge did just that after Minneapolis officials sought an injunction against Jay Near's weekly newspaper, the *Saturday Press*. Near's inflammatory newspaper routinely disparaged Catholics, Jews, African Americans, and labor unions, but its content was challenged only after it claimed that the mayor of Minneapolis and other public officials had connections to organized crime in the area.

The state court told Near to cease publication of his paper, stipulating that any effort on his part to resume operations would be viewed as contempt of the judge's order, for which he would be punished with a fine of $1,000 or a year in jail. By a 5–4 margin, the Court deemed the law an unconstitutional infringement on the freedom of the press. While the Court recognized that there were some situations that justified censorship of the press, such as forbidding information about troop or warship movements, protecting the reputations of public officials was not one of them. Rather than resorting to fines and imprisonment to restrain publishers who make defamatory statements about them, the Court ruled that public officials could simply turn to state civil libel laws for redress. The Court's opinion in this historic case is best known for its rejection of prior restraints on the press, but *New York Times v. Sullivan* would build on it, in part, by questioning whether massive damage awards in civil cases could just as effectively stifle speech as the criminal penalties addressed in *Near*.

In a brief comment in a 1942 case, the Court pronounced that libel, along with the "lewd and obscene, the profane, . . . and the insulting or 'fighting' words" is not constitutionally protected speech.[25] Ten years later, a Chicago man published and disseminated racist material and was convicted of violating an Illinois law that criminalized the defamation of groups based on their race, color, creed, or religion. By a 5–4 margin, the Court again declared that "libelous utterances [are] not . . . within the area of constitutionally protected speech" in holding that states could enforce some criminal libel laws to preserve peace and good order.[26] Finally, in a subsequent obscenity case in 1957, the author of the *New York Times* decision himself left no doubt as to the constitutional status of libel. Distinguishing it from the sexually explicit materials at issue in that case, Justice William Brennan declared that "the unconditional phrasing of the First Amendment was not intended to protect every utterance. . . . [Libel is] "outside the protection intended for speech and press."[27]

Taken together, these and other related cases essentially cemented the status of libel in America: that it was a matter for state regulation, and that those charged with it could defend themselves by demonstrating the truth of their statements, but the Constitution would not otherwise shield them. In short, by the time the *New York Times* case appeared before the Supreme Court, there was simply no precedent for invoking First Amendment protection for those charged with libel. With this unambiguous legal history before them, Sullivan and his lawyer had every right to be confident in their case. As Rod Nachman told his daughter just prior to the Court's decision in *New York Times v. Sullivan*, "Either I win the case or they will change the law of the land."[28]

THE LITIGATION

Aware that they were likely to lose in Alabama because of its strict liability standard for libel, attorneys for the *New York Times* devoted the summer of

1960 to attempting to get the trial moved to federal court by raising jurisdictional questions. As a New York company, the *Times*, they argued, barely had a presence in Alabama. More than half a million copies of the *New York Times* were published every day, but only 394 copies were sent to Alabama. The newspaper employed no full time staff there and had no direct operations in the state whatsoever.

Judge Jones rejected all of those arguments, however, after determining that the *Times* had periodically deployed reporters to the state, paid local journalists for stories it published, accepted advertisements from the state, and had business arrangements with news dealers and individual subscribers who received the newspapers shipped to Alabama every day. Jones thereby retained jurisdiction of the case and scheduled the trial for the following November.

During those proceedings, attorneys for Sullivan repeatedly emphasized the careless nature of the ad. The *Times* failed to follow its own policies, they argued, for ensuring that the content of advertisements was not misleading. In addition, it had made no effort to contact any of the eighty signatories to verify their endorsement of the ad.[29] Perhaps most significant was the fact that after Sullivan had asked for a retraction, the *Times* commissioned a report from an Alabama journalist about the events at Alabama State, the results of which clearly demonstrated that the ad's claims were false. The *Times*, however, completely ignored the findings of its own report.

During his trial testimony, John Murray, the author of the ad, admitted that its purpose "was to get money and to . . . project [the described events] in the most appealing form from the material we were getting."[30] When asked whether questions were raised about the accuracy of the claims he was provided to use in the ad, he replied, "[I]t did not enter into consideration at all except that we took it for granted that it was accurate. . . . We had every reason to believe it."[31] Such casual treatment of the truth, Sullivan's attorneys argued to the jury, demanded a strong response. "Towards the close of his argument," the *Montgomery Advertiser* reported, "Nachman turned toward the table where the lawyers for the *Times* were seated, pointed his finger and exclaimed: 'When you write about a citizen of this town, you tell the truth, Mr. *New York Times*—the whole truth—and you won't have to face suit in this county!'"[32]

Attorneys for the *Times* admitted that the ad contained some inaccuracies but argued that Sullivan had simply shown no proof of any injury to his reputation. The six witnesses who testified on his behalf had told the court they could understand how someone could come away with a negative impression of Sullivan and the police if they believed the ad. However, all of them expressly testified that they did not believe the ad or think poorly of Sullivan for it. In addition, four admitted they had never even seen the ad until Sullivan's lawyer showed it to them.

As the three-day trial concluded, Judge Jones explained to the jury exactly what Alabama libel law entailed. He told them that Sullivan was only required to demonstrate that a reasonable person who saw the ad would believe it to be defamatory of him. Jones also told the jury that Alabama law viewed the portions of the ad pertaining to Sullivan as "libelous per se," meaning that if the jurors found the material defamatory, they need not also determine whether or not it was false and malicious; it was automatically assumed to be so. He reminded the jury that the law permitted punitive damages, which were designed to punish as well as to deter, without Sullivan having to provide proof of any injury. Truth was a defense for the *Times*, Jones added, but only if the ad was true in all of its particulars. A little more than two hours after receiving these instructions, the jury returned to the courtroom and announced that it had found the *New York Times* guilty of libel. In a very strong message to the newspaper, the jury also awarded L. B. Sullivan the $500,000 he sought in damages. It was the largest civil libel award in Alabama history.

On appeal, the Alabama Supreme Court affirmed the verdict and award while stating that the "First Amendment of the U.S Constitution does not protect libelous publication."[33] The Alabama Supreme Court also strongly rebuked the *Times* for its "irresponsibility in printing the advertisement and scattering it to the four winds."[34] It was obvious, the court declared, that the ad was "'revved up' to make it more 'appealing.'"[35] The newspaper had information from its Alabama reporter that clearly showed that many of the ad's assertions were false, but chose to ignore it. The paper had issued a retraction on Governor Patterson's request, but refused to do so for Sullivan even though both officials thought the ad defamatory and neither had been specifically named. In addition, despite all the evidence to the contrary, an executive with the *Times* still insisted at the trial "that the advertisement was 'substantially correct.'"[36] Given such actions, the state court held, the *Times* should not have been surprised at the verdict or the damage award. "In the face of this cavalier ignoring of the falsity of the advertisement," the court explained, "the jury could not have but been impressed with the bad faith of the *Times* and its maliciousness inferable therefrom."[37] The *Times* immediately appealed to the United States Supreme Court.

Although not a major argument in the lower courts, attorneys for the *Times* stressed in their briefs to the Supreme Court that the case was less about Sullivan's reputation than the First Amendment right to criticize the government and its officials. They claimed that the state court decisions turned traditional defamation doctrine on its head by transforming it "from a method of protecting private reputation to a device for insulating government against attack."[38] That simply was not consistent with the purposes and ideals of the First Amendment. "Speech or publication that is critical of governmental or official action," they added, "may not be repressed upon the ground that it diminishes the reputation of the officers whose conduct it deplores."[39] If the decision and sizeable award stood, the attorneys warned, "the ability and willingness of publications to give voice to grievances against the agencies of governmental power" would be significantly curtailed as publishers silenced their criticism of the government for fear of losing a libel action.[40]

The *Times* was not completely unmindful of the importance of preserving the reputation of public officials but encouraged the Court to consider other alternatives. For example, some states had modified their laws to hold libel of public officials to a different standard than libel of private individuals. Attorneys for the newspaper suggested that rather than applying the strict liability standard with its burden on publishers to prove the truthfulness of every word and all of its chilling consequences for the First Amendment, the Court should consider whether malice was evident. Under this formulation, the *Times* argued, the burden would be on the aggrieved official to demonstrate that there was a reckless disregard for the truth behind a critic's defamatory publications in order to win a libel action. This approach would preserve the First Amendment rights of government critics while still providing an avenue for public officials to hold people responsible for what they published.

For their part, Sullivan's attorneys blasted the *Times*, noting that truth is always a defense against libel claims, and yet the newspaper never argued that the ad's allegations were true. They reminded the justices that even strict liability standards for libel offered other options to the *Times* and every other publication charged with libel: if the newspaper could not demonstrate the truthfulness of the things it printed, it could show its good faith by retracting the material in question, just as it had done when Governor Patterson complained. The *Times*'s refusal to do so for Sullivan underscored his belief that the ad was "a willful, deliberate and reckless attempt to portray . . . rampant, vicious, terroristic and criminal police action in Montgomery, Alabama, to a nationwide public of 650,000."[41]

They also reminded the Court that at trial the author of the ad admitted that his purpose was simply to raise money, and the accuracy of their characterization of the incidents at Alabama State had not been considered at all. In short, Sullivan's lawyers argued, "Truth, accuracy and long-accepted standards of journalism were not criteria for the writing or publication of this advertisement."[42] Further, the sizeable award against the *Times* was admittedly intended to send a message: that the knowing publication of defamatory material would not be tolerated.

As compelling as they believed their arguments to be, Sullivan's attorneys knew that their strongest claim lay in the simple fact that the Court itself had repeatedly and consistently refused to grant any First Amendment protection to libel. On March 9, 1964, the Supreme Court announced its unanimous opinion in the case.

THE DECISION

New York Times v. Sullivan (9–0)
376 U.S. 254 (1964)

JUSTICE BRENNAN delivered the opinion of the Court.

We are required in this case to determine for the first time the extent to which the constitutional protections for speech and press limit a State's power to award damages in a libel action brought by a public official against critics of his official conduct.

Respondent L. B. Sullivan is one of the three elected Commissioners of the City of Montgomery, Alabama. . . . He brought this civil libel action against the four individual petitioners, who are Negroes and Alabama clergymen, and against petitioner the *New York Times* Company, a New York corporation which publishes the *New York Times*, a daily newspaper. A jury in the Circuit Court of Montgomery County awarded him damages of $500,000, the full amount claimed, against all the petitioners, and the Supreme Court of Alabama affirmed.

Respondent's complaint alleged that he had been libeled by statements in a full-page advertisement that was carried in the *New York Times* on March 29, 1960. Entitled "Heed Their Rising Voices," the advertisement began by stating that "As the whole world knows by now, thousands of Southern Negro students are engaged in widespread non-violent demonstrations in positive affirmation of the right to live in human dignity as guaranteed by the U.S. Constitution and the Bill of Rights." It went on to charge that "in their efforts to uphold these guarantees, they are being met by an unprecedented wave of terror by those who would deny and negate that document which the whole world looks upon as setting the pattern for modern freedom. . . ." Succeeding paragraphs purported to illustrate the "wave of terror" by describing certain alleged events. The text concluded with an appeal for funds for three purposes: support of the student movement, "the struggle for the right-to-vote," and the legal defense of Dr. Martin Luther King, Jr., leader of the movement, against a perjury indictment then pending in Montgomery.

The text appeared over the names of 64 persons, many widely known for their activities in public affairs, religion, trade unions, and the performing arts. Below these names, and under a line reading "We in the south who are struggling daily for dignity and freedom warmly endorse this appeal," appeared the names of the four individual petitioners and of 16 other persons, all but two of whom were identified as clergymen in various Southern cities. The advertisement was signed at the bottom of the page by the "Committee to Defend Martin Luther King and the Struggle for Freedom in the South," and the officers of the Committee were listed.

Of the 10 paragraphs of text in the advertisement, the third and a portion of the sixth were the basis of respondent's claim of libel. They read as follows:

Third paragraph:

> In Montgomery, Alabama, after students sang "My Country, 'Tis of Thee" on the State Capitol steps, their leaders were expelled from school, and truckloads of police armed with shotguns and tear-gas ringed the Alabama State College Campus. When the entire student body protested to state authorities by refusing to re-register, their dining hall was padlocked in an attempt to starve them into submission.

Sixth paragraph:

> Again and again the Southern violators have answered Dr. King's peaceful protests with intimidation and violence. They have bombed his home almost killing his wife and child. They have assaulted his person. They have arrested him seven times—for "speeding," "loitering" and similar "offenses." And now they have charged him with "perjury"—a felony under which they could imprison him for ten years. . . .

Although neither of these statements mentions respondent by name, he contended that the word "police" in the third paragraph referred to him as the Montgomery Commissioner who supervised the Police Department, so that he was being accused of "ringing" the campus with police. He further claimed that the paragraph would be read as imputing to the police, and hence to him, the padlocking of the dining hall in order to starve the students into submission. As to the sixth paragraph, he contended that since arrests are ordinarily made by the police, the statement "They have arrested [Dr. King] seven times" would be read as referring to him. . . .

It is uncontroverted that some of the statements contained in the paragraphs were not accurate descriptions of events which occurred in Montgomery. Although Negro students staged a demonstration on the State Capitol steps, they sang the National Anthem and not "My Country, 'Tis of Thee." Although nine students were expelled by the State Board of Education, this was not for leading the demonstration at the Capitol, but for demanding service at a lunch counter in the Montgomery County Courthouse on another day. Not the entire student body, but most of it, had protested the expulsion, not by refusing to register, but by boycotting classes on a single day; virtually all the students did register for the ensuing semester. The campus dining hall was not padlocked on any occasion, and the only students who may have been barred from eating there were the few who had neither signed a preregistration application nor requested temporary meal tickets. Although the police were deployed near the campus in large numbers on three occasions, they did not at any time "ring" the campus, and they were not called to the campus in connection with the demonstration on the State Capitol steps, as the third paragraph implied. Dr. King had not been arrested seven times, but only four. . . .

Respondent made no effort to prove that he suffered actual pecuniary loss as a result of the alleged libel. One of his witnesses, a former employer, testified that if he had believed the statements, he doubted whether he "would want to be associated with anybody who would be a party to such things that are stated in that ad," and that he would not re-employ respondent if he believed "that he allowed the Police Department to do the things that the paper say he did." But neither this witness nor any of the others testified that he had actually believed the statements in their supposed reference to respondent. . . .

The trial judge submitted the case to the jury under instructions that the statements in the advertisement were "libelous per se" and were not privileged, so that petitioners might be held liable if the jury found that they had published the advertisement and that the statements were made "of and concerning" respondent. The jury was instructed that, because the statements were libelous per se, "the law . . . implies legal injury from the bare fact of publication itself," "falsity and malice are presumed," "general damages need not be alleged or proved but are presumed," and "punitive damages may be awarded by the jury even though the amount of actual damages is neither found nor shown." . . .

We reverse the judgment. We hold that the rule of law applied by the Alabama courts is constitutionally deficient for failure to provide the safeguards for freedom of speech and of the press that are required by the First and Fourteenth Amendments in a libel action brought by a public official against critics of his official conduct. . . .

Under Alabama law as applied in this case, a publication is "libelous per se" if the words "tend to injure a person . . . in his reputation" or to "bring [him] into public contempt"; the trial court stated that the standard was met if the words are such as to "injure him in his public office, or impute misconduct to him in his office, or want of official integrity, or want of fidelity to a public trust. . . ." The jury must find that the words were published "of and concerning" the plaintiff, but where the plaintiff is a public official his place in the governmental hierarchy is sufficient evidence to support a finding that his reputation has been affected by statements that reflect upon the agency of which he is in charge. Once "libel per se" has been established, the defendant has no defense as to stated facts unless he can persuade the jury that they were true in all their particulars. . . . Unless he can discharge the burden of proving truth, general damages are presumed, and may be awarded without proof of pecuniary injury.

The question before us is whether this rule of liability, as applied to an action brought by a public official against critics of his official conduct, abridges the freedom of speech and of the press that is guaranteed by the First and Fourteenth Amendments. . . .

[W]e consider this case against the background of a profound national commitment to the principle that debate on public issues should be uninhibited, robust, and wide-open, and that it may well include vehement, caustic, and sometimes unpleasantly sharp attacks on government and public officials. The present advertisement, as an expression of grievance and protest on one of the major public issues of our time, would seem clearly to qualify for the constitutional protection. The question is whether it forfeits that protection by the falsity of some of its factual statements and by its alleged defamation of respondent.

Authoritative interpretations of the First Amendment guarantees have consistently refused to recognize an exception for any test of truth—whether administered by judges, juries, or administrative officials—and especially one that puts the burden of proving truth on the speaker. The constitutional protection does not turn upon "the truth, popularity, or social utility of the ideas and beliefs which are offered." . . .

Injury to official reputation affords no more warrant for repressing speech that would otherwise be free than does factual error. Where judicial officers are involved, this Court has held that concern for the dignity and reputation of the courts does not justify the punishment as criminal contempt of criticism of the judge or his decision. This is true even though the utterance contains "half-truths" and "misinformation." . . . If judges are to be treated as 'men of fortitude, able to thrive in a hardy climate,' surely the same must be true of other government officials, such as elected city commissioners. Criticism of their official conduct does not lose its constitutional protection merely because it is effective criticism and hence diminishes their official reputations.

If neither factual error nor defamatory content suffices to remove the constitutional shield from criticism of official conduct, the combination of the two elements is no less inadequate. This is the lesson to be drawn from the great controversy over the Sedition Act of 1798, which first crystallized a national awareness of the central meaning of the First Amendment.

Although the Sedition Act was never tested in this Court, the attack upon its validity has carried the day in the court of history. Fines levied in its prosecution were repaid by Act of Congress on the ground that it was unconstitutional. . . . Jefferson, as President, pardoned those who had been convicted and sentenced under the Act and remitted their fines. . . .

There is no force in respondent's argument that the constitutional limitations implicit in the history of the Sedition Act apply only to Congress and not to the States. It is true that the First Amendment was originally addressed only to action by the Federal Government, . . . [b]ut this distinction was eliminated with the adoption of the Fourteenth Amendment and the application to the States of the First Amendment's restrictions.

What a State may not constitutionally bring about by means of a criminal statute is likewise beyond the reach of its civil law of libel. The fear of damage awards under a rule such as that invoked by the Alabama courts here may be markedly more inhibiting than the fear of prosecution under a criminal statute. Alabama, for example, has a criminal libel law which subjects to prosecution "any person who speaks, writes, or prints of and concerning another any accusation falsely and maliciously importing the commission by such person of a felony, or any other indictable offense involving moral turpitude," and which allows as punishment upon conviction a fine not exceeding $500 and a prison sentence of six months. Presumably a person charged with violation of this statute enjoys ordinary criminal-law safeguards such as the requirements of an indictment and of proof beyond a reasonable doubt. These safeguards are not available to the defendant in a civil action. The judgment awarded in this case—without the need for any proof of actual pecuniary loss—was one thousand times greater than the maximum fine provided by the Alabama criminal statute, and one hundred times greater than that provided by the Sedition Act. . . . Whether or not a newspaper can survive a succession of such judgments, the pall of fear and timidity imposed upon those who would give voice to public criticism is an atmosphere in which the First Amendment freedoms cannot survive. . . .

The state rule of law is not saved by its allowance of the defense of truth. . . . A rule compelling the critic of official conduct to guarantee the truth of all his factual assertions—and to do so on pain of libel judgments virtually unlimited in amount—leads to a comparable "self-censorship." Allowance of the defense of truth, with the burden of proving it on the defendant, does not mean that only false speech will be deterred. . . . Under such a rule, would-be critics of official conduct may be deterred from voicing their criticism, even though it is believed to be true and even though it is in fact true, because of doubt whether it can be proved in court or fear of the expense of having to do so. They tend to make only statements which "steer far wider of the unlawful zone." The rule thus dampens the vigor and limits the variety of public debate. It is inconsistent with the First and Fourteenth Amendments.

The constitutional guarantees require, we think, a federal rule that prohibits a public official from recovering damages for a defamatory falsehood relating to his official conduct unless he proves that the statement was made with "actual malice"—that is, with knowledge that it was false or with reckless disregard of whether it was false or not. . . .

Such a privilege for criticism of official conduct is appropriately analogous to the protection accorded a public official when he is sued for libel by a private citizen. In *Barr v. Matteo* [1959], this Court held the utterance of a federal official to be absolutely privileged if made "within the outer perimeter" of his duties. The States accord the same immunity to statements of their highest officers, although some differentiate their lesser officials and qualify the privilege they enjoy. But all hold that all officials are protected unless actual malice can be proved. The reason for the official privilege is said to be that the threat of damage suits would otherwise "inhibit the fearless, vigorous, and effective administration of policies of government" and "dampen the ardor of all but the most resolute, or the most irresponsible, in the unflinching discharge of their duties." Analogous considerations support the privilege for the citizen-critic of government. It is as much his duty to criticize as it is the official's duty to administer. As Madison said, "the censorial power is in the people over the Government, and not in the Government over the people." It would give public servants an unjustified preference over the public they serve, if critics of official conduct did not have a fair equivalent of the immunity granted to the officials themselves.

We conclude that such a privilege is required by the First and Fourteenth Amendments.

We hold today that the Constitution delimits a State's power to award damages for libel in actions brought by public officials against critics of their official conduct. Since this is such an action, the rule requiring proof of actual malice is applicable. . . .

Applying these standards, we consider that the proof presented to show actual malice lacks the convincing clarity which the constitutional standard demands, and hence that it would not constitutionally sustain the judgment for respondent under the proper rule of law. . . .

We think the evidence against the *Times* supports at most a finding of negligence in failing to discover the misstatements, and is constitutionally insufficient to show the recklessness that is required for a finding of actual malice.

We also think the evidence was constitutionally defective in another respect: it was incapable of supporting the jury's finding that the allegedly libelous statements were made "of and concerning" respondent. . . . There was no reference to respondent in the advertisement, either by name or official position. A number of the allegedly libelous statements—the charges that the dining hall was padlocked and that Dr. King's home was bombed, his person assaulted, and a perjury prosecution instituted against him—did not even concern the police; despite the ingenuity of the arguments which would attach this significance to the word "They," it is plain that these statements could not reasonably be read as accusing respondent of personal involvement in the acts in question. . . .

The judgment of the Supreme Court of Alabama is reversed and the case is remanded to that court for further proceedings not inconsistent with this opinion.

Reversed and remanded.

THE AFTERMATH AND SIGNIFICANCE OF *NEW YORK TIMES V. SULLIVAN*

In this landmark decision, the Court held that public officials could not succeed in libel actions simply because something was inaccurate. Instead, they had to demonstrate "actual malice" on the part of the party they accused of libel.[43] While not defined precisely, actual malice suggests knowledge that statements are false or made with reckless disregard for whether or not they are false. The burden of proof to meet this standard is entirely on the public officials who believe they have been libeled. It is admittedly a very high standard to meet because of the difficulty of proving that another person knew their statements were false or acted with reckless disregard for the truth.[44]

Shortly after *Sullivan*, the Court expanded the application of this test to libel claims involving public figures so that they, like government officials, would also have to demonstrate actual malice in order to win their libel claim.[45] This expansion was problematic, however, because the Court failed to define precisely what constituted a public figure. Entertainers, professional athletes, and other well-known people certainly fall into the "public figure" category, but what about others who find themselves, for whatever reason, in the spotlight? What recourse does a small-town businessman, college student-athlete, crime victim, or even an alleged perpetrator have against defamatory statements if they are viewed as public figures because of press coverage?

The Court weighed these questions for a decade before deciding in 1974 that greater protection was needed for private individuals who had been libeled. The Court held that individuals who had made no effort to place themselves in the public eye need not meet the actual malice standard required of public officials and figures. Since they typically lacked the resources of politicians, celebrities, and other public figures to win back their good name, the Court reasoned, private individuals only need to show that the person who made the defamatory statement was negligent; that is, he or she failed to exercise normal care to ensure that a statement was accurate before publishing it.[46] Because negligence is a lower threshold to meet than actual malice, it is much easier for private individuals to win a libel action than for public figures.

The significance of *New York Times v. Sullivan* cannot be overstated. The ruling was a victory for the *New York Times*, of course, but also for other papers that reported on the civil rights movement in the South. National newspapers played a critical role at the time in educating the country about attempts in the South to deny constitutionally protected rights to African Americans. Had the damage award against the *Times* been sustained, and if other news organizations whose reporting was not error free faced similar penalties under the libel laws of Alabama and other southern states, the power of the press to report on civil rights violations would have been vastly impeded. As First Amendment attorney Floyd Abrams said, "Without the ruling in the *Sullivan* case, all reporting on the civil rights movement in the South would have been constricted in a fashion unrecognizable today."[47]

It is no exaggeration to say that subsequent civil rights victories may owe as much to those in the North who wrote about the movement as to those in the South who actually participated in it.

The case is also significant, and most widely known, for its protections for the press. The *New York Times* itself, on the fiftieth anniversary of the decision, editorialized that the case "still represents the clearest and most forceful defense of press freedom in American history."[48] It granted the press far more freedom to investigate and report on public officials and public figures with a reduced fear of being sued. While not granting constitutional protection to libel, the Court nevertheless fundamentally altered the law surrounding it by removing the requirement that publishers vouch for the truthfulness of every statement they print and by requiring the person bringing the libel action to demonstrate that actual malice was behind the creation or dissemination of the material in dispute.

The most important outcome of *New York Times v. Sullivan*, however, is related to the very issue that brought about the dispute in the first place. As First Amendment scholar Harry Kalven Jr. wrote in the wake of the Court's opinion, "Political freedom ends when government can use its powers and its courts to silence its critics."[49] History is replete with examples of government officials who punished their critics; something that still happens around the world today. These realities make it very difficult to imagine a modern America without this ruling.

How might recent American history, politics, and society have been different if journalists had been unable to investigate and if people had been unable to criticize Lyndon Johnson's escalation of the Vietnam War; Richard Nixon and Watergate; Bill Clinton's affair with White House intern Monica Lewinsky; George W. Bush's military response to the attacks of September 11, 2001; and Barack Obama's promises about the Affordable Care Act? To what extent would the protests and criticism directed at Donald Trump since his inauguration have been possible without this ruling? Further, in the digital age, how much public dialogue would be suppressed if newspapers were held responsible for every online comment their websites hosted or if social media platforms were responsible for everything posted by their users?

However, the decision is not without its critics. While acknowledging the First Amendment rights it protects, some have complained that the Court's ruling permits and perhaps even encourages disrespect for public officials, with two important consequences. The first is that with the high unlikelihood of a public official proving actual malice, harsh words against government policies and leaders (and often their supporters) have come to pervade contemporary political discussions. From late night television comedy shows to social media and internet blogs, from talk radio to cable news channels, and from public demonstrations in Washington, DC, to town hall meetings, one of the legacies of *New York Times v. Sullivan* is an environment at the national, state, and increasingly local levels of government where, exactly as Justice Brennan described in that ruling, "vehement, caustic, and sometimes unpleasantly sharp attacks on government and public officials" take place.[50] Without a modicum of civility in our civil discourse, partisan tendencies harden, compromise becomes unattainable, and the potential for the type of significant social, economic, and political progress that results from common goals, concerted effort, and shared sacrifice goes unrealized.

A related consequence is the way that very environment discourages prospective candidates from seeking public office. Given the likely impact on their family, friends, and good name, even people with vision, leadership ability, demonstrated skill in working with diverse groups, and tremendous talent in solving larger problems can be dissuaded from running for office. *New York Times v. Sullivan* certainly is not responsible for all that is ugly in contemporary politics, but its protection for any statement made about a public officials that cannot be linked to actual malice has been a contributing factor.

Although Americans bemoan the loss of civil discourse in their discussions of political policies, parties, and leaders, the alternative of government regulation of speech and press through criminal and civil defamation laws is worse—something the founders knew and appreciated as well. Addressing the Virginia General Assembly shortly after the passage of the Sedition Act of 1798, James Madison noted that the liberty to criticize the government and its leaders "is often carried to excess; that it has sometimes degenerated into licentiousness, is seen and lamented, but the remedy has not yet been discovered."[51] He went on to argue that "uninhibited, robust, and wide-open" discourse—the type authorized by *New York Times v. Sullivan* (including hostile and even abusive statements about the government and public officials)—was a necessary by-product of freedom. "Perhaps," he observed, "[such criticism] is an evil inseparable from the good with which it is allied; perhaps it is a shoot which cannot be stripped from the stalk without wounding vitally the plant from which it is torn."[52] Madison understood more than most that however much modern Americans deplore the incivility of their political dialogue, its very presence is a reminder that they still live in a free society.

4

SCOTTSBORO

The Right to Effective Counsel and *Powell v. Alabama* (1932)

The American judicial system has witnessed many prominent legal cases throughout its history, but few compare to the trial that was held in Scottsboro, Alabama, in 1931. It was a singular event for several reasons: First, but for a bizarre twist of fate, the eleven principal individuals involved might have lived out their lives in complete anonymity. Instead, although unremarkable in nearly every way, their names became known to hundreds of thousands around the world within a matter of months.

Second, the social conventions of that era practically guaranteed that the circumstances surrounding the alleged crime would exacerbate existing racial tensions and stereotypes. That did occur, but reaction to the jury verdicts in the first round of trials also brought white and black Americans together in a common cause and in such numbers as had rarely, if ever, been seen in this country.

Third, the constitutional protections recognized in this case and affirmed in subsequent rulings by the United States Supreme Court have helped untold numbers of Americans involved in the criminal justice process. Yet, while those protections saved the defendants in this case from execution, they arguably did little else for the nine young African Americans who were both vilified and immortalized collectively as the Scottsboro Boys.

THE STORY

The saga of the Scottsboro Boys began on the afternoon of March 25, 1931, when nine young black men were pulled from a train and arrested in

Figure 4. The Scottsboro Boys and their second attorney, Samuel Leibowitz, 1933. *Standing left to right*: Olen Montgomery, Clarence Norris, Willie Roberson (*front*), Andrew Wright (*partially obscured*), Ozie Powell, Eugene Williams, Charlie Weems, and Roy Wright. Haywood Patterson is seated next to Leibowitz. Courtesy of the Morgan County Archives, Decatur, Alabama.

Paint Rock, Alabama. The eldest, Charlie Weems, was twenty years old. The youngest, Leroy "Roy" Wright, was just thirteen and on his first trip away from home. The other seven, all in their early to late teens, were Olen Montgomery, Clarence Norris, Haywood Patterson, Ozie Powell, Willie Roberson, Eugene Williams, and Andy Wright, Roy's older brother. Patterson, Williams, and the Wrights were friends from Chattanooga. Norris and Weems were acquaintances in Georgia but had boarded at different points and neither knew the other was on the train. The rest had never met any of the others before that day. Looking for work, the nine joined several other people who had "hoboed" their way onto a Chattanooga freight train bound for Memphis.

Just after the train dipped into northern Alabama on its way west, a fight broke out between the freight-hoppers, although accounts differ as to what precipitated it. Haywood Patterson, perhaps the most well known of the Scottsboro Boys, recounted that as a group of white youths were walking across the top of the train, one of them deliberately stepped on his hand, causing him to nearly topple from his narrow perch aboard a tank car. He protested, saying, "The next time you want by, just tell me you want by and I let you by."[1] The young white man retorted, "I don't ask you when I want by. What you doing on this train anyway . . . ? This is a white man's train. You better get off."[2]

Clarence Norris remembered that he and several other black men found themselves together in a gondola or open-aired car in the middle of the train when trouble broke out: "Now, there was some white boys on this train. They must have seen us getting into this gondola. In any case, one of them stuck his head over the edge of the car, and when he saw us laying about, he called back to some others, '[L]et's get them off.'"[3]

However it started, the fight that ensued saw most of the white youth either thrown from the moving train or jump off of their own accord. Several of them proceeded back to the town of Stevenson and told the stationmaster there that a gang of armed blacks had started a fight and had thrown them from the train. One claimed that gunshots were fired at him as he was being flung overboard.[4]

The stationmaster telegraphed the information to officials at the next station, who notified Jackson County sheriff Matt Wann. Thirty minutes later, when the train pulled into Paint Rock, Alabama, to take on water, it was met by Charlie Latham, Wann's deputy who lived in the area, and a mob. Unsure of what they would encounter aboard the train and having been told that those they were to arrest were armed, Sheriff Wann had ordered Latham to deputize every man in the town if necessary and have them be prepared for anything when the train arrived. The other African Americans involved in the fight had already disembarked by this point, leaving only nine young black men scattered throughout the various cars of the train when it pulled to a stop. Of that moment Clarence Norris later recalled, "When the train arrived, it was immediately surrounded by a mob. I mean, man, there was nothing but white people with sticks, guns, pitchforks, and every damn thing you could think of. . . . All of us thought for sure we would be lynched right there, with no questions asked."[5]

Against the vigorous protests of the gathered crowd, the nine were loaded onto the back of a flatbed truck, tied together, and quickly taken to the Jackson County Jail in Scottsboro. At the time, they were under the impression that they could be charged with assault and even attempted murder because of the fight aboard the train. Such charges were serious anyway, but particularly so given the racial climate that existed in Alabama at the time and the fact that white men had made the allegations.

Two white women dressed in men's clothing were also found on the train, but Deputy Latham paid scant attention to them until he had secured the young men. He then briefly met with one of the women, seventeen-year-old Ruby Bates, who claimed that the nine African Americans he had just sent off to Scottsboro had raped her and her friend, Victoria Price, aboard the train. Had they not been gone by that time, the young men almost certainly would have been lynched at the scene. Instead, they were safe but completely oblivious to what lay ahead of them. Indeed, they would be the last to find out. Deputy Latham apparently "made no effort to keep the [rape] charge confidential, and news of the alleged attacks spread throughout and beyond Scottsboro within the hour."[6]

By dusk a crowd of some three hundred people had formed outside the Jackson County Jail, many of whom were armed and shouting racial epithets. They demanded that Sheriff Wann turn the boys over. He steadfastly refused, but he knew there was little he and his deputies could do should the mob decide to rush the jail. The situation grew increasingly tense as the evening wore on. As Norris later described it, "You could hear a change in the mob's attitude without even seeing them, and then you could actually sense they were ready to try it. You knew they were coming. Everybody in the cell knew things were getting tight."[7]

To his credit, Sheriff Wann did all he could to keep the mob at bay, including at one point stepping out of the jail brandishing his pistol and declaring to the restless mob, "If you come any further, I'll blow your damn brains out. You boys understand me, there ain't nobody coming in here. If you try, if you put your feet in this door, I'm gonna blow your . . . brains out."[8] Doubting that even this threat could hold back the mob for long, Wann contacted Governor Benjamin Meek Miller, who responded by immediately mobilizing around one hundred members of the National Guard. By the time they arrived in Scottsboro around midnight, only a few people were still milling around the jail, the unusually cold temperature that evening having forced most of the crowd to disperse.

Alabama circuit judge Alfred E. Hawkins then ordered the removal of the young men from Scottsboro to Gadsden, where they were taken for their safety the next day by military escort. Newspapers around the country rightfully heralded Sheriff Wann's "heroic efforts in protecting [the Scottsboro Boys] from mob violence," as did Clarence Norris, who later declared that Wann was "the only man that kept us from getting lynched."[9] However, Wann did the young men no favors by also telling the local press that six of them had either already confessed to the rape charge or had implicated the others.

All nine of the Scottsboro Boys were subsequently indicted by a grand jury on March 31, and Judge Hawkins set their trial for the next week on April 6, 1931. Hawkins had indicated that he would appoint counsel for the young men and sought to have all seven members of the local bar assigned to their defense.[10] Conflicts of interest such as assisting the prosecution in the same case and other obligations ultimately lessened the number of available Scottsboro attorneys to just one, the aged Milo Moody, who was described at the time as a "doddering, extremely unreliable, senile individual who is losing whatever ability he once had."[11] On the morning of the trial, however, an additional attorney was present.

The young men were not allowed to contact relatives after they were apprehended in Paint Rock, but their families evidently found out about their situation from the explosive newspaper coverage. Yet, as the parents of the four friends from Chattanooga (Patterson, Williams, and the Wright brothers) all later testified, they made no attempt to try and visit their sons because they were too afraid to come to Alabama.[12] On their behalf, several notable black citizens and ministers in Chattanooga approached Stephen Roddy, a local white attorney who served both black and white clients, about participating in the case. Roddy was a real estate lawyer with no experience in criminal law, but he agreed to observe the proceedings for $120. He dutifully made the sixty-mile trip to Scottsboro to be present in the courtroom when the trial began. With essentially no prior knowledge of the case, he must have been astonished at what he found when he arrived there.

By April 6, a national audience was already following the story of the purported crime and the potential sentence for those found guilty: rape in Alabama was punishable from ten years imprisonment to death. The *Chicago Daily Tribune* offered its readers this description of the morning of the trial:

"The Negroes were brought to Scottsboro from Gadsden before six o'clock this morning, accompanied by a hundred National Guardsmen, whose glistening bayonets were a novelty to the mountain folks already swarming into this small town. They came from as far as seventy miles away, in automobiles—ancient and modern—trucks, buggies, wagons, by muleback, afoot."[13] The first day of the trial also happened to be the first Monday of the month, the traditional market and trading day for area farmers. Consequently, some ten thousand people were in Scottsboro for market day and the trial, dwarfing the town's population of 2,300.[14]

The National Guard had more than just the "glistening bayonets," noted by the Chicago paper, at its disposal. Affirming his responsibility to protect the young men while transporting them from the more secure facilities in Gadsden to their trial in Scottsboro, Major Joe Starnes also equipped his men with machine guns and tear gas bombs. The presence of such a large and heavily armed military contingent certainly protected the defendants, but it also conveyed the impression that these nine young men were unusually dangerous.

When all the parties were in place, Judge Hawkins proceeded to call up the case and asked whether counsel was ready to begin, to which the prosecution replied in the affirmative. However, when no one answered for the defense, Stephen Roddy stood and, in what turned out to be a critically important exchange with Judge Hawkins, sought to clarify his role with respect to the Scottsboro Boys.

He began by explaining that he had not actually been formally retained as their attorney but was merely there at the behest of some people interested in the case. Nevertheless, he acknowledged that he was willing to assist whomever Judge Hawkins had already appointed to defend the young men. Hawkins apparently took Roddy's presence to mean that he would be lead counsel with members of the local bar (now only the elderly Mr. Moody) to assist him as needed. Roddy then asked him directly, "Your Honor has appointed counsel, is that correct?"[15] Judge Hawkins responded that he had appointed all the members of the Scottsboro bar to assist and expected them to continue in that capacity "if no counsel appears."[16] Roddy again stressed, "I don't appear then as counsel but I do want to stay in and not be ruled out of this case."[17] At least three times, Roddy stated that he was willing and ready to serve alongside counsel already appointed by the Court.

Judge Hawkins, however, proceeded to ask Moody if he would be willing to assist Roddy, which he agreed to do. Sensing that he was about to become the lead attorney in his first capital case, Roddy exclaimed, "[I]f I was paid down here and employed, it would be a different thing, but I have not prepared this case for trial and have only been called into it by people who are interested in these boys from Chattanooga. Now, they have not given me an opportunity to prepare the case and I am not familiar with the procedure in Alabama."[18] He went on to plead with the judge, "I am merely here at the solicitation of people who have become interested in this case without any payment of fee and without any preparation for trial and I think the boys would be better off if I step entirely out of the case according to my way of looking at it and according to my lack of preparation of it and not being familiar with the procedure in Alabama."[19] Believing that Milo Moody could provide the necessary details of Alabama criminal procedure, Judge Hawkins again asked Moody if he was willing to help Roddy. When he agreed, the judge granted the attorneys a mere twenty-five minutes to meet with their clients and then proceeded to trial.[20]

As a Tennessee real estate attorney making his criminal law debut in an Alabama capital rape trial, Roddy was clearly out of his element, and he knew it. In addition, his legal skills, which were characterized as only "modest," were further hampered by his apparent "inability to remain sober."[21] Upon arriving in the courtroom on April 6, one of the prosecuting attorneys noted that Roddy was so "stewed, he could scarcely walk straight."[22] This characterization of a drunken Roddy on the morning of the first trial is included in nearly every account of the Scottsboro case, all presumably based on the prosecuting attorney's comment.[23] However, a review of the trial transcript that day fails to confirm any indication that Roddy was alcohol impaired. His admitted failure to provide an adequate defense was the result of his own very limited legal talents, the environment in which the trial was held, the lack of preparation time permitted him, and the prosecution's objections (nearly all of which were sustained by Judge Hawkins) whenever Roddy asked a probing question. It is difficult to imagine how even a seasoned—or sober—criminal defense attorney could have prevailed in similar circumstances.[24]

Judge Hawkins later stated that his order removing the young men to Gadsden for their safety, his insistence on an indictment by a grand jury as opposed to the decision of a lynch mob, and his appointment of counsel all reflected his desire to ensure that proper legal processes were followed. Once counsel was appointed and the trial began, however, he seemed far less concerned about other aspects of due process.

For example, searching for any advantage he could find, Roddy immediately motioned for a change of venue. He provided the judge with a number of local newspaper clippings and cited the inflammatory nature of their coverage. In the nearly two weeks that had transpired since the Scottsboro

Boys had been arrested, both local and regional newspapers had printed details of the alleged crime and other related pieces filled with rumor and speculation. The two female accusers, as well as some of the young white men thrown from the train, had already given several newspaper interviews setting forth their version of the events. Roddy argued that such media coverage made it impossible to convene an unbiased jury, particularly in light of the girls' allegations and the speed with which initial news of the purported attack had spread. He thought it unlikely that there was any person in the surrounding area who had not heard of the Scottsboro Boys' alleged crime. Judge Hawkins overruled the motion, however, after pressing Roddy to conclusively demonstrate that the newspaper articles had actually influenced public opinion and the lawyer was unable to do so.

The prosecution then asked Roddy if he would like to pursue separate trials for the defendants instead of having them tried together. When he declined, the prosecution team asked that Weems, Norris, and Roy Wright stand trial first. Roddy objected to Wright's inclusion in this group because of his age, and both Judge Hawkins and the prosecution agreed to remove him for the time being. Prosecutors then requested to try Patterson alone and Montgomery, Powell, Roberson, Williams, and Andy Wright together. Judge Hawkins granted the severances in each instance and proceeded to the first trial of Charlie Weems and Clarence Norris.

Victoria Price was the first to testify in the Weems-Norris trial and made a lengthy and graphic statement to the court describing the events of March 25. Several times during his cross-examination of Price, Roddy sought to establish that, contrary to the media reports describing her as a proper southern woman, she had, in fact, a rather sordid past, which made the reliability of her testimony suspect. The prosecution objected to this line of inquiry several times, with Judge Hawkins sustaining each one, and Roddy sat down, having made little impact on either Price's testimony or image.

The doctors who examined Price and Bates after they left the train were the next to take the stand. They stated that both women exhibited signs of recent sexual activity, but acknowledged there was little evidence of their having been raped or physically abused in any other way. Rather than capitalize on this admission, Roddy asked whether the doctors had questioned the girls about their sexual habits or had examined them for venereal diseases. Again, the prosecution objected to the questioning and Judge Hawkins refused to let the doctors answer.

The trial was bound over for the next day when Ruby Bates would testify. She unwittingly contradicted Price's earlier testimony on several points, but Roddy failed to press her about these inconsistencies. After several other witnesses for the prosecution testified, Roddy called Charlie Weems and Clarence Norris to the witness stand. Weems recounted his version of the events and vehemently denied, even under heavy questioning from the prosecution, that he had done anything to the women. Norris, on the other hand, testified that all of the young black men, except for himself, had, in fact, raped the girls. Upon cross-examination from Roddy, however, Norris was unable to provide even the barest details of the rape allegations his testimony had just corroborated.[25] The state quickly rested its case, and Roddy, out of frustration with Norris's shortsighted attempt to save himself, elected not to give a closing statement.

When the prosecution stood to offer its final summation, however, Roddy objected. He believed that since he had not offered a closing statement, the court should not allow prosecutors to give one since such a one-sided presentation "would be harmful and prejudicial to the interest of the defendants."[26] Judge Hawkins overruled the objection, and after the prosecution ended its thirty-minute summary, he turned the case over to the jury.

As the Weems-Norris jury filed out of the courtroom, jury selection in the trial of Haywood Patterson began immediately. When his trial commenced shortly thereafter, its proceedings largely mirrored that of the earlier trial. Victoria Price again offered a vivid account of the alleged crime while Roddy was again stymied in every attempt to discredit her character. However, during Ruby Bates's testimony, he was able to get her to admit that she could not be certain that Patterson (as had been charged by Price) was the first one to assault them.

Just as Bates ended her testimony, Judge Hawkins received word that the Weems-Norris jury had reached a verdict. Patterson's jury was escorted to an adjoining room while the other jury returned to the courtroom. When the court clerk read the words, "We find the defendants guilty of rape and fix their sentence at death," the courtroom broke into loud applause.[27] Seconds later, the massive crowd of people outside the courthouse heard the news and roared their approval, accompanied by music from a local car dealer's amplified gramophone playing "There'll be a Hot Time in the Old Town Tonight."[28] When Haywood Patterson's trial resumed, Roddy quickly motioned for a mistrial arguing that the Patterson jury had clearly heard the celebration and might have been influenced by it. Judge Hawkins denied his request.

Roddy then called Patterson and the remaining Scottsboro Boys to testify. Like Norris, Patterson implicated several of the others but said he had never seen the girls until he was pulled from the train at Paint Rock. Roy Wright testified that he too had seen five of the Scottsboro Boys rape the girls, but he and the Chattanooga group of boys were all innocent. When Andy Wright, Williams, Ozie Powell, and Olen Montgomery testified, however, they each said they had seen neither the rape nor the girls while on the train.

At the conclusion of their testimony and after Roddy again declined to offer a closing statement, the case was given to the jury, and trial proceedings for the remaining five began. However, just twenty-five minutes after it had left the courtroom, the Patterson jury announced that it had already reached a decision. Judge Hawkins sternly warned those in the room against making any noise when the verdict was read. They complied as the jury declared Patterson guilty and sentenced him to death.

At the third trial, Price, Bates, the examining doctors, and others again offered their testimony. Despite the fact that Montgomery was nearly blind; Roberson had a painful venereal disease that left him scarcely able to walk; and the consistent denials of Powell, Andy Wright, and Williams under vigorous cross-examination, their jury reached the same verdict as had been twice rendered earlier: guilty of rape and sentenced to death.

Young Roy Wright remained to stand trial. Rather than wait for the matter to be tried in juvenile court, the prosecution offered Roddy a deal. The state was prepared to only ask for life imprisonment if Wright pled guilty. Roddy refused but at the end of the short trial proceedings asked the jury to consider life imprisonment because of Wright's age. Later that night, the jury announced it was deadlocked: seven of its members insisted on the death penalty for the thirteen-year-old. Believing that the matter could not be resolved, Judge Hawkins ordered a mistrial.

On April 9, 1931, the eight who had been convicted were again brought before Judge Hawkins, who set their execution date in Kilby Prison's electric chair just ninety days later. The *Atlanta Constitution* reported, "Judge J. A. Hawkins' eyes were wet with tears, as upon one after the other he pronounced sentence. It was the first death sentence he had pronounced in his five years on the bench."[29] Notwithstanding this tearful display, Hawkins fairly bristled at any suggestion that he had conducted the trials unfairly. On the day of sentencing, the *New York Times* reported the judge's angry response to such criticism: "[The young men] were given every opportunity to provide themselves with counsel," he retorted, "and I appointed able members of the Jackson County bar to represent them. . . . I personally will welcome any investigation of the trial."[30] Roddy and Moody immediately appealed the Scottsboro verdicts to the Alabama Supreme Court, which stayed the July executions pending the outcome of the appeal.

THE CONSTITUTIONAL BACKGROUND

The United States Constitution references counsel just once, in the Sixth Amendment's declaration that "in all criminal prosecutions, the accused shall enjoy the right . . . to have the assistance of counsel for his defense." As originally interpreted, this clause did not require that an attorney be retained or appointed; it merely acknowledged the right to use counsel if one so chose and at his or her own expense. The Supreme Court has significantly strengthened the right to counsel clause over the past fifty years, but even the less than robust original version recognized the importance of counsel far more than had been the case in England, from where so much of America's legal heritage derives.

In 1695, for the first time and as part of a series of criminal procedure reforms, Parliament formally granted defendants a right to counsel at their own expense. Only those accused of treason were able to avail themselves of this right, however, as all others charged with felonies defended themselves. In fact, until the mid-eighteenth century, English law expressly forbade the assistance of counsel for those charged with serious crimes other than treason. A variety of justifications for this ban have been offered, but most appeared to be grounded in the fear that a defense attorney might actually win an acquittal and thus frustrate the time, money, and effort the government and its lawyers had invested in the prosecution.

The British colonies in America had a better appreciation for the role of counsel in the criminal justice system wherein the accused, if found guilty, would be punished with a fine and/or be deprived of his life, liberty, or property. The 1641 Massachusetts Body of Liberties, the first legal code in New England, proclaimed, "Every man that findeth himself unfit to plead his own cause in any Court shall have liberty to employ any man . . . to help him."[31] Other colonies and the early states followed with similar statements, such as Delaware's 1776 Declaration of Rights, which declared "that in all prosecutions for criminal offenses, every man hath a right . . . to be allowed counsel," and Vermont's Constitution of 1777, which stated that in all criminal trials "a man hath a right to be heard, by himself and his counsel."[32] All thirteen states, and later the First Congress, in the Federal Crimes Act of 1790, required counsel to be provided for all accused of capital crimes. Four early states went even further, providing counsel in noncapital cases to those too poor to secure it on their own.

However, from the early statehood era until the Supreme Court's decision in *Powell v. Alabama* in 1932, there was little significant expansion of the right to counsel. Those accused of capital crimes were guaranteed legal representation, but all others generally had access to an attorney only insofar as they could pay for one themselves. This obvious disparity in representation between those charged with noncapital and capital crimes and between the rich and poor was exacerbated by the adversarial system of justice in American law.

A cornerstone of English common law, the adversarial system is well known to even the most disinterested legal observer because of pop culture. Law-themed television shows and movies regularly depict courtroom opponents working to win their case by the evidence they introduce, the witnesses they question, and the arguments they make. They zealously work for the interests they represent, and they win their cases not so much on the grounds that they were "right" or that the "truth" was on their side as on the overall quality of their advocacy. Presiding over it all is a neutral and detached magistrate who rarely intervenes other than to ensure that proper courtroom procedure is followed. This is in direct contrast to the inquisitorial system used in some countries in Europe, Africa, and South America where the judge dominates the proceedings and takes an active role in the investigation and evidence gathering, up to and including questioning witnesses. For good or bad, judges in inquisitorial systems oversee every aspect of the process to determine the "facts" or the "truth" to his or her satisfaction.

Given the contested nature of trials in the adversarial system, it is not difficult to appreciate the importance of access to effective counsel. With the two sides pitted against each other, the procedural elements with which a layman would not likely be familiar, and a presiding judge who is loath to intervene even when one side may be clearly outmatched, unprepared, or incompetent, it is obvious why effective counsel is necessary. For the Scottsboro Boys, effective counsel was a matter of life and death.

THE LITIGATION

By the time the Scottsboro Boys' appeal was argued before Alabama's highest court, several significant developments had taken place. The most important of these was the entry into the case of the International Labor Defense (ILD) organization, the legal arm of the American Communist Party, which took up the young men's defense.[33] The ILD's support helped draw worldwide attention to the plight of the Scottsboro Boys. However, its involvement also raised questions about whether the organization truly wanted to help the young men or simply use them to further its own agenda. Such criticisms were leveled almost from the moment the ILD entered the case.

For example, the same group of Chattanooga ministers who had sent Stephen Roddy to Scottsboro later issued a statement charging that the ILD's participation was "mainly for the purpose of drawing Negroes of the South into the Communist organization."[34] Critics in Alabama agreed, arguing that "with its large and, in many instances, illiterate Negro population, [Alabama] presented a fertile field for Communism's insidious arguments and propaganda and since no opportunity to ostensibly 'aid the underdog' had presented itself for a long time, it isn't difficult to picture the jubilance with which the organization seized the Scottsboro case."[35]

While the presence of the ILD did indeed provoke controversy throughout the South, it also helped unite the efforts of whites and blacks in a common cause on a scale never before seen in America. Beginning in the late 1920s, American Communists had made a concerted effort to attract blacks to their organization by protesting housing conditions, police brutality, lynchings, and other issues of concern to African Americans. They also "staged interracial meetings, socials, and dances as well as demonstrations and get-togethers in all regions of the nation."[36]

Adopting the slogan, "They Shall Not Die," the Communist Party organized dozens of protests and parades throughout the country in which thousands of people, black and white, participated in support of the Scottsboro Boys. The media coverage that accompanied the demonstrations also ensured that the case would not be forgotten. As ACLU attorney Arthur Garfield Hays noted at the time, "The fact remains that, in spite of their blustering threats which probably do harm, [ILD leaders] have stirred up tremendous excitement all over the world, so that no court, judge, or even private citizen is likely to overlook the Scottsboro case."[37] Indeed, over the course of the next year, Communists protested on behalf of the Scottsboro Boys in demonstrations throughout the United States as well as overseas in such cites as Berlin, Vienna, Paris, Havana, and Buenos Aires.

On March 24, 1932, a divided Alabama Supreme Court affirmed all of the convictions and sentences except for that of Eugene Williams. It reversed the decision in his case and remanded it back to the trial court to determine whether Williams was under sixteen years of age. If so, his case was to be reheard in juvenile court.[38] As for the others, the majority found nothing in the lower court record to suggest that the young men had not received a fair trial. One by one, the court reviewed and dispensed with each of the arguments raised on appeal: the inflammatory newspaper coverage, Roddy's lack of time to prepare, the absence of any black jurors, the refusal of Judge Hawkins to permit questions regarding Price's character, the Patterson jury overhearing the crowd celebrating the convictions of

Weems and Norris, and the speed with which the entire process had been conducted.

Chief Justice John C. Anderson was the only member of the Alabama Supreme Court to disagree. The opening sentence of his dissent minced no words: "While the Constitution guarantees to the accused a speedy trial, it is of greater importance that it should be by a fair and impartial jury . . . , a jury free from bias or prejudice, and, above all, from coercion and intimidation."[39] Like the majority opinion, his dissent also addressed several of the points raised on appeal. He refused to believe, for example, that the ubiquitous and heavily armed military guard accompanying the boys, and other factors, had not unduly influenced those chosen for jury service. How could the jury possibly consider the young men innocent until proven guilty seeing how heavily guarded they were, he questioned. What were jury members to infer from Judge Hawkins's appointment of a Tennessee real estate lawyer on the morning of the first trial or from the judge's denial of practically every one of Roddy's motions while sustaining the motions and objections of the prosecution? What were the jurors in the Patterson trial supposed to think when they heard the courtroom and the crowd outside erupt in applause and cheers at the guilty verdict and sentence of death in the Weems-Norris case?

Chief Justice Anderson expressed particular concern with the juries' collective verdicts and punishments that were both quick and extreme, affixing death for the convicted when Alabama rape law provided for a range of penalties that spanned from ten years imprisonment to capital punishment. Why, he questioned, had the juries not looked at such things "as difference in age, leadership, etc. that would render the conduct of some less culpable than others[?]"[40] Anderson went on to stress that the guilt of the young men was really of secondary importance. The real question was, "Did they get a fair and impartial trial as contemplated by the [B]ill of [R]ights?"[41] He concluded that they had not, and that they had been "deprived of this right when the jury [became] overawed or coerced by outside influence, pressure, or conduct."[42] He argued that the Scottsboro Boys could and ought to be retried, but only "after some months of cooling time have elapsed" and after the young men had secured "vigilant employed counsel."[43]

One week after the Alabama Supreme Court upheld the Scottsboro Boys' convictions and again sentenced them to death, the United States Supreme Court granted certiorari. The Court consolidated the three cases involving the young men and scheduled oral arguments on the matter for October 10, 1932.[44] A month later, the Supreme Court issued its ruling in the case with Justice George Sutherland writing for the seven-member majority.

THE DECISION

Powell v. Alabama (7–2)
287 U.S. 45 (1932)

JUSTICE SUTHERLAND delivered the opinion of the Court.

The petitioners, hereinafter referred to as defendants, are [N]egroes charged with the crime of rape, committed upon the persons of two white girls. The crime is said to have been committed on March 25, 1931. The indictment was returned in a state court of first instance on March 31, and the record recites that on the same day the defendants were arraigned and entered pleas of not guilty. There is a further recital to the effect that upon the arraignment they were represented by counsel. But no counsel had been employed, and aside from a statement made by the trial judge several days later during a colloquy immediately preceding the trial, the record does not disclose when, or under what circumstances, an appointment of counsel was made, or who was appointed. During the colloquy referred to, the trial judge, in response to a question, said that he had appointed all the members of the bar for the purpose of arraigning the defendants and then of course anticipated that the members of the bar would continue to help the defendants if no counsel appeared. Upon the argument here both sides accepted that as a correct statement of the facts concerning the matter.

There was a severance upon the request of the state, and the defendants were tried in three several groups, as indicated previously. As each of the three cases was called for trial, each defendant was arraigned, and, having the indictment read to him, entered a plea of not guilty. Whether the original arraignment and pleas were regarded as ineffective is not shown. Each of the three trials was completed within a single day. Under the Alabama statute the punishment for rape is to be fixed by the jury, and in its discretion may be from ten years imprisonment to death. The juries found defendants guilty and imposed the death penalty upon all. The trial court overruled motions for new trials and sentenced the defendants in accordance with the verdicts. The judgments were affirmed by the state supreme court. . . .

It is perfectly apparent that the proceedings from beginning to end, took place in an atmosphere of tense, hostile, and excited public sentiment. During the entire time, the defendants were closely confined or were under military guard. The record does not disclose their ages, except that one of them was nineteen; but the record clearly indicates that most, if not all, of them were youthful, . . . ignorant[,] and illiterate. . . .

However guilty defendants, upon due inquiry, might prove to have been, they were, until convicted, presumed to be innocent. It was the duty of the court having their cases in charge to see that they were denied no necessary incident of a fair trial. With any error of the state court involving alleged contravention of the state statutes or [c]onstitution we, of course, have nothing to do. The sole inquiry which we are permitted to make is whether the federal Constitution was contravened; and as to that, we confine ourselves . . . to the inquiry whether the defendants were in substance denied the right of counsel, and if so, whether such denial infringes the due process clause of the Fourteenth Amendment.

First. The record shows that immediately upon the return of the indictment defendants were arraigned and pleaded not guilty. Apparently they were not asked whether they had, or were able to employ, counsel, or wished to have counsel appointed; or whether they had friends or relatives who might assist in that regard if communicated with. That it would not have been an idle ceremony to have given the defendants reasonable opportunity to communicate with their families and endeavor to obtain counsel is demonstrated by the fact that very soon after conviction, able counsel appeared in their behalf. . . .

It is hardly necessary to say that the right to counsel being conceded, a defendant should be afforded a fair opportunity to secure counsel of his own choice. Not only was that not done here, but such designation of counsel as was attempted was either so indefinite or so close upon the trial as to amount to a denial of effective and substantial aid in that regard. . . .

[U]ntil the very morning of the trial[,] no lawyer had been named or definitely designated to represent the defendants. Prior to that time, the trial judge had "appointed all the members of the bar" for the limited "purpose of arraigning the defendants." Whether they would represent the defendants thereafter, if no counsel appeared in their behalf, was a matter of speculation only, or, as the judge indicated, of mere anticipation on the part of the court. Such a designation, even if made for all purposes, would, in our opinion, have fallen far short of meeting, in any proper sense, a requirement for the appointment of counsel. How many lawyers were members of the bar does not appear; but, in the very nature of things, whether many or few, they would not, thus collectively named, have been given that clear appreciation of responsibility or impressed with that individual sense of duty which should and naturally would accompany the appointment of a selected member of the bar, specifically named and assigned.

That this action of the trial judge in respect of appointment of counsel was little more than an expansive gesture, imposing no substantial or definite obligation upon any one, is borne out by the fact that prior to the calling of the case for trial on April 6, a leading member of the local bar accepted employment on the side of the prosecution and actively participated in the trial. It is true that he said that before doing so he had understood Mr. Roddy would be employed as counsel for the defendants. This the lawyer in question, of his own accord, frankly stated to the court; and no doubt he acted with the utmost good faith. Probably other members of the bar had a like understanding. In any event, the circumstance lends emphasis to the conclusion that during perhaps the most critical period of the proceedings against these defendants, that is to say, from the time of their arraignment until the beginning of their trial, when consultation, thorough-going investigation and preparation were vitally important, the defendants did not have the aid of counsel in any real sense, although they were as much entitled to such aid during that period as at the trial itself.

Nor do we think the situation was helped by what occurred on the morning of the trial. At that time . . . , Mr. Roddy stated to the court that he did not appear as counsel, but that he would like to appear along with counsel that the court might appoint; that he had not been given an opportunity to prepare the case; that he was not familiar with the procedure in Alabama, but merely came down as a friend of the people who were interested; that he thought the boys would be better off if he should step entirely out of the case. Mr. Moody, a member of the local bar, expressed a willingness to help Mr. Roddy [saying,] . . . "I am willing to do that for him as a member of the bar; I will go ahead and help do anything I can do." With this dubious understanding, the trials immediately proceeded. The defendants, young, ignorant, illiterate, surrounded by hostile sentiment, haled back and forth under guard of soldiers, charged with an atrocious crime regarded with especial horror in the community where they were to be tried, were thus put in peril of their lives within a few moments after counsel for the first time charged with any degree of responsibility began to represent them.

It is not enough to assume that counsel thus precipitated into the case thought there was no defense, and exercised their best judgment in proceeding to trial without preparation. Neither they nor the court could say what a prompt and thorough-going investigation might disclose as to the facts. No attempt was made to investigate. No opportunity to do so was given. Defendants were immediately hurried to trial. . . . Under the circumstances disclosed, we hold that defendants were not accorded the right of counsel in any substantial sense. To decide otherwise, would simply be to ignore actualities.

It is true that great and inexcusable delay in the enforcement of our criminal law is one of the grave evils of our time. Continuances are frequently granted for unnecessarily long periods of time, and delays incident to the disposition of motions for new trial and hearings upon appeal have come in many cases to be a distinct reproach to the administration of justice. The prompt disposition of criminal cases is to be commended and encouraged. But in reaching that result a defendant, charged with a serious crime, must not be stripped of his right to have sufficient time to advise with counsel and prepare his defense. To do that is not to proceed promptly in the calm spirit of regulated justice but to go forward with the haste of the mob. . . .

Second. The Constitution of Alabama provides that in all criminal prosecutions the accused shall enjoy the right to have the assistance of counsel; and a state statute requires the court in a capital case, where the defendant is unable to employ counsel, to appoint counsel for him. The state Supreme Court held that these provisions had not been infringed, and with that holding we are powerless to interfere. The question, however, which it is our duty, and within our power, to decide, is whether the denial of the assistance of counsel contravenes the due process clause of the Fourteenth Amendment to the Federal Constitution. . . .

Historically and in practice, in our own country at least, [the right to a hearing] has always included the right to the aid of counsel when desired and provided by the party asserting the right. The right to be heard would be, in many cases, of little avail if it did not comprehend the right to be heard by counsel. Even the intelligent and educated layman has small and sometimes no skill in the science of law. If charged with crime, he is incapable, generally, of determining for himself whether the indictment is good or bad. He is unfamiliar with the rules of evidence. Left without the aid of counsel he may be put on trial without a proper charge, and convicted upon incompetent evidence, or evidence irrelevant to the issue or otherwise inadmissible. He lacks both the skill and knowledge adequately to prepare his defense, even though he have a perfect one. He requires the guiding hand of counsel at every step in the proceedings against him. Without it, though he be not guilty, he faces the danger of conviction because he does not know how to establish his innocence. If that be true of men of intelligence, how much more true is it of the ignorant and illiterate, or those of feeble intellect. If in any case, civil or criminal, a state or federal court were arbitrarily to refuse to hear a party by counsel, employed by and appearing for him, it reasonably may not be doubted that such a refusal would be a denial of a hearing, and, therefore, of due process in the constitutional sense. . . .

In the light of the facts outlined in the forepart of this opinion—the ignorance and illiteracy of the defendants, their youth, the circumstances of public hostility, the imprisonment and the close surveillance of the defendants by the military forces, the fact that their friends and families were all in other states and communication with them necessarily difficult, and above all that they stood in deadly peril of their lives—we think the failure of the trial court to give them reasonable time and opportunity to secure counsel was a clear denial of due process.

But passing that, and assuming their inability, even if opportunity had been given, to employ counsel, as the trial court evidently did assume, we are of opinion that, under the circumstances just stated, the necessity of counsel was so vital and imperative that the failure of the trial court to make an effective appointment of counsel was likewise a denial of due process within the meaning of the Fourteenth Amendment. Whether this would be so in other criminal prosecutions, or under other circumstances, we need not determine. All that it is necessary now to decide, as we do decide, is that in a capital case, where the defendant is unable to employ counsel, and is incapable adequately of making his own defense because of ignorance, feeble-mindedness, illiteracy, or the like, it is the duty of the court, whether requested or not, to assign counsel for him as a necessary requisite of due process of law; and that duty is not discharged by an assignment at such a time or under such circumstances as to preclude the giving of effective aid in the preparation and trial of the case. To hold otherwise would be to ignore the fundamental postulate, already adverted to, "that there are certain immutable principles of justice which inhere in the very idea of free government which no member of the Union may disregard." In a case such as this, whatever may be the rule in other cases, the right to have counsel appointed, when necessary, is a logical corollary from the constitutional right to be heard by counsel. . . .

The United States by statute and every state in the Union by express provision of law, or by the determination of its courts, make it the duty of the trial judge, where the accused is unable to employ counsel, to appoint counsel for him. In most states the rule applies broadly to all criminal prosecutions, in others it is limited to the more serious crimes, and in a very limited number, to capital cases. A rule adopted with such unanimous accord reflects, if it does not establish the inherent right to have counsel appointed at least in cases like the present, and lends convincing support to the conclusion we have reached as to the fundamental nature of that right.

The judgments must be reversed and the causes remanded for further proceedings not inconsistent with this opinion.

Justice Butler (with Justice McReynolds), dissenting.

If correct, the ruling that the failure of the trial court to give petitioners time and opportunity to secure counsel was denied of due process is enough, and with this the opinion should end. But the Court goes on to declare that

> "the failure of the trial court to make an effective appointment of counsel was likewise a denial of due process within the meaning of the Fourteenth Amendment." This is an extension of federal authority into a field hitherto occupied exclusively by the several States. Nothing before the Court calls for a consideration of the point. It was not suggested below and petitioners do not ask for its decision here. The Court, without being called upon to consider it, adjudges without a hearing an important constitutional question concerning criminal procedure in state courts.

THE AFTERMATH AND SIGNIFICANCE OF *POWELL V. ALABAMA*

The Supreme Court's decision in *Powell* can scarcely be compared to any of its other rulings detailed in this volume because it was at once both so sweeping in its pronouncement and so narrow in its specific application; it has been of great consequence to many Americans and yet was relatively meaningless for the Scottsboro Boys themselves. Such a result was perhaps to be expected given the bizarre and tragic circumstances that accompanied this case. As one legal commentator aptly put it, "no crime in American history—let alone a crime that never occurred—produced as many trials, convictions, reversals, and retrials" as the Scottsboro Boys case.[45]

The larger significance of *Powell v. Alabama* lay in the fact that it was the first time that the Supreme Court had held any of the criminal law procedures guaranteed in the Constitution to be applicable against the states. From the founding era onward, Supreme Court precedent had consistently held that the provisions of the Bill of Rights, including the Sixth Amendment's right to counsel, protected citizens against national government action only and were thus not binding on the states. Indeed, it was Chief Justice John Marshall himself who declared in 1833, "[that the Bill of Rights contains] no expression indicating an intention to apply them to the state governments. This court cannot so apply them."[46] Successive justices followed Marshall's lead, and Justice Sutherland's opinion for the Court in *Powell* did not depart from that line of precedents.

However, it did find the denial of an effective appointment of counsel by Alabama courts as a violation of the due process clause of the Fourteenth Amendment, which, unlike the Bill of Rights, specifically forbids certain actions taken by states against their citizens. In other words, Alabama's appointment of unprepared and ineffective attorneys in Scottsboro violated fundamental principles of fairness and justice that were guaranteed by the Fourteenth Amendment, even if not applicable at the time by the Sixth. Importantly, however, it was the blatant disregard for fundamental rights exhibited at the Scottsboro trials that further spurred the constitutional conversation that had been taking place between members of the Court for nearly fifty years.

Since the 1880s, several justices had openly wondered how an egregious action by the national government would result in a violation of the Bill of Rights but could be permissible if undertaken by the states. In 1897, Justice John Marshall Harlan I, who had long argued unsuccessfully that the Bill of Rights applies to state government as well as to national government action, delivered an opinion for the Court that did just that in a case arising out of Chicago's condemnation of private property so that it could widen and lengthen a public road. Harlan argued that eminent domain protections, enjoyed by citizens against the national government by the Fifth Amendment, limited state governments as well. He wrote, "Private property [that] is taken for the state or under its direction for public use, without compensation made or secured to the owner, is, upon principle and authority, wanting in the due process of law required by the [F]ourteenth [A]mendment of the constitution of the United States."[47]

Justice William Henry Moody later suggested in his 1908 opinion for the Court in *Twining v. New Jersey* that some rights were so fundamental to liberty and justice that infringement on them by any level of government was unconstitutional. He explained, "[I]t is possible that some of the personal rights safeguarded by the first eight Amendments against National action may also be safeguarded against state action, because a denial of them would be a denial of due process of law. If this is so, it is not because those rights are enumerated in the first eight Amendments, but because they are of such a nature that they are included in the conception of due process of law."[48]

Writing for the Court in *Gitlow v. New York* (1925), Justice Edward Sanford singled out the freedoms of speech and press in particular in opining that they were "among the fundamental personal rights and 'liberties' protected by the due process clause of the Fourteenth Amendment from impairment by the States."[49] The Court continued to reiterate the fundamental nature of First Amendment rights against both national and state government infringement over the next decade.[50]

Finally, in its landmark 1937 decision in *Palko v. Connecticut*, the Court assembled these and other similar rulings, including *Powell*, to compile a list of those rights that it deemed to "have been found to be implicit in the concept of ordered liberty, and thus, through the Fourteenth Amendment, become valid against the states."[51] Writing for the Court, Justice Benjamin Cardozo specifically identified the First Amendment's protections for religion, speech, press, and assembly and the Sixth Amendment's right to counsel as being "so rooted in the traditions and conscience of our people as to be ranked fundamental."[52] In other words, these specific rights were believed to be so important that any infringement on them by government at any level was a constitutional violation. He went on to imply that the Fifth Amendment's eminent domain clause should also be treated accordingly.[53]

This "doctrine of incorporation" (making applicable the guarantees of the Bill of Rights against the states), as it came to be known, was controversial from the beginning because other rights that had not made it onto Cardozo's select list could still be infringed on by the states. It would take several more decades and the persistent effort of Justice Hugo Black, the third Alabamian appointed to the Supreme Court and a champion of incorporating all of the Bill of Rights against state and local government action, before the Supreme Court expanded *Palko*'s limited "honor roll" of rights.

Yet, even after the Court identified fundamental rights, some of these were constrained by later decisions. *Powell*, for example, was later interpreted to require the appointment of legal counsel only in cases in which capital punishment might be imposed or those involving the sort of unique circumstances present in the Scottsboro case.[54] Not until 1963, in its *Gideon v. Wainwright* decision, would the Court declare that the Sixth Amendment, by way of the Fourteenth Amendment's due process clause, requires that states make an effective appointment of counsel for any criminal felony defendant unable to retain an attorney on his or her own.[55] In so doing, the Court relied heavily on *Powell* and its emphasis on the fundamental nature of counsel. A decade later, the Court extended the right to counsel to include all offenses involving the possibility of imprisonment.[56]

The Court's decision in *Powell* saved the Scottsboro Boys from execution, but it had little other practical impact on their lives. With the Supreme Court's reversal and remand, the cases were sent back to Alabama where the young men were to be retried individually and with the benefit of qualified counsel.[57] Yet, even with the assistance of some of the best defense lawyers in the country and a change of venue to Decatur, the second round of trials largely mirrored the originals. There were, however, two important developments that occurred during the second trial of Haywood Patterson, the first of the Scottsboro Boys to be retried.

One of these was the fact that Patterson's defense team received nearly as much unfavorable attention as the purported incident aboard the train. Attorneys for the state, in addition to taking continued advantage of the racial divide that was so pronounced in the original trials, also chose to highlight the fact that the Scottsboro Boys' ILD attorneys were Jewish and from New York. Patterson's second trial was thus permeated not only by race and rape but also by religious intolerance and regional hatred still simmering from the Civil War. It was also noteworthy for the testimony of Ruby Bates, this time for the defense, who disavowed her earlier allegations of rape. Unable to challenge successfully her revised account of the events that had occurred aboard the train, attorneys for the state focused instead on how a poor, uneducated girl from Huntsville could afford to live in New York City while the case was on appeal and purchase the fashionable clothing she wore at Patterson's trial.

It was in this spirit that Morgan County solicitor Wade Wright, in seeking to undermine the credibility of Bates and others, laid his memorable question before the Patterson jury: "Don't you know that these people—these defense witnesses are bought and paid for? Now the question in this case is, 'Is justice in this case going to be bought and sold in Alabama with Jew money from New York?'"[58] As the ACLU's Arthur Garfield Hays put it at the time, the second round of trials had "ignorant, illiterate Negroes on one side, identified with Northerners, Communists, and Jews! The State of Alabama on the other!"[59] Not surprisingly, Patterson was again found guilty and sentenced to death.

The second important difference was the notable and heroic action of Circuit Judge James E. Horton Jr., who had been selected by the Alabama Supreme Court to preside at the second round of trials in Decatur because of his sterling reputation. At the conclusion of Patterson's trial and mindful of the tactics the state's attorneys had used, Horton went to some length in his instructions to the jury to remind them what the trial was all about: "You are not trying whether the defendant is white or black. . . . You are not trying lawyers, you are not trying State lines; but you are here at home as jurors . . . under oath sitting in the jury box taking the evidence and considering it, leaving out any outside influences."[60] When the jury again returned a guilty verdict and sentence of death, Patterson's attorneys motioned for a new trial. Horton did not grant the motion immediately, and in light of his concerns about proceeding ahead in the still tense environment, postponed the remaining trials of the other Scottsboro Boys until a future date.[61]

On June 22, 1933, two and a half months after the Patterson jury rendered its verdict, Judge Horton granted the defense motion for a new trial and did so by reading his lengthy and detailed opinion from the bench. He began by stating that "social order is based on law, and its perpetuity on its fair and impartial administration."[62] He then went on to consider the evidence and testimony presented at trial. Point by point, he described the evidence that had been presented: no testimony from credible witnesses about the purported fight between the Scottsboro Boys and the young white men on the train; no evidence that the young women had been physically assaulted with rocks and knives; no evidence of rape; clear evidence of Victoria Price's questionable morals; clear evidence that she lied under oath; clear evidence that two of the young men could not possibly have committed the crime of rape because of physical disabilities.

For Judge Horton, the Patterson case was about basic due process and the jury's role in truly listening to testimony, truly evaluating evidence, and taking seriously its role in determining guilt or innocence and in seeing lives spared or taken. The jury's apparent failure to consider any of these things, in Horton's judgment, violated the due process rights of the Scottsboro Boys. He concluded his twenty-six-page opinion by declaring that Victoria Price's testimony was "not only uncorroborated, but it also bears on its face indications of improbability and is greatly contradicted by other evidence."[63] Horton then proceeded to set aside the jury's guilty verdict and sentence and ordered a new trial. That decision created a firestorm of controversy, and he was removed by the Alabama Supreme Court from presiding over any further hearings on the matter. The remaining Scottsboro Boys' trials required by the Supreme Court's decision in *Powell* were transferred to the court of Judge William Callahan.

Judge James Horton seemed destined for political greatness given his important family connections and the high regard in which power brokers in Montgomery held him ever since his service in the state legislature. His decision to frame Patterson's case against the bold outlines of due process, however, cost him reelection in 1934. Having run unopposed in his previous bids for office, he was defeated in a primary election less than a year after setting aside the Patterson jury's verdict. He retired to his farm, never to step back into the public eye for the remaining four decades of his life.

In November 1933, Haywood Patterson and Clarence Norris were again convicted and sentenced to death in Judge Callahan's courtroom. Their attorneys again filed an appeal to the United States Supreme Court claiming that racial discrimination pervaded the jury selection process such that local black citizens were not even considered for the jury. The Court agreed and overturned their convictions, unanimously holding that "the long-continued, systematic, and arbitrary exclusion of qualified Negro citizens from service on juries solely because of their race and color [was a] violation of the Constitution of the United States."[64]

Patterson was tried for the fourth time in January 1936 and was again convicted of rape. This time, however, the jury sentenced him to seventy-five years in prison. It was reportedly the first time that a black man convicted of raping a white woman in Alabama had received anything other than a death sentence. He escaped from an Alabama prison farm in 1948 and made his way to Detroit, where he was able to avoid detection while living with his sister. While there, and with the assistance of noted American author Earl Conrad, Patterson wrote a short memoir. *Scottsboro Boy* is a first-person account of Patterson's experiences aboard the train and in the courtroom that also offers graphic and often horrifying details about Alabama prison conditions at the time. Upon the book's publication in 1950, FBI agents quickly apprehended Patterson. The state of Alabama sought to have him returned, but Michigan governor G. Mennan Williams refused the extradition request. In 1951, Patterson was convicted of manslaughter after stabbing a man in a barroom fight. He died of cancer the next year in a Michigan prison at the age of thirty-nine.

The day after Patterson's fourth conviction, Ozie Powell, Clarence Norris, and Roy Wright were being transported from Decatur back to jail in Birmingham when one of the two sheriffs accompanying them suddenly struck Powell in the face. Although manacled to the other two young men, the enraged Powell responded by slashing the officer's throat with a smuggled knife, whereupon the other officer present shot Powell through the head. Both the officer and Powell survived their injuries, but Powell was left with serious brain damage and partial paralysis. In July 1937, the rape charges against Powell were dropped when he pled guilty to assaulting the officer. He was sentenced to twenty years imprisonment but was paroled in 1946. He returned to Georgia and quickly disappeared from public view.

Also in July 1937, and after six and a half years in prison, all rape charges were suddenly dropped against Olen Montgomery, Willie Roberson, Eugene Williams, and Roy Wright. The Associated Press reported that prosecutors for the state were willing to admit that Roberson was so incapacitated from venereal disease and Montgomery so nearly blind that neither of them could have committed the alleged crime and that their female accusers must have made a mistake in identifying them. As for Williams and Wright, the state merely said that "the ends of justice would be met at this time by releasing these two juveniles, on condition that they leave the state, never to return."[65] Roy Wright, incidentally, was never retried after his mistrial in Scottsboro but remained incarcerated with the other young men, spending all of his teenage years in prison. With the help of the ILD, the NAACP, and the ACLU, the four embarked on a national tour, where they spoke to crowds of thousands to bring attention to the plight of the remaining imprisoned Scottsboro Boys. As both support from their sponsors and public interest in their case waned, however, the four went their separate ways.

Williams joined his family in St. Louis, later reportedly enrolled in a California college for a time, and then moved to Tennessee where he too faded from public consciousness. Montgomery moved to Detroit, where he was accused of attempted rape, and then to New York City, where he worked as a dishwasher and waiter while trying to break into the entertainment business. Cab Calloway, a prominent bandleader during the Swing era, even helped pay for his musical training, but Montgomery was never able to launch the career he had envisioned while incarcerated with the other Scottsboro Boys. He struggled with alcoholism and was arrested for public disorder several times before returning to live in Georgia in the late 1950s.

Roberson married, went by the names of Willie Robertson and Willie Robinson, and worked as a doorman and janitor in New York City. He served a ninety-day sentence in jail for accosting a woman on a subway car while he was drunk and then following her off the train. His boyhood asthma had been seriously aggravated during his years in prison, and he died in Brooklyn in 1959 of an asthma attack.

Roy Wright appeared to have the most promising future. He caught the attention of Bill "Bojangles" Robinson, the most celebrated African American entertainer of that era, and his wife, who treated him like their own son. In addition to providing Wright with a private tutor, they later financed his education at a vocational school where he studied to become a furrier. Using his full name of Arthur Leroy Wright, he served a successful stint in the army, married, and later joined the merchant marine. In 1959, after having been at sea for an extended period, he came home to New York believing that his wife had been unfaithful. After a heated argument, he shot his wife to death and then committed suicide. His brother Andy identified the bodies for the police.

Charlie Weems, Clarence Norris, and Andy Wright were each convicted again in 1937. Weems was sentenced to seventy-five years in prison but was paroled in 1943. Making good on his promise to "forget all about that part of my life which is past, work hard, and make a man of myself," Weems returned to the Atlanta area, found work in a laundry, married, and was never heard from publicly again.[66]

Norris was again sentenced to death, but his sentence was commuted to life the following year, and he was paroled in 1944. His parole was revoked when he left the state without permission; he spent two more years in Kilby State Prison before being paroled again in 1946. Wright was sentenced to ninety-nine years, but was paroled in 1943. He remained in Alabama, married, and had two children, but his parole was revoked in 1946, when, like Norris, he left the state without permission. He returned to prison until being paroled again in 1950, the last of the Scottsboro Boys to be imprisoned for the events of March 25, 1931.

Wright left Alabama for New York State where he hoped to earn enough money to enable his family to join him. In 1951, he was working as a weaver in a knitting mill in Albany, using his full name of James Andrew Wright, when he was accused of raping a thirteen-year-old girl. He spent eight months in jail before being acquitted by an all-white jury after just an hour and twenty minutes of deliberation. Three years later, he was charged with second-degree assault for nicking his estranged second wife about the hands and neck with a butcher knife in a fit of anger.[67] He received a suspended sentence and moved to New York City.

In identifying his brother's body for the police in August 1959, Andy also told them that "Arthur Wright" was the Roy Wright of the Scottsboro Boys, inadvertently drawing public attention to himself as well. Two weeks later, the influential black newspaper, the *New York Age*, interviewed Wright, who was now forty-seven-years old, suffering from painful circulatory and neurological conditions, jobless, nearly friendless, and about to be evicted from the rented room he had occupied for more than five years now that his identity had been made public. When asked if he harbored any ill will, Wright replied, "Not today I don't. But I am concerned about the way people feel. Since last week they seem to shun me. They should realize that innocent or guilty, any person deserves a chance to live. All I want is a chance to live—a chance I've been fighting for for nearly 30 years."[68] Andy reportedly moved to Connecticut shortly thereafter and then slipped from public view. He is buried in an unmarked grave beside his brother Roy in a Chattanooga cemetery.

Norris moved to Ohio and then New York, married three times, had two children, and assumed his brother's name for many years to avoid questions about his past. He was arrested for gun possession and gambling, but he also held relatively steady employment for the next thirty years. In the early 1970s, he quietly began working with the NAACP to win a pardon from the state of Alabama. Attorneys in New York and Alabama worked with the Alabama Attorney General's office to produce the required clear and convincing evidence of Norris's innocence required by state law. The board could grant the pardon only if the members of the state Board of Pardons and Paroles and the governor unanimously agreed to the finding of innocence.

On November 29, 1976, and not without some trepidation, sixty-four-year-old Clarence Norris returned to Alabama for the first time in three decades to receive his pardon certificate from the parole board and meet with Governor George C. Wallace. At a subsequent press conference, he expressed his satisfaction with the outcome and that he felt no bitterness toward anyone. Although surrounded by a large throng of well-wishers, both black and white, it was clear that Norris's thoughts were with those who were not there that day. With tears streaming down his face, he declared, "I'm glad to be free," but then quietly added, "I just wish those other eight boys were around."[69] He died twelve years later, the last of the Scottsboro Boys, in January 1989.

More than eighty years after the nine young men were pulled from the train at Paint Rock, the state officially closed the legal chapter on the Scottsboro Boys. On November 21, 2013, the Alabama Board of Pardons and Paroles granted posthumous pardons to Haywood Patterson, Charlie Weems, and Andy Wright, the last of the nine who had not already been pardoned or had the charges of rape dropped.

5

TRANSFORMING TUSKEGEE

Racial Redistricting and *Gomillion v. Lightfoot* (1960)

As a child growing up in Johnston, South Carolina, Charles Gomillion could not have imagined the impact he would one day have on Alabama and the nation as a whole. His father was born a slave and could neither read nor write, and his mother was barely literate. Nevertheless, both parents urged Gomillion and his three younger siblings to become educated. That was no easy task because Johnston's local elementary school for African American children only operated from three to five months a year, and there was no high school for black students in the entire county. Gomillion later estimated that he received just over two years of formal education before leaving home to attend high school in Augusta, Georgia. He took his parents' advice to heart, however, by graduating from college and subsequently earning his PhD at Ohio State University.

In 1928, Gomillion began a forty-year teaching career at the Tuskegee Institute. There he joined a community improvement organization called the Tuskegee Men's Club. For ten years, Gomillion worked with the group as it sought road paving, increased street lighting, garbage pickup, and other city services for black neighborhoods—services that were already provided to the white areas of town. In 1939, after four years of trying, he received his Certificate of Registration to vote. His work to encourage other African Americans in the area to do the same helped them to realize that the power to vote meant the power to change their community. The success of those efforts also became the catalyst to one of the most significant voting rights cases in American history.

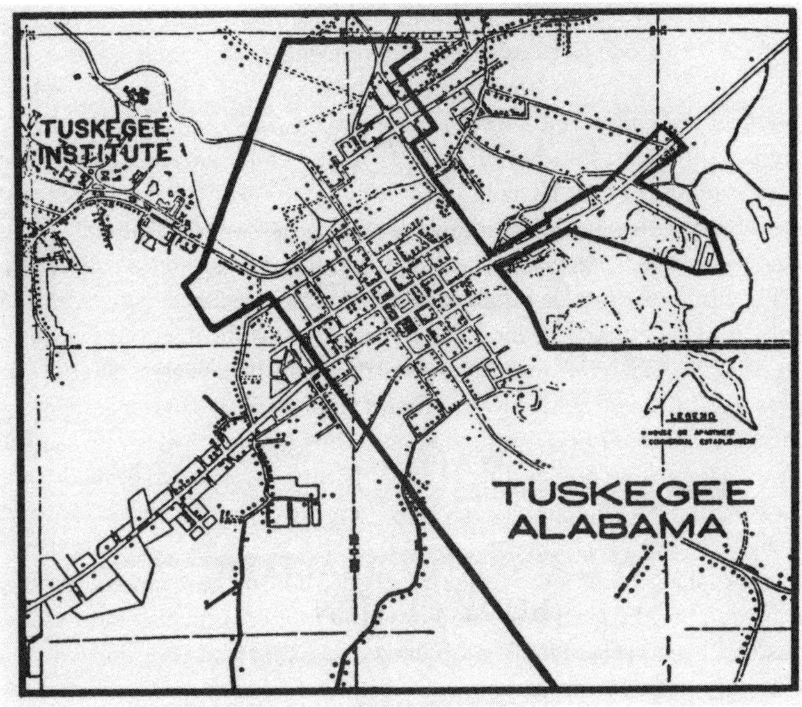

Figure 5. Tuskegee's original borders formed a simple square (everything within this map). The state legislature later changed those boundaries into a twenty-eight-sided figure (the heavy lines within the square) designed to exclude all but a few African American voters. This map was created for Fred Gray in 1958. A poster-sized version was displayed in the Supreme Court during oral argument and Justice Frankfurter included it in an appendix to his opinion for the majority.

THE STORY

One could argue that this case began with the 1619 arrival in Jamestown, Virginia, of twenty African slaves aboard a Dutch trading ship. It is equally plausible to contend that the southern secession movement, the Civil War, or Reconstruction was responsible for the circumstances that led to this dispute. The most precise point of origin for what would become *Gomillion v. Lightfoot*, however, is May 22, 1901, in Montgomery, Alabama. There, at exactly 11:00 A.M., with 155 delegates assembled, the convention to revise and amend the Alabama state constitution was called to order, and the first full day of business began. After a brief invocation and roll call of members, the president of the state constitutional convention, John B. Knox of Calhoun County, stood to address his fellow delegates and remind them of the task that lay ahead. "In my judgment," he began, "the people of Alabama have been called upon to face no more important situation than now confronts us, unless it be when they, in 1861, stirred by the momentous issue of impending conflict between the North and the South, were forced to decide whether they would remain in or withdraw from the Union."[1] "Then, as now," he added, "the Negro was the prominent factor in the issue."[2]

The ultimate purpose of the convention, Knox declared, was "within the limits imposed by the Federal Constitution, to establish white supremacy in this State."[3] In order to do so, he encouraged the delegates to craft measures to ensure that, regardless of their actual numbers in the general populace, blacks would never be able to politically dominate Alabama. As Knox put it, "There is no higher duty resting upon us . . . [than] to embody in the fundamental law such provisions as will enable us to protect the sanctity of the ballot."[4]

He recalled the bitterness that resulted from the government set up in Alabama after the Civil War and how Reconstruction institutions and policies had been viewed as illegitimate because they had been foisted on an unwilling citizenry. Thus, it was critical, he explained, "if we would have white supremacy, we must establish it by law—not by force or fraud."[5] Knox directed the delegates to look to the constitutions of Mississippi, Louisiana, the Carolinas, and Massachusetts for guidance as each had successfully implemented measures to restrict the vote in their states.

The 1901 Constitutional Convention ultimately adopted three voting-related requirements: the payment of a $1.50 poll tax; residency in the county, precinct, or ward in which one wished to vote; and formal voter registration. In order to register, a prospective voter had to own personal property of more than $300, or forty acres of land on which taxes had been paid, or pass a literacy test to the satisfaction of the local voting registrar.[6]

The voter qualifications authorized by Alabama's controversial 1901 Constitution were "race-neutral" on their face in that the poll tax, property, and literacy requirements also affected poor and illiterate whites. As Knox anticipated, however, and as could clearly be seen in states that had already enacted similar measures, such restrictions had a devastating impact on black voters. Some one hundred thousand African Americans voted in Alabama's state and federal elections of 1900. By 1904, just one year after the new constitution went into effect, there were only 3,654 qualified black voters left in the entire state.[7]

In 1945, the Alabama legislature removed the property option for voter registration, while making the literacy requirement considerably more difficult. Voters signaled their approval of this action by amending the state constitution the following year to reflect these changes. The so-called Boswell Amendment to the constitution of Alabama required prospective voters to "read and write, understand and explain any article of the Constitution of the United States in the English language." In addition, potential registrants also had to "understand the duties and obligations of good citizenship under a republican form of government."

The substantive aspects of the new literacy requirements alone made them difficult to meet. Whereas registrants were previously required to only read and copy passages from the US Constitution, the Boswell Amendment required them to have a basic understanding of the three branches of government, federalism, the constitutional amendment process, the supremacy clause, and other features of the Constitution in order to vote. The main difficulty of these heightened requirements, however, lay not with the people taking the literacy test but with those who administered it. The amendment did not stipulate the specific questions to be asked or set a minimum level of understanding to be met for passage. It also left the interpretation of such words as "understand" and "explain" completely up to the discretion of local voting registrars whose own knowledge and understanding of the Constitution might well have been suspect.

A federal court struck down the Boswell Amendment two years later in 1949 and, on appeal, the US Supreme Court upheld the decision.[8] Alabama responded by requiring prospective voters to again demonstrate their literacy by reading and copying passages of the US Constitution and to be of good character. White voters who were incapable of meeting Alabama's poll tax, literacy, and other requirements were permitted to be grandfathered in if they or their ancestors were veterans. Some were also just simply registered and permitted to vote anyway by white registrars—a privilege rarely accorded black voters. It was against this history that Charles Gomillion sought to give African Americans in Tuskegee a voice in their government.

In a 1985 interview, Gomillion recalled that, for all of its other community improvement efforts, the Tuskegee Men's Club rarely addressed the issue of voting. He implored his fellow members to register, but it was an unusually difficult and discouraging process in large measure because blacks more than doubled the white population of Tuskegee and outnumbered whites in Macon County by a 5–1 margin. Both races knew that even slight increases in black voters threatened white control of the local government.

At the time of Gomillion's lawsuit, Macon County required two white people to vouch for any African American seeking to register to vote. The first voucher was rather easily obtained, because the person wanting to register only had to give the names of qualified white voters whom they knew personally and who would certify that the prospective voter lived at the address he or she had listed on the application form. The second, however, was far more difficult to acquire because the white person had to personally go to the county courthouse and sign a document vouching for the black applicant.

Gomillion learned that few white people in the area were willing to list their names publicly for such a purpose. In his own case, he found one person to vouch for him in 1935, but four years passed before he was able to find another. Gomillion's second voucher happened to be a white contractor interested in building a home for him. As Gomillion later recalled, "I told him I had not received my Certificate of Registration, and he said 'Well, I'll see that you get it very shortly.' And so, three days later my Certificate of Registration came through the mail. . . . And I gave him a contract to build the house."[9]

In 1941, Gomillion joined with several other city residents to reorganize the Tuskegee Men's Club into the Tuskegee Civic Association (TCA), of which he would serve as president for much of the next thirty years. The TCA provided civic education to Tuskegee residents in weekly and monthly community meetings held in local churches. The participation of Tuskegee's churches was critical, as black pastors announced TCA initiatives from their pulpits and encouraged the members of their congregations to participate. Jessie P. Guzman later acknowledged in her history of the Tuskegee Civic Association that it "was only through the churches that the widest and most direct and continuous publicity could be obtained. Without the cooperation of these institutions, . . . the TCA's program would have been seriously handicapped."[10] In these meetings, Tuskegee residents learned about democracy, the importance of participating in local government, and the power of voting. Members were also encouraged to qualify for the vote, pay their poll taxes, and register.

As African American interest in civic affairs and voter registration increased, so too did opposition from local government leaders. Macon County officials instituted a number of formal and informal measures that made it very difficult for black voters to register. White citizens who sought to register to vote were quickly and professionally accommodated. Black citizens, on the other hand, faced extraordinary delays.

African Americans who had experienced no problems registering to vote in other states found themselves required by Macon County officials to read and copy extensive sections of the US Constitution for hours on end. One Tuskegee Institute professor declared, "I can understand why one must demonstrate his literacy, . . . [but it] didn't take me that long to demonstrate my competence in French—and German as well, for that matter—when I took my PhD exams at Boston University."[11] Prospective black voters signed up on a waiting list, received a number, and then patiently waited their turn or showed up at a later registration date when their number might be called. According to one account, a Tuskegee woman who had been assigned the number "17" in June was still waiting for her number to be called in mid-October.[12] Black voters joked that their high registration numbers actually stood for the year they would get registered or would be used by their children since they would likely die of old age before their numbers were called.

Officials tasked with registering black voters were accused of calling in sick on registration days as well as holding truncated business hours by arriving late and leaving early. Registrars were known to abruptly change registration locations without providing notice to black voters. In one oft-cited example, after searching all over the county courthouse on the designated registration day, black voters finally found registrars conducting their business in the probate judge's office—inside his walk-in vault.[13] Sudden resignations from the county Board of Registrars would further slow voter registration, if not stop it altogether, for months at a time until new members could be appointed to form the necessary quorum. Indeed, in 1957 just before the legislative action at issue in *Gomillion v. Lightfoot*, the Macon County Board of Registrars had met and registered voters just once in eighteen months.[14] The following year the entire board resigned and new registrars appointed by the governor to fill those vacancies refused to serve, which meant no new voters could be added.

In the mid-1950s, Macon County's population stood at just over 30,000, with more than 27,000 African Americans. White voters, however, outnumbered black voters by a 2–1 margin. The burgeoning civil rights movement saw African Americans throughout the South become increasingly vocal about their right to participate in the political process, and notwithstanding the dilatory tactics of local registrars, the number of black voters in Tuskegee and Macon County had actually increased, and would continue to do so.

To prevent the likelihood of Macon County or Tuskegee being the "first to fall under control of Negroes," as he put it, state senator Sam Engelhardt of Macon County oversaw the passage of two bills in the state legislature during the summer of 1957.[15] Identified by the *Montgomery Advertiser* as the "number one segregationist in the State Senate," Engelhardt explained the need for his legislation by saying, "I have known for some time prior to the introduction of my bill[s] . . . that the master plan for this area was to register as many Negroes as possible. That was their way of taking over city government."[16]

His first bill, later known as Act 140, would effectively gerrymander black voters out of Tuskegee by taking what had been the two-and-a-half-mile-square boundary of the city and transform it into a twenty-eight-sided figure that excluded black neighborhoods, the famed Tuskegee Institute, and all but a handful of the city's four hundred qualified black voters. Engelhardt's second bill was a backup plan that would take effect in the event that the gerrymander somehow failed. It proposed to dissolve Macon County entirely and thus dissipate black political influence into the six surrounding counties. Engelhardt and his supporters were confident that both proposals would survive judicial scrutiny in the federal courts because the Supreme Court had plainly stated its reluctance to get involved in state-level boundary-drawing decisions.[17]

Charles Gomillion and the TCA responded to these legislative proposals with ads in the state's major newspapers asking Alabamians to contact their state legislators and ask them to vote against the gerrymander bill. The ad pled with white voters to consider what was at stake if legislators could use race alone to "throw out of the city limits of Tuskegee hundreds of patriotic, law-abiding and well-educated families, their schools, churches, and the world-renowned Tuskegee Institute."[18] Later, at a rally attended by some 2,500 people at the Butler Chapel AME Zion Church in Tuskegee, Gomillion denounced both the gerrymander and the cumulative effect of everything that had preceded it, which had trapped African Americans "in a political situation," he said, that "is now desperate."[19] "All members of any board—education, welfare, recreation—in Macon County are white and in complete control over us," he declared. "We have been thwarted when we try to register ourselves and to vote. . . . We have to hunt and find a board of registrars in their hiding places."[20] He lamented the entire situation but was unapologetic about what he and other African Americans were ultimately seeking: "The time will come when they will have to respect us. They may hate our guts, but they will respect us."[21]

When the Tuskegee gerrymander bill became law in July 1957, without hearings, debate, or a single dissenting vote in either house of the Alabama legislature, Gomillion's group resolved on a two-part strategy. The first and broader-based plan called on the very African Americans who had just lost their ability to cast a political vote in Tuskegee to vote instead with their pocketbooks and wallets. If the city did not want them, then they would take their money and shop elsewhere. "Trade With Your Friends" became the theme of this extremely effective campaign that ran for nearly four years. It targeted white establishments in the area that required African Americans to use rear entrances or that had only served them after first attending to white customers. "We will buy goods and services from only those who will recognize us as first-class citizens," Gomillion proclaimed, "and who help rather than oppress us."[22] Martin Luther King Jr. came to Tuskegee to offer his support. Before a crowd of some two thousand people at a weekly TCA meeting, he said he was "happy [that] the day has come when you no longer pay to be mistreated."[23] His cause, like theirs, he said, was not "to put the stores out of business but to put justice into business."[24]

As area merchants began to feel the effect of the boycott, the sponsor of the gerrymander, Senator Engelhardt, announced that he would do everything within his power to strip the famed Tuskegee Institute of all state appropriations until black shoppers returned to downtown Tuskegee. In addition, after raiding the offices of the TCA in late July, Attorney General John Patterson sought an injunction from Circuit Judge Will O. Walton forbidding the TCA from engaging in any activity that might force or coerce others to boycott Tuskegee establishments. Judge Walton subsequently denied Patterson's request stating that Alabama citizens, regardless of color, had a right to trade with whomever they pleased.[25]

The TCA's second and more targeted effort was a federal court challenge to Act 140 and the Tuskegee gerrymander. Filing suit in the US District Court in Montgomery against Tuskegee mayor Philip M. Lightfoot, members of the city council, and others, Gomillion and the TCA argued that the action violated the Fourteenth Amendment's due process and equal protection clauses and the Fifteenth Amendment's right to vote.

THE CONSTITUTIONAL BACKGROUND

Despite the obvious racial intent behind the 1901 Alabama Constitution, the decades of concerted effort by Macon County officials to make voter registration difficult for African Americans, and the Tuskegee gerrymander law, federal judges at the time could not simply declare these governmental actions and practices unconstitutional. The constraints of Supreme Court precedent made it very difficult (attorneys for the Tuskegee gerrymander law believed it to be nearly impossible) to upend race-based voting practices.

For example, in the early twentieth century, poll taxes were not generally regarded as a tool of discrimination. In fact, the United States Supreme Court unanimously upheld their use in the 1937 case of *Breedlove v. Suttles*.[26]

There the Court ruled that a Georgia law requiring poll taxes of all citizens between the ages of twenty-one and sixty, except for women and the blind, did not unconstitutionally discriminate against the male voter who brought the case because it was the states that conferred on their citizens the right to vote. The Fifteenth Amendment, the Court held, requires only that suffrage not be denied "on account of race, color, or previous condition of servitude." States could, therefore, restrict voting privileges to those above a certain age, to those free of mental disabilities or felony convictions, or to those who paid a poll tax. In other words, the Court said, "save as restrained by the Fifteenth and Nineteenth Amendments and other provisions of the Federal Constitution, the State may condition suffrage as it deems appropriate."[27]

Poll taxes obviously affected all citizens who were too poor to pay the amount, regardless of their race. However, the impact of this and other voting requirements on African American voters was staggering. As mentioned earlier, prior to the passage of the 1901 Constitution, blacks in Alabama had voted in the tens of thousands. Within four years of the new constitution taking effect, however, and with nearly a million African Americans living in the state, fewer than four thousand were registered to vote.[28]

With the ratification of the Twenty-Fourth Amendment in January 1964, the levying of poll taxes against those wishing to vote in federal elections became unconstitutional. At that time, however, several states, including Alabama, still made use of poll taxes in both state and local elections. Under the authority of the Voting Rights Act of 1965, the United States Department of Justice took Alabama to federal court over its continued use of the poll tax as a violation of the Fifteenth Amendment.

In its argument in *United States v. Alabama* (1966), the state advanced several reasons for its reliance on the poll tax. The tax, it argued, served as a test of good citizenship, reflected a concern about public education (since that is where poll tax proceeds were directed), and properly denied a voice in governance to those too lazy or too apathetic to raise the money to pay the toll.[29] Mindful of the reasons behind the 1901 Constitutional Convention's adoption of the poll tax requirement in the first place, the district court that heard the case rejected the ostensibly race-neutral justifications the state offered. Declaring the poll tax to be "one of the last great pillars of racial discrimination," the lower court struck the state's practice down as unconstitutional on March 3, 1966.[30] Three weeks later, the US Supreme Court's decision in *Harper v. Virginia Board of Elections* banned the practice in all elections.[31]

Prospective voters who were able to pay the poll tax still confronted other registration requirements, such as literacy tests, which the US Supreme Court had also previously upheld. As late as 1959, the Court affirmed the constitutionality of a North Carolina law that required all potential voters to be able to read and write in English any section of the state constitution. Writing for a unanimous Court in *Lassiter v. Northampton County Board of Elections*, Justice William O. Douglas noted, "Literacy and illiteracy are neutral on race, creed, color, and sex . . . , [and] a State might conclude that only those who are literate should exercise the franchise. . . . We do not sit in judgment of the wisdom of that policy. We cannot say, however, that it is not an allowable one measured by constitutional standards."[32] So long as officials administered the test to all prospective voters regardless of race, the Court reasoned, it was constitutional.

Over time, and as the Supreme Court confronted the selective application of certain voting requirements to deter black voters, it began to strike down such practices by looking to the Fourteenth and Fifteenth Amendments.[33] The Tuskegee gerrymander, however, forced the Court to turn its attention to its own role in a constitutional system of federalism and separate institutions sharing power.

During its first 150 years, the Supreme Court largely avoided deciding questions that it thought were more properly resolved by the other branches of government. What such "political questions" as the Court termed them entailed, of course, was in the eye of the beholder. Still, the Court generally held true to Chief Justice John Marshall's guiding observation in *Marbury v. Madison* (1803): "The province of the court is, solely, to decide on the rights of individuals, not to inquire how [government] officers, perform duties in which they have a discretion. Questions, in their nature political, . . . can never be made in this court."[34]

While never explicitly defined, the political question doctrine suggests that disputes that come before the Court that are rooted more in politics than in law should be reserved for the executive and legislative branches to decide. Of course, the Court has more than dabbled in areas that might conceivably be thought of as political questions, but for most of its history, the Court assiduously avoided disputes in one particular area: that of legislative apportionment and redistricting. Which voters were drawn into (or out of) a voting district and how seats in Congress or a state legislature were apportioned were generally viewed by the Court as political questions and therefore nonjusticiable.

In 1946, the Court considered a challenge to badly malapportioned congressional districts in Illinois. The state created those districts in 1901 but failed to update them to reflect the massive shifts in population that occurred during the intervening forty years. Thus, where two members of Congress from Illinois may have both represented 10,000 people in 1901, four decades later one member might still represent 10,000 people while the other represented 100,000. Voters challenged the law stating that malapportionment diluted the votes of those who lived in more populous areas.

In writing for a narrow majority in *Colegrove v. Green* (1946), Justice Felix Frankfurter invoked the political question doctrine to declare there was nothing the Court could do to help the Illinois voters. "Nothing is clearer than that this controversy concerns matters that bring courts into immediate and active relations with party contests. . . . It is hostile to a democratic system to involve the judiciary in the politics of the people."[35] Citizens, political parties, and even Congress could properly intervene to correct this acknowledged wrong, but "[c]ourts," Frankfurter warned, "ought not to enter this political thicket."[36] This historical and judicial background convinced Sam Engelhardt and proponents of the Tuskegee gerrymander that the Supreme Court would do nothing to undermine their actions.

THE LITIGATION

In retrospect, Charles Gomillion and the TCA could not have hoped for a federal judge more sympathetic to their concerns than US district judge Frank M. Johnson. He would serve more than forty years on the federal bench, handing down several important rulings that fundamentally transformed Alabama. When the Tuskegee gerrymander case came before him, however, he had only been on the bench for a little more than two years, and his ruling was a major disappointment to Tuskegee's African Americans.

Johnson's brief opinion in the case never reached the questions regarding racial discrimination or access to the ballot box. Instead, he focused on the authority of the legislature to change Tuskegee's square boundaries to a figure that more perfectly resembled, in Johnson's words, the outline of "a sea dragon."[37] In reviewing the Alabama Constitution of 1901, Johnson found clear authority for the state legislature to alter municipal boundaries, including those of Tuskegee. He then considered whether the legislators could change such boundaries arbitrarily. He concluded that they could so long as the authorized lawmakers did so through the proper legislative process. Johnson did not attempt to hide or ignore the purpose behind the Tuskegee gerrymander, but he ruled that, regardless of the motive, he simply had "no control, no supervision over, and no power to change any boundaries . . . fixed by a duly convened and elected legislative body."[38]

On appeal, a Fifth Circuit panel of judges upheld the district court's opinion, but could not agree as to why. The majority opinion basically mirrored Johnson's view that so long as the gerrymander was within the power of the legislature to enact, and barring any explicit racial discrimination on its face (specifically stating, for example, that it was targeted at African Americans), it could not prevent the new Tuskegee boundaries.

Judge John Minor Wisdom wrote a separate concurrence that clearly acknowledged the real effect of the gerrymander: "In a democratic country nothing is worse than disfranchisement. And there is no such thing as being just a little bit disfranchised. A free man's right to vote is a full right to vote or it is no right to vote."[39] However, he also believed that what Gomillion and the Tuskegee Civic Association sought might well be "a cure worse than the disease."[40] To invite the federal judiciary "to control a state legislature's right to fix the boundaries of a political subdivision," he wrote, "carries consequences even more serious and far-reaching than . . . disfranchisement."[41] It was not just the fact that judges were being asked to enter *Colegrove*'s "political thicket," it was also that they really were not qualified to help. As Wisdom put it, "Courts, any courts, are incompetent to remap city limits. And any decree in this case purporting to give relief will be a sham: the relief sought will give no relief."[42]

In dissent, Circuit Judge John Robert Brown went to great lengths to reframe the dispute as one pertaining more to individual rights than to separation of powers. What was really at stake, he argued, was not so much whether the Alabama legislature was authorized to create the new Tuskegee boundaries or whether the gerrymander constituted the type of political question that lay outside of the court's jurisdiction. The problem, he argued, was the effect of the gerrymander on African Americans who had formerly been citizens of Tuskegee and to whom the law was directed. He gently chided his colleagues for ignoring the real issue in the case when he wrote, "We need not be that 'blind' Court that Mr. Chief Justice Taft described as unable to see what 'all others can see and understand.'"[43]

Gomillion pressed ahead with an appeal of the Fifth Circuit's decision, and in March 1960, the US Supreme Court agreed to hear the case. In their briefs for the Court, attorneys for Gomillion argued that the gerrymander was just the latest in a long line of discriminatory practices that African Americans in Tuskegee had experienced. They acknowledged that a full hearing on the matter might result in the emergence of other plausible reasons for such irregular boundaries. But, in light of the pattern of voting-related difficulties in Macon County, they pled with the Court to see the gerrymander for what it was: purposeful discrimination in violation of the

Fourteenth Amendment's due process and equal protection clauses, and the Fifteenth Amendment's protection for voting.

For their part, attorneys for the city questioned how this could even be a justiciable issue given previous state laws incorporating Tuskegee and fixing its boundaries at two and half miles square. Subsequent state laws reduced those boundaries to a mile square and then later expanded them again. They argued that the gerrymander was just another boundary shift for Tuskegee by the state legislature. Further, they questioned the wisdom and propriety of any court informing a legislature that municipal boundaries are fixed and thus can never be altered. The city's attorneys also stressed that the law did not deprive anyone of their vote. Granted, the gerrymander would not permit previous Tuskegee citizens to vote in city elections as they had in the past, but they possessed their full voting rights in all forthcoming federal, state, and county elections.

The following October, the Court heard oral arguments on the matter. The justices authorized a rare visual aid in their courtroom by permitting Fred Gray, one of Gomillion's attorneys, to display an oversized map of Tuskegee that reflected the city's boundaries before and after the gerrymander. Gray situated the map in full view of the Court, and the justices were fascinated by it. From the minute Gray stood up, they subjected him to a number of probing questions about the map, such as how far city services extended, whether police or fire protection went beyond the city boundaries, and if the changes would affect the public schools.

As Gray discussed the formerly square boundaries of the city and contrasted them with the bizarre shape created by the gerrymander, Justice Felix Frankfurter, the author of *Colegrove* and the political thicket doctrine, asked him where the famed Tuskegee Institute was located. Gray pointed to its location on the map and replied, "Tuskegee Institute is here, in the northwest corner. It is no longer in the city." Frankfurter quietly mused, "That's now outside." To which Gray responded, "It is now outside, yes sir."[44] Gray later wrote that it was at that moment that he knew he had Justice Frankfurter's vote.[45]

When asked about the population of Tuskegee, Gray responded that within its former boundaries, the city was home to approximately 6,700 people, 5,397 of whom were African American with about 400 of that number registered as qualified voters. He admitted to having no idea of the city's population under the new boundary but did offer that, to his knowledge, all of the 1,310 whites in the city and the 600 qualified white voters among them still lived within Tuskegee's borders. He urged the justices to consider the Tuskegee border action against the broader backdrop of

Macon County where, during the previous four years, the board of registrars had qualified only three black voters.

Robert Carter, one of the NAACP's lead attorneys who assisted with the case, then rose to address the Court. "Our position in this case is quite simple," he said. "We take the position that this is purely a case of racial discrimination, solely and simply racial discrimination."[46] He presented hypothetical scenarios where Alabama disenfranchised all blacks or passed a law denying African Americans the right to live in Tuskegee. The Court would rightly deem each of those unconstitutional, he argued, and the gerrymander law was no different.

Justice Black pressed him directly about whether the justices should overrule *Colegrove*. Well aware of the Court's historical reluctance in the area, Carter replied, "[W]e're not asking [you] to overrule *Colegrove v. Green*. Our contention is that this is not a reapportionment case and that the *Colegrove* doctrine has nothing to do with the problems which are raised here. We take the position that this is purely a race discrimination case."[47]

Representing Tuskegee's mayor and city council, James G. Carter then stood and immediately took issue with the "sea dragon" characterization of Tuskegee's new borders. He said the previous night he had picked up a roadmap and viewed the boundaries of several major cities in the United States. They reminded him of when he was a boy and lay on the grass looking at clouds and deciphering shapes of them. It really did not matter what Tuskegee looked like, he reminded the justices, because the Court's own precedents had clearly established that states have "a sovereign right to extend corporate limits, to draw them in, to consolidate cities, or to abolish them."[48]

When the justices asked if a state could use its legitimate, lawful power to accomplish an unconstitutional end, Carter acknowledged that it could. He added, however, that the intent and the context of the allegedly unconstitutional action would have to be considered. "To get to the racial angle . . . we would have to go back and see what the legislature meant," he declared.[49] He added, "[There is also] ambiguous legislation, where we always go back to committee reports."[50] He then said, perhaps revealing the reason why there had been neither hearings nor debate in the Alabama state legislature on the Tuskegee gerrymander, "Here there is none. There's nothing in the Act. There's nothing to construe in this statute from that end. These are the boundary lines, period."[51]

He concluded by reminding the justices about *Colegrove*. To insert the Court in the boundary drawing of municipalities "is about as highly political a thing as anybody can get into. . . . If we start drawing boundary lines as such for every ward and every precinct and everything, there's going to be question after question."[52] The *Montgomery Advertiser* echoed that sentiment in an editorial just before oral arguments: "The Tuskegee case, whatever its own importance, may open the way for judicial changes in the voting patterns of the nation. Whether these changes are for good or ill, they will certainly have wide impact."[53] Less than a month later, the Court issued its unanimous opinion in the case.

THE DECISION

Gomillion v. Lightfoot, Mayor of Tuskegee (9–0)
364 U.S. 339 (1960)

JUSTICE FRANKFURTER delivered the opinion of the Court.

This litigation challenges the validity, under the United States Constitution, of Local Act No. 140, passed by the Legislature of Alabama in 1957, redefining the boundaries of the City of Tuskegee. . . . Petitioners' claim is that enforcement of the statute, which alters the shape of Tuskegee from a square to an uncouth twenty-eight-sided figure, will constitute a discrimination against them in violation of the Due Process and Equal Protection Clauses of the Fourteenth Amendment to the Constitution and will deny them the right to vote in defiance of the Fifteenth Amendment.

The respondents moved for dismissal of the action for failure to state a claim upon which relief could be granted and for lack of jurisdiction of the District Court. The court granted the motion, stating, "This Court has no control over, no supervision over, and no power to change any boundaries of municipal corporations fixed by a duly convened and elected legislative body, acting for the people in the State of Alabama." On appeal, the Court of Appeals for the Fifth Circuit, affirmed the judgment, one judge dissenting. We brought the case here, since serious questions were raised concerning the power of a State over its municipalities in relation to the Fourteenth and Fifteenth Amendments.

At this stage of the litigation, we are not concerned with the truth of the allegations, that is, the ability of petitioners to sustain their allegations by proof. The sole question is whether the allegations entitle them to make good on their claim that they are being denied rights under the United States Constitution. The complaint, charging that Act 140 is a device to disenfranchise Negro citizens, alleges the following facts: prior to Act 140, the City of Tuskegee was square in shape; the Act transformed it into a strangely irregular twenty-eight-sided figure as indicated in the diagram appended to this opinion. The essential inevitable effect of this redefinition of Tuskegee's boundaries is to remove from the city all save four or five of its 400 Negro voters while not removing a single white voter or resident. The result of the Act is to deprive the Negro petitioners discriminatorily of the benefits of residence in Tuskegee, including, *inter alia*, the right to vote in municipal elections.

These allegations, if proven, would abundantly establish that Act 140 was not an ordinary geographic redistricting measure, even within familiar abuses of gerrymandering. If these allegations, upon a trial, remained uncontradicted or unqualified, the conclusion would be irresistible, tantamount for all practical purposes to a mathematical demonstration, that the legislation is solely concerned with segregating white and colored voters by fencing Negro citizens out of town so as to deprive them of their pre-existing municipal vote.

It is difficult to appreciate what stands in the way of adjudging a statute having this inevitable effect invalid in light of the principles by which this Court must judge, and uniformly has judged, statutes that, howsoever speciously defined, obviously discriminate against colored citizens. "The [Fifteenth] Amendment nullifies sophisticated as well as simple-minded modes of discrimination" *Lane v. Wilson* (1939).

The complaint amply alleges a claim of racial discrimination. Against this claim the respondents have never suggested, either in their brief or in oral argument, any countervailing municipal function which Act 140 is designed to serve. The respondents invoke generalities expressing the State's unrestricted power—unlimited, that is, by the United States Constitution—to establish, destroy, or reorganize by contraction or expansion its political subdivisions, to wit, cities, counties, and other local units. We freely recognize the breadth and importance of this aspect of the State's political power. To exalt this power into an absolute is to misconceive the reach and rule of this Court's decisions. . . .

[The] Court has never acknowledged that the States have power to do as they will with municipal corporations regardless of consequences. Legislative control of municipalities, no less than other state power, lies within the scope of relevant limitations imposed by the United States Constitution. . . .

[I]t should be equally true that . . . such power, extensive though it is, is met and overcome by the Fifteenth Amendment to the Constitution of the United States, which forbids a State from passing any law which deprives a citizen of his vote because of his race. The opposite conclusion, urged upon us by respondents, would sanction the achievement by a State of any impairment of voting rights whatever so long as it was cloaked in the grab of the realignment of political subdivisions. . . .

The respondents find another barrier to the trial of this case in *Colegrove v. Green* (1946). . . . The decisive facts in this case, which at this stage must be taken as proved, are wholly different from the considerations found controlling in *Colegrove*.

That case involved a complaint of discriminatory apportionment of congressional districts. The appellants in *Colegrove* complained only of a dilution of the strength of their votes as a result of legislative inaction over a course of many years. The petitioners here complain that affirmative legislative action deprives them of their votes and the consequent advantages that the ballot affords. When a legislature thus singles out a readily isolated segment of a racial minority for special discriminatory treatment, it violates the Fifteenth Amendment. In no case involving unequal weight in voting distribution that has come before the Court did the decision sanction a differentiation on racial lines whereby approval was given to unequivocal withdrawal of the vote solely from colored citizens. Apart from all else, these considerations lift this controversy out of the so-called "political" arena and into the conventional sphere of constitutional litigation.

In sum, as Mr. Justice Holmes remarked, when dealing with a related situation, in *Nixon v. Herndon* (1927) "Of course the petition concerns political action," but "The objection that the subject matter of the suit is political is little more than a play upon words." A statute which is alleged to have worked unconstitutional deprivations of petitioners' rights is not immune to attack simply because the mechanism employed by the legislature is a redefinition of municipal boundaries. According to the allegations here made, the Alabama Legislature has not merely redrawn the Tuskegee city limits with incidental inconvenience to the petitioners; it is more accurate to say that it has deprived the petitioners of the municipal franchise and consequent rights and to that end it has incidentally changed the city's boundaries. While in form this is merely an act redefining metes and bounds, if the allegations are established, the inescapable human effect of this essay in geometry and geography is to despoil colored citizens, and only colored citizens, of their theretofore enjoyed voting rights. That was not *Colegrove v. Green*.

When a State exercises power wholly within the domain of state interest, it is insulated from federal judicial review. But such insulation is not carried over when state power is used as an instrument for circumventing a federally protected right. This principle has had many applications. It has long been recognized in cases which have prohibited a State from exploiting a power acknowledged to be absolute in an isolated context to justify the imposition of an "unconstitutional condition." What the Court has said in those cases is equally applicable here, viz., that "Acts generally lawful may become unlawful when done to accomplish an unlawful end [see *United States v. Reading Co.* (1913)], and a constitutional power cannot be used by way of condition to attain an unconstitutional result" (*Western Union Telegraph Co. v. Foster* [1918]). The petitioners are entitled to prove their allegations at trial.

For these reasons, the principal conclusions of the District Court and the Court of Appeals are clearly erroneous and the decision below must be

Reversed.

Justice Whittaker, concurring.

I concur in the Court's judgment, but not in the whole of its opinion. It seems to me that the decision should be rested not on the Fifteenth Amendment, but rather on the Equal Protection Clause of the Fourteenth Amendment to the Constitution. I am doubtful that the averments of the complaint, taken for present purposes to be true, show a purpose by Act No. 140 to abridge petitioners' "right . . . to vote," in the Fifteenth Amendment sense. It seems to me that the "right . . . to vote" that is guaranteed by the Fifteenth Amendment is but the same right to vote as is enjoyed by all others within the same election precinct, ward or other political division. . . .

But it does seem clear to me that accomplishment of a State's purpose—to use the Court's phrase—of "fencing Negro citizens out of" Division A and into Division B is an unlawful segregation of races of citizens, in violation of the Equal Protection Clause of the Fourteenth Amendment, and, as stated, I would think the decision should be rested on that ground—which, incidentally, clearly would not involve, just as the cited cases did not involve, the *Colegrove* problem.

THE AFTERMATH AND SIGNIFICANCE OF *GOMILLION V. LIGHTFOOT*

The Court's decision had a twofold impact. The first and most immediate was the February 1961 restoration of the original Tuskegee boundaries by US district judge Frank Johnson who, acting on the principles set forth in the Court's *Gomillion* decision, invalidated the state law authorizing the gerrymander. A month later, he issued a stern decree to Macon County registrars to cease "such acts and practices [that] have brought about and perpetuated the disparity between the relative percentages" of black and white voters.[54]

The second impact was far more consequential. *Gomillion* was the Supreme Court's first step into the previously forbidden area of legislative districting and apportionment. The Court firmly rooted its *Gomillion* opinion in the Fifteenth Amendment, which categorically forbids the denial or abridgement of the right to vote based on race. As Justice Frankfurter's decision for the Court indicated, depriving practically the entire African American population of Tuskegee of their right to vote was simply too egregious for the Court to ignore. However, several other justices believed that there was little difference between depriving citizens of their vote entirely and diluting their vote to such an extent that it robbed them of any efficacy whatsoever. Over the next few years, in landmark cases such as *Baker v. Carr* (1962), *Wesberry v. Sanders* (1964), *Reynolds v. Sims* (1964), and others, the Court asserted its authority to review legislative districts and require states to redraw or reapportion those that it found unsatisfactory.[55]

Acclaimed southern historian Robert J. Norrell wrote in his classic work on Tuskegee and the civil rights movement, "*Gomillion* . . . set a precedent for the Court's negating a political boundary fixed by a state. . . . [The] 'one-man, one-vote' decisions did not follow directly from *Gomillion*, but the Tuskegee case ushered the Court into the political thicket that the justices previously avoided. Once there, they stayed."[56] Indeed, no more reluctant to engage in issues surrounding legislative districts, the Court has found itself dealing with the most political of all political questions: gerrymandering for partisan advantage.

In 1986, the Court ruled in *Davis v. Bandemer* that political gerrymandering was justiciable, but the seven justices in the majority were unable to agree on a standard by which to adjudicate claims that a majority party's power to redraw legislative districts to its advantage discriminated against the minority party.[57] Nearly two decades later, with six justices appointed since *Bandemer*, and having considered several other redistricting cases in the meantime without having made any progress toward securing a standard, a plurality of justices announced in *Vieth v. Jubelirer* (2004) that the Court simply could not adjudicate political gerrymandering.[58] Because that opinion did not command a majority, the Court continues to be caught in the political thicket of redistricting with no clear path either forward or back. The Court underscored its indecision in the area again recently in *Gill v. Whitford* (2018) and *Rucho v. Common Cause* (2019).[59]

Although he is best known for his untiring efforts to win and protect the right to vote for African Americans in Tuskegee, Charles Gomillion's actual job was as a professor of sociology. He would go on to serve as chair of the Division of Social Sciences at the Tuskegee Institute and later as dean of students and dean of the College of Arts and Sciences. He retired in 1970, and spent much of the remaining twenty-five years of his life in Washington, DC, and New Jersey.

Gomillion died in Montgomery on October 4, 1995. Newspapers from around the country recounted his life and legacy, but one of the more notable tributes published by the *New York Times* was entered into the *Congressional Record* by Senator Howell Heflin of Alabama, who prefaced the article with these remarks: "Mr. Charles Goode Gomillion, who passed away on October 4 at the age of 95, will go down in history as the leader of the struggle to bring political power to the black majority of citizens in Tuskegee, Alabama. The case *Gomillion v. Lightfoot* ultimately yielded a landmark U.S. Supreme Court decision on the issue of redistricting. The decision in the case is also recognized by legal scholars as a major step forward in the dual causes of civil and voting rights."[60] Heflin added, "Charles Gomillion will long be remembered as a pioneer who took a firm stand on principle and by so doing paved the way for major advances in the cause of equality."[61]

Gomillion's view of his life was far more modest. When asked in a 1985 interview what he had accomplished in his life, he did not mention the challenges facing black voters in Macon County, the Tuskegee Civic Association, or even the Supreme Court case that bears his name. Instead, reflecting on his forty years at the Tuskegee Institute, he responded, "What have I accomplished? I think my major contribution was in the enlightenment of students. . . . I think when any of them have endeavored to put into practice some of the things which they learned in some of . . . (our) courses . . . , I am happier about my association with them."[62]

6

EQUAL PROTECTION, EQUAL BENEFITS

Women's Rights and *Frontiero v. Richardson* (1973)

On its surface, this case hardly seemed worthy of the Supreme Court's attention. The circumstances involved a young, newly married couple struggling to make ends meet who sought additional financial assistance and benefits from the primary wage earner's employer. What made this very common scenario unique at the time, however, was that the employer was the United States Air Force and the primary wage earner was female. Furthermore, the US Air Force's denial of the assistance she requested was not based on the availability of funds or the worthiness of her claim, but on her gender alone.

The subsequent lawsuit brought by the twenty-three-year-old, publicity-shy air force officer coincided with a constitutional question that was being passionately argued in the courts by one of America's most famous female attorneys and debated across the country by the public at large because of the pending Equal Rights Amendment.[1] That question was simply this: does the Constitution permit the government to treat men and women differently? While the Supreme Court's decision in *Frontiero v. Richardson* did not fully answer that question, it was nevertheless a major victory for Lieutenant Sharron Frontiero; Joseph Levin, the Montgomery attorney who took the case; Ruth Bader Ginsburg, who made her first appearance before the Supreme Court in the case, and for all women in America.

THE STORY

Sharron Perry's connection to Alabama came by way of a military assignment. She was born and raised in Massachusetts and attended the University of

Figure 6. US Air Force lieutenant Sharron Frontiero, ca. 1969–73. Courtesy of the Southern Poverty Law Center.

Connecticut where she joined the US Air Force in October of her senior year. Upon graduating in the spring of 1969, she received her commission and her first assignment to Maxwell Air Force Base in Montgomery, where she worked as a physical therapist at the base hospital for most of the next four years. While in Montgomery, she renewed a friendship with Joseph Frontiero, who had attended her Gloucester, Massachusetts, high school. He had previously served in the US Navy, but was then enrolled as a full-time student at Huntingdon College. On December 27, 1969, they married and, like many young couples, began to struggle financially.

Between Sharron's military pay, Joseph's $205 monthly veterans' benefits, and his $30 per month part-time job, the young couple found it difficult to cover their rent and other basic living expenses. Their situation continued unchanged for nearly a year before Sharron learned that her married male counterparts in the military received $120 monthly to assist with the expenses of their off-base housing.

In the fall of 1970, she contacted Maxwell Air Force Base officials about the Basic Allowance for Quarters (BAQ). These were supplemental funds to offset the cost of housing in the local community when base accommodations were not available.[2] She also applied for the comprehensive medical benefits offered to dependents of military personnel.[3] The federal law governing military housing and benefits stipulated that a "married female member may claim her husband and . . . minor children upon a showing that they are in fact dependent on her."[4] Military authorities accordingly asked Sharron to prove her husband's dependency status by demonstrating that she provided more than one-half of his support. Joseph's own expenses were estimated at $354 a month, but between the veterans' benefits that he received monthly and the additional income he earned from his part-time job, it was obvious that Sharron did not supply more than one-half of Joseph's support. Unable to recognize Joseph as her dependent, the air force denied Sharron's requests for the housing allowance and medical benefits.

The explanation officials gave for the rejection was clear, concise, and an accurate reflection of the dependency provisions of the applicable law: different standards applied to male and female service members. With regard to men, the law simply stipulated that "a married male may claim his wife and . . . minor children regardless of whether those persons are dependent in fact."[5] In other words, unlike Frontiero, a male member of the military who asked for the BAQ and/or extended medical and dental benefits for his family would essentially receive them automatically without having to demonstrate that he provided more than one-half of their support.

Frontiero initially believed that the discrepancy in the regulations relative to male and female service members was little more than an overlooked clerical error. With an estimated nine thousand married women serving in the military at the time, she believed that once military authorities found out about the problem, they would move quickly to correct it.[6] When she subsequently learned that there had been no clerical error, that the gender distinctions governing the extension of housing allowances and medical benefits were, in fact, written into law, she turned to Montgomery lawyer Joe Levin for help.[7]

On December 23, 1970, just four days before they celebrated their first wedding anniversary, Sharron and Joseph Frontiero filed suit in US District Court in Montgomery against Secretary of Defense Melvin R. Laird, Secretary of the Air Force Robert C. Seamans Jr., and Colonel Charles G. Weber, the commanding officer of Maxwell Air Force Base. The Frontieros argued that the "different treatment for female and male members of the uniformed services, arbitrarily and unreasonably discriminate[d] against [them]" and was therefore unconstitutional.[8] They not only wanted the discriminatory regulations to end, they also sought to have the housing allowance made retroactive to the date of their marriage. Interviewed about the lawsuit two weeks later while on leave in Massachusetts, Sharron explained,

"This is a last ditch attempt to get the allowances. We tried for a year to go through the proper channels, but everyone kept saying, 'We've got regulations. It just can't be helped.'"[9]

THE CONSTITUTIONAL BACKGROUND

The Supreme Court's role in protecting female citizens against discrimination is relatively, and surprisingly, recent despite the fact that gender-based laws denying rights and privileges to women were in place from the moment the United States declared its independence from Great Britain. For example, the new country retained the British common law rules of coverture, which created a single legal entity out of a married couple. Once a woman married, her own legal identity was subsumed into that of her husband's, and thus she could no longer enter into contracts, sue or be sued, or, except in special circumstances, own property in her own name. The Supreme Court dealt with coverture in one well-known instance but grounded its decision more in federalism than in individual rights.

In 1873, the Court considered the case of Myra Bradwell, the first woman to pass the Illinois bar exam, the founder and editor of the influential *Chicago Legal News*, and the wife of a prominent state judge. When she applied for her own license to practice law in 1869, the Illinois Supreme Court denied the request because, given coverture, "as a married woman [she] would be bound neither by her express contracts nor by those implied contracts which it is the policy of the law to create between attorney and client."[10] Bradwell appealed to the United States Supreme Court, which upheld the lower court decision by an 8–1 margin. In so doing, the Court explained that the Fourteenth Amendment's privileges and immunities clause that Bradwell had invoked in her claim did not govern "the right to control and regulate the granting of license to practice law in the courts of a State."[11] Law licensure, the Court concluded, "is one of those powers which are not transferred [from the states] to the Federal government," which meant there was no protection in the Constitution against Illinois's disparate treatment of women and men.[12]

As another example of early gender-based laws, women were almost categorically excluded from voting. Twelve of the thirteen original state constitutions restricted voting to men only. New Jersey's however, stipulated that "all [adult] inhabitants" were entitled to vote. Women in New Jersey were thus empowered to vote and did so in local, state, and national elections for the next three decades until the state legislature restricted voting to men in 1807. Women were also able to vote in several western territories and states in the late nineteenth century, but most of the states entering the Union followed the example of the founding generation and denied women the vote.

The Court had an opportunity to rectify this inequality and extend voting to women nearly fifty years before the ratification of the Nineteenth Amendment. When Virginia Minor was blocked in her attempt to register to vote in the 1872 presidential election, her husband sued the registrar on her behalf. Writing for a unanimous Supreme Court in *Minor v. Happersett* (1875), Chief Justice Morrison Waite went to some length to assure Virginia that "[T]here is no doubt that women may be citizens" and that "[a woman] has always been a citizen from her birth and entitled to the privileges and immunities of citizenship."[13] However, the Court questioned whether voting was protected by the privileges and immunities clause of the Fourteenth Amendment. It acknowledged that ever since the founding, states had indeed restricted voting on the basis of gender, but also on the basis of property, race, age, residency, and servitude as well as on one's debtor and taxpayer status. Given that such restrictions narrowed the field of qualified voters even among men, the Court questioned the plausibility of Virginia Minor's claim to a "right" to vote that was free from state regulation. Surely, the Court reasoned, if voting were one of the privileges and immunities protected by the Fourteenth Amendment, that amendment would have specifically said so. In fact, the Court added, if voting was already a protected right under the Fourteenth, then why was the Fifteenth Amendment adopted, which stipulates that the vote cannot be denied on the basis of "race, color, or previous condition of servitude[?]"[14] The Court concluded, "If the courts can consider any question settled, this is one . . . [:] the Constitution of the United States does not confer the right of suffrage upon any one, and that the constitutions and laws of the several States which commit that important trust to men alone are not necessarily void."[15]

The Court's opinion in *Happersett* did three things: First, as in *Bradwell*, it sidestepped the actual issue of whether the government can permissibly treat women differently from men by focusing on whether the rights women claimed were protected by the Constitution. Second, it further narrowed the definition of the Fourteenth Amendment's privileges and immunities clause beyond that articulated in *Bradwell* and the Court's 1873 decision in the *Slaughterhouse Cases*.[16] The clause has never recovered from the contracted interpretation this trio of rulings in the 1870s gave to it and is essentially meaningless today. Third, it strongly checked the momentum of the women's suffrage movement at the time. It would require nearly five more decades before women won the right to vote with the ratification of the Nineteenth Amendment in 1920.

During the early twentieth century, the Court had other opportunities to consider cases where women were treated differently from men. Most of these cases were workplace related and stemmed from state legislation forbidding women from working more than a certain number of hours, in certain conditions, or at night. Viewing such laws as beneficial to the welfare of women, their homes, and their families, the Court sided with these statutes. The practical effect of these state laws in many instances, however, was to cordon off whole professions for men only since they were not subject to the same restrictions. In short, the Court's holdings to this point and its insistence on appealing to federalism, an enervated privileges and immunities clause, and the health and welfare of women yielded few, if any, benefits for women. That all began to change in 1938 with a Supreme Court decision that had absolutely nothing to do with gender.

In that year, the Court heard a case involving a federal law prohibiting the shipment of filled milk (skimmed milk mixed with vegetable oil) across state lines. The Court's decision in *U.S. v. Carolene Products*, like so many other regulatory cases from the New Deal era, upheld Congress's power to enact such a law.[17] In a nod to previous rulings limiting government intervention into business matters, Justice Harlan Stone's opinion for the majority suggested that from that time forth, at least where economic regulations were concerned, "the existence of facts supporting the legislative judgment is to be presumed . . . [and the law] is not to be pronounced unconstitutional."[18] So long as there was a rational basis for such governmental regulations, the Court held, the judiciary should defer to the legislative branch.

However, in perhaps the most important footnote in Supreme Court history, Justice Stone's opinion in *Carolene Products* also stated that there may be other instances in which judicial deference was not appropriate and which would require the Court to look at legislation much more closely. Stone offered examples of when this might be necessary, such as when governmental action clearly violates the provisions of the Bill of Rights, restricts the processes by which citizens might bring about political change, or is targeted at "discrete and insular minorities." This last category referred to those who may be so politically powerless relative to the legislative and executive branches that the courts would be their only prospect for relief from laws and policies that discriminated against them.[19]

Footnote 4 of *Carolene Products* thus became the foundation on which the Court subsequently erected its equal protection jurisprudence. The equal protection clause, like the privileges and immunities clause discussed previously, is found in the Fourteenth Amendment and forbids a state from "deny[ing] to any person within its jurisdiction the equal protection of the laws."[20] Previous generations of Supreme Court justices had largely failed to explicate and apply the equal protection clause to the claims of discriminatory treatment that came before them. Only in the mid-1950s did members of the Warren Court (1953–69) finally begin to invest this clause with authority. Yet that authority was also accompanied by confusion as the Court came to embrace a two-tiered approach to discrimination—an approach that despite the express wording of the equal protection clause permitted similarly situated people to be treated differently by their government.[21]

The first tier of the Court's equal protection analysis encompasses most claims of discrimination. Just as *Carolene Products*' footnote 4 recognized that economic regulations resting "upon some rational basis" would generally be upheld, so too has the Court acknowledged that laws that discriminate between citizens for some rational reason might also be permissible. The "rational basis test" for determining the constitutionality of such governmental action is simply that there must be a legitimate government interest at stake and the law must be rationally related to achieving that interest. For example, laws governing the issuance of driver's licenses, alcohol and tobacco sales, and age of consent for sexual activity are all age-based. The government treats similarly situated people in these instances differently depending on their age. While this is discriminatory, it is not unconstitutional because the Court has acknowledged the rational basis for such laws. Because rational basis presumes that the governmental action, even when discriminatory, is rationally related to a legitimate government interest, most challenged laws and policies in this tier are upheld.

The second tier requires that there must be a compelling state interest for the government action in question and even then, that action must use the least restrictive means possible to achieve that interest. This approach is known as "strict scrutiny" for the "searching judicial inquiry" it entails as noted in *Carolene Products*' footnote 4. The Court has applied strict scrutiny to claims of infringement on fundamental rights and claims of discrimination from the "suspect" classes of race, religion, and nationality. Strict scrutiny essentially questions whether there can ever be a government interest compelling enough to justify laws that discriminate on the basis of race, for example. It is an exceedingly difficult standard to meet, which means the Court will usually strike down laws touching on fundamental rights or affecting suspect classes.

During the decades the Court was fashioning and refining its rational basis and strict scrutiny standards of review, a single question continued to loom over the equal protection debate: Where exactly did gender fit? That is, was gender like age and thus there were reasonable, rational explanations for laws and policies that discriminated against women? Given the history of gender-based laws in the United States, critics wondered how the Court could continue to defer to the same government entities that had enacted previous laws detrimental to women in light of an increasingly robust equal protection clause?

Or was gender more like race where there could be simply no justification to ever treat similarly situated men and women differently? This was problematic as well since women, as fully half of the nation's population, could not claim to be the type of "discrete and insular minority" referenced in footnote 4. In addition, strict scrutiny arguments that recognized no difference between blacks and whites or Christians and Jews could not be fully relied on because of the biological differences between men and women.

In 1971, the Court finally signaled that something needed to be done about gender, as it did not squarely fit into either level of the Court's two-tiered equal protection analysis. In *Reed v. Reed*, the Court was asked to consider a century-old Idaho law that gave preference to a father over a mother in the administration of their deceased son's estate.[22] When Richard "Skip" Reed killed himself at age sixteen, both of his parents applied to be named administrator of his estate, which consisted primarily of his high school band clarinet, a few records, clothing, and about $500 he had been saving for college. Sally and Cecil Reed's stormy marriage had ended in divorce shortly after they adopted Skip into the family. Sally had gone on to support herself and her son by doing odd jobs and caring for disabled veterans and the elderly in her Boise home. Given the fact that she had raised Skip on her own, she was deeply disappointed when she was not named administrator of his meager estate. She was surprised to learn that the only reason her ex-husband had been designated was because Idaho law required that when more than one qualified person sought to be named estate administrator, "males must be preferred to females."[23]

Attorneys for the state of Idaho would later argue that the preference for men was simply to ease the administrative workload of probate courts dealing with multiple petitions to be named executor of the same estate. However, in its brief opinion striking down the law, a unanimous Supreme Court questioned how reducing administrative burdens was a legitimate state interest and how excluding women was rationally related to that interest. "To give a mandatory preference to members of either sex over members of the other," the Court concluded, "merely to accomplish the elimination of hearings on the merits, is to make the very kind of arbitrary legislative choice forbidden by the Equal Protection Clause of the Fourteenth Amendment."[24]

Because *Reed* resulted not from a political or social movement but from a grieving mother's quiet but determined quest to be named administrator of her son's estate, it is tempting to overlook the importance of this case. The significance of the Court's decision in *Reed* lay in the fact that, for the first time in its history, the Supreme Court struck down a state law that discriminated on the basis of gender. The Court grounded its short opinion in the rational basis test because the Idaho law simply made no sense, but it also clearly indicated that sex discrimination that resulted from seemingly "arbitrary legislative choice[s]" would thereafter be scrutinized very carefully. It was clear that after *Reed*, gender was not yet a suspect class like race, but claims of gender discrimination could no longer be relegated to rational basis either.

Sharron Frontiero's dispute with the US Air Force would yield further guidance on the issue since it involved the federal government. Most claims of discrimination look to the Fourteenth Amendment's equal protection clause for relief. However, the specific language of that amendment prohibiting states from denying "to any person within [their] jurisdiction the equal protection of the laws" does not apply to the federal government. When questions arise about federal government action thought to be discriminatory, the Court has found a guarantee of equal treatment to be implicit in the Fifth Amendment's due process clause. In short, whether protected by the Fifth or Fourteenth Amendments, equal protection suggests "that persons subject to the law will be treated equally by those who make and administer the laws."[25]

THE LITIGATION

At the federal level, cases are typically initiated in one of ninety-four US district courts where a single judge oversees the proceedings and renders an opinion. Until 1976, however, when constitutional questions arose regarding a state or federal government action, a three-judge district court was routinely convened to hear the initial dispute.[26] The Frontieros' case was heard by district judges Frank H. McFadden and Frank M. Johnson Jr., and by circuit judge Richard T. Rives. Johnson and Rives were among a handful of southern judges who used the law to protect the civil rights of African Americans in the face of both societal pressure and personal death threats. It would presumably be only a short step from their previous equal protection decisions on race to recognize Sharron Frontiero's plea for equal treatment of women.

Yet, when the court announced its ruling on April 5, 1972, Johnson and

Rives found themselves on opposing sides. Rives's opinion for the majority went to some length to suggest that the challenged statutes did not constitute gender discrimination per se. The court acknowledged that male service members could claim their wives and children without having to prove their dependency status. But so too, the court added, were female members exempt from proving the dependency of the "unmarried, legitimate, minor children" they claimed.[27] Similarly, just as women had to demonstrate the dependency status of anyone other than their minor children, so too did men who sought military benefits for their "adult children, parents, and parents-in-law."[28] Thus, the majority argued, "the availability of the presumption does not turn exclusively on the basis of the member's sex but rather on the nature of the relationship between the member and the claimed dependent."[29]

The district court opinion then went on to consider, albeit mostly for the sake of argument, the heart of Frontiero's claim: that women in the military were treated differently than men. Using the rational basis test, the court concluded that there was a reasonable justification for the gender bias in the legislation governing military housing and benefits. "It seems clear," the majority declared, "that the reason Congress established a conclusive presumption in favor of married servicemen was to avoid imposing . . . a substantial administrative burden of requiring actual proof from some 200,000 male officers and over 1,000,000 enlisted men that their wives were actually dependent upon them."[30] The practical result, the district court went on to say, was "a considerable saving of administrative expense and manpower."[31]

In dissent, Judge Frank M. Johnson argued that the majority opinion had simply ignored both the question of "whether Congress may legitimately distinguish between men and women" with regard to spousal dependency and the Supreme Court's ruling in *Reed*.[32] That decision had explicitly rejected administrative convenience as a justifiable basis for gender discrimination, and there was no constitutional protection for either Congress or the United States military, any more than there had been for the state of Idaho in that case, to treat men and women differently.

The Frontieros appealed the district court opinion to the Supreme Court and were ecstatic when the Court agreed to hear the case. However, there was some question as to who would actually represent them there. Montgomery attorney Joe Levin and the Southern Poverty Law Center had led the effort to this point, but sensing the enormous potential of the case, the ACLU Women's Rights Project in New York, and particularly its cofounder and director, Columbia Law School professor Ruth Bader Ginsburg, sought to direct the litigation as it moved to the Supreme Court. Levin consulted with Ginsburg's group for advice, coordination of briefs, and preparation for oral argument, but he was unwilling to relinquish control of the case. At one point, ironically, Levin and Ginsburg were involved in a gender-related dispute of their own over who would argue the case before the justices.

In a letter to the Southern Poverty Law Center, Ginsburg expressed her desire to argue the case not only because of the singular "knowledge of the women's rights area [she had] developed" but also because of the symbolic "importance of argument by a woman attorney in a case of this significance."[33] Levin responded, "There is nothing chauvinistic in our desire to present oral argument. We have carried this case from its inception and do not intend to lose control over it at this stage. I do not think it makes one iota of difference whether a male or female makes the argument."[34] Eventually, they agreed that ten minutes, a third of the oral argument time, would be reserved for Ginsburg.

Those who attended the *Frontiero v. Richardson* oral arguments on January 17, 1973, witnessed three remarkable things in the Supreme Court that day. The first was, after thirty-five years of a two-tiered system for assessing equal protection claims, a third standard of review began to emerge. Joe Levin argued that the rational basis standard of review and its general deference to governmental authority was simply inappropriate where widespread and ongoing gender discrimination was concerned. He also acknowledged that strict scrutiny might not be appropriate either as there could be limited instances where men and women must be treated differently. He argued instead for a third way that placed demands on the government as well as on the person claiming discrimination. "We feel that a burden should be placed on both the Government . . . to show a legitimate governmental interest, and on the appellant to show that there is discrimination," he explained. "We think that there should be equal burdens."[35]

In response, Assistant Solicitor General Samuel Huntington argued that the dispute was much ado about nothing particularly since Congress had already addressed the military housing and benefits at issue in the case a few months earlier. In September 1972, the Senate passed a bill giving female service members the same benefits accorded male service members. Congress had adjourned before a similar measure could pass in the House, but the government fully expected that it would be reintroduced. Huntington also encouraged the Court to not extend strict scrutiny to gender since the Equal Rights Amendment then under consideration throughout the country would accomplish the same thing. That proposed constitutional amendment would have prohibited any level of government from discriminating on the basis of gender and, at the time of oral arguments, had already been approved by twenty-two of the thirty-eight states necessary for ratification.

The second significant thing to occur during the *Frontiero* oral arguments was Ruth Bader Ginsburg's debut before the Supreme Court. As director of the ACLU's Women's Rights Project, she would go on to argue six landmark gender-related cases before the Supreme Court, prevailing in five of them. Relatedly, and the third thing that made the oral arguments in *Frontiero* particularly memorable, was that during Ginsburg's presentation, the entire bench was quiet.

Oral arguments before the Supreme Court consist of lawyers from both sides standing before a wooden lectern in front of the nine justices and pleading their case for typically thirty minutes per side. Because the case arrives on appeal, there can be hundreds of pages of briefs, lower court opinions, and other materials that the justices and their clerks have reviewed prior to oral arguments. With so much information already in possession of the justices and with so little time to present their position, attorneys at oral argument know they must focus only on the key aspects of their case. That task is made considerably more difficult, however, by the fact that the justices constantly interrupt oral arguments to pose questions of counsel. What usually follows is a rapid-fire exchange as attorneys respond to questions while desperately trying to stay on track and make their point before their allotted time runs out.

In *Frontiero*, the justices interrupted Levin twenty-one times and Huntington nearly fifty times during their combined fifty minutes before the Court. But at Ginsburg's first appearance before the Supreme Court, the justices were silent as she argued that gender discrimination deserved strict scrutiny consideration. "Sex, like race," she explained, "is a visible, immutable characteristic, bearing no necessary relationship to a body. Sex, like race, has been made the basis for unjustified, or at least unproved, assumptions concerning an individual's potential to perform or contribute to society."[36] For ten uninterrupted minutes, Ginsburg captivated the Court while challenging the justices to protect Frontiero and all women from discriminatory laws and policies.

After hearing oral arguments, the justices later meet together in conference to discuss the case, vote whether to affirm or reverse the lower court opinion, and assign a justice to write the majority opinion. Informal conference notes taken by Justices William O. Douglas and William Brennan reveal that the Court was prepared by an 8–1 margin to uphold Frontiero's claim, although there was no consensus as to why.[37] Assigned to write the opinion for the Court, Justice Brennan circulated a draft to his colleagues that would have reversed the lower court opinion, to which nearly all of them agreed. However, mirroring much of what Ruth Bader Ginsburg had included in her written briefs and oral arguments before the Court, his draft also declared gender a suspect class like race and elevated discrimination on that basis to strict scrutiny. This portion of the draft opinion, however, won the support of only three other members of the Court. One vote shy of the majority necessary to give Brennan's opinion the force of law, the justices technically left the larger issue of gender discrimination where they found it after *Reed*: not at strict scrutiny, but not at merely rational basis either. On May 14, 1973, the Court announced its decision.

THE DECISION

Frontiero v. Richardson (8–1)
411 U.S. 677 (1973)

JUSTICE BRENNAN delivered the plurality opinion for the Court.

The question before us concerns the right of a female member of the uniformed services to claim her spouse as a "dependent" for the purposes of obtaining increased quarters allowances and medical and dental benefits under 37 U.S.C. 401, 403, and 10 U.S.C. 1072, 1076, on an equal footing with male members. Under these statutes, a serviceman may claim his wife as a "dependent" without regard to whether she is in fact dependent upon him for any part of her support. A servicewoman, on the other hand, may not claim her husband as a "dependent" under these programs unless he is in fact dependent upon her for over one-half of his support. Thus, the question for decision is whether this difference in treatment constitutes an unconstitutional discrimination against servicewomen in violation of the Due Process Clause of the Fifth Amendment. A three-judge District Court for the Middle District of Alabama, one judge dissenting, rejected this contention and sustained the constitutionality of the provisions of the statutes making this distinction. . . . We reverse. . . .

Appellant Sharron Frontiero, a lieutenant in the United States Air Force, sought increased quarters allowances, and housing and medical benefits for her husband, appellant Joseph Frontiero, on the ground that he was her "dependent." Although such benefits would automatically have been granted with respect to the wife of a male member of the uniformed services, appellant's application was denied because she failed to demonstrate that her husband was dependent on her for more than one-half of his support. Appellants then commenced this suit, contending that, by making this distinction, the statutes unreasonably discriminate on the basis of sex in violation of the Due Process Clause of the Fifth Amendment. In essence, appellants asserted that the discriminatory impact of the statutes is twofold: first, as a procedural matter, a female member is required to demonstrate her spouse's dependency, while no such burden is imposed upon male members; and, second, as a substantive matter, a male member who does not provide more than one-half of his wife's support receives benefits, while a similarly situated female member is denied such benefits. Appellants therefore sought a permanent injunction against the continued enforcement of these statutes and an order directing the appellees to provide Lieutenant Frontiero with the same housing and medical benefits that a similarly situated male member would receive.

Although the legislative history of these statutes sheds virtually no light on the purposes underlying the differential treatment accorded male and female members, a majority of the three-judge District Court surmised that Congress might reasonably have concluded that, since the husband in our society is generally the "breadwinner" in the family—and the wife typically the "dependent" partner—"it would be more economical to require married female members claiming husbands to prove actual dependency than to extend the presumption of dependency to such members." Indeed, given the fact that approximately 99% of all members of the uniformed services are male, the District Court speculated that such differential treatment might conceivably lead to a "considerable saving of administrative expense and manpower."

At the outset, appellants contend that classifications based upon sex, like classifications based upon race, alienage, and national origin, are inherently suspect and must therefore be subjected to close judicial scrutiny. We agree and, indeed, find at least implicit support for such an approach in our unanimous decision only last Term in *Reed v. Reed* (1971). . . .

The Court noted that the Idaho statute "provides that different treatment be accorded to the applicants on the basis of their sex; it thus establishes a classification subject to scrutiny under the Equal Protection Clause." Under "traditional" equal protection analysis, a legislative classification must be sustained unless it is "patently arbitrary" and bears no rational relationship to a legitimate governmental interest. . . .

[T]he Court held the statutory preference for male applicants unconstitutional. In reaching this result, the Court implicitly rejected appellee's apparently rational explanation of the statutory scheme, and concluded that, by ignoring the individual qualifications of particular applicants, the challenged statute provided "dissimilar treatment for men and women who are . . . similarly situated." The Court therefore held that, even though the State's interest in achieving administrative efficiency "is not without some legitimacy," "[t]o give a mandatory preference to members of either sex over members of the other, merely to accomplish the elimination of hearings on the merits, is to make the very kind of arbitrary legislative choice forbidden by the [Constitution]. . . ." This departure from "traditional" rational-basis analysis with respect to sex-based classifications is clearly justified.

There can be no doubt that our Nation has had a long and unfortunate history of sex discrimination. Traditionally, such discrimination was rationalized by an attitude of "romantic paternalism" which, in practical effect, put women, not on a pedestal, but in a cage. . . .

As a result . . . , our statute books gradually became laden with gross, stereotyped distinctions between the sexes and, indeed, throughout much of the 19th century the position of women in our society was, in many respects, comparable to that of blacks under the pre–Civil War slave codes. Neither slaves nor women could hold office, serve on juries, or bring suit in their own names, and married women traditionally were denied the legal capacity to hold or convey property or to serve as legal guardians of their own children. And although blacks were guaranteed the right to vote in 1870, women were denied even that right—which is itself "preservative of other basic civil and political rights"—until adoption of the Nineteenth Amendment half a century later.

It is true, of course, that the position of women in America has improved markedly in recent decades. Nevertheless, it can hardly be doubted that, in part because of the high visibility of the sex characteristic, women still face pervasive, although at times more subtle, discrimination in our educational institutions, in the job market and, perhaps most conspicuously, in the political arena.

Moreover, since sex, like race and national origin, is an immutable characteristic determined solely by the accident of birth, the imposition of special disabilities upon the members of a particular sex because of their sex would seem to violate "the basic concept of our system that legal burdens should bear some relationship to individual responsibility." [See *Weber v. Aetna Casualty & Surety Co.* (1972).] And what differentiates sex from such nonsuspect statuses as intelligence or physical disability, and aligns it with the recognized suspect criteria, is that the sex characteristic frequently bears no relation to ability to perform or contribute to society. As a result, statutory distinctions between the sexes often have the effect of invidiously relegating the entire class of females to inferior legal status without regard to the actual capabilities of its individual members.

We might also note that, over the past decade, Congress has itself manifested an increasing sensitivity to sex-based classifications. In Title VII of the Civil Rights Act of 1964, for example, Congress expressly declared that no employer, labor union, or other organization subject to the provisions of the Act shall discriminate against any individual on the basis of "race, color, religion, sex, or national origin." Similarly, the Equal Pay Act of 1963 provides that no employer covered by the Act "shall discriminate . . . between employees on the basis of sex." And Section 1 of the Equal Rights Amendment, passed by Congress on March 22, 1972, and submitted to the legislatures of the States for ratification, declares that "[e]quality of rights under the law shall not be denied or abridged by the United States or by any State on account of sex." Thus, Congress itself has concluded that classifications based upon sex are inherently invidious, and this conclusion of a coequal branch of Government is not without significance to the question presently under consideration.

With these considerations in mind, we can only conclude that classifications based upon sex, like classifications based upon race, alienage, or national origin, are inherently suspect, and must therefore be subjected to strict judicial scrutiny. Applying the analysis mandated by that stricter standard of review, it is clear that the statutory scheme now before us is constitutionally invalid.

The sole basis of the classification established in the challenged statutes is the sex of the individuals involved. Thus, under 37 U.S.C. 401, 403, and 10 U.S.C. 1072, 1076, a female member of the uniformed services seeking to obtain housing and medical benefits for her spouse must prove his dependency in fact, whereas no such burden is imposed upon male members. In addition, the statutes operate so as to deny benefits to a female member, such as appellant Sharron Frontiero, who provides less than one-half of her spouse's support, while at the same time granting such benefits to a male member who likewise provides less than one-half of his spouse's support. Thus, to this extent at least, it may fairly be said that these statutes command "dissimilar treatment for men and women who are . . . similarly situated" [*Reed v. Reed* (1971)].

Moreover, the Government concedes that the differential treatment accorded men and women under these statutes serves no purpose other than mere "administrative convenience." In essence, the Government maintains that, as an empirical matter, wives in our society frequently are dependent upon their husbands, while husbands rarely are dependent upon their wives. Thus, the Government argues that Congress might reasonably have concluded that it would be both cheaper and easier simply conclusively to presume that wives of male members are financially dependent upon their husbands, while burdening female members with the task of establishing dependency in fact.

The Government offers no concrete evidence, however, tending to support its view that such differential treatment in fact saves the Government any money. In order to satisfy the demands of strict judicial scrutiny, the Government must demonstrate, for example, that it is actually cheaper to grant increased benefits with respect to all male members, than it is to determine which male members are in fact entitled to such benefits and to grant increased benefits only to those members whose wives actually meet the dependency requirement. Here, however, there is substantial evidence that, if put to the test, many of the wives of male members would fail to qualify for benefits. And in light of the fact that the dependency determination with respect to the husbands of female members is presently made solely on the basis of affidavits, rather than through the more costly hearing process, the Government's explanation of the statutory scheme is, to say the least, questionable.

In any case, our prior decisions make clear that, although efficacious administration of governmental programs is not without some importance, "the Constitution recognizes higher values than speed and efficiency" [*Stanley v. Illinois* (1972)]. And when we enter the realm of "strict judicial scrutiny," there can be no doubt that "administrative convenience" is not a shibboleth, the mere recitation of which dictates constitutionality. On the contrary, any statutory scheme which draws a sharp line between the sexes, solely for the purpose of achieving administrative convenience, necessarily commands "dissimilar treatment for men and women who are . . . similarly situated," and therefore involves the "very kind of arbitrary legislative choice forbidden by the [Constitution] . . ." [*Reed v. Reed* (1971)]. We therefore conclude that, by according differential treatment to male and female members of the uniformed services for the sole purpose of achieving administrative convenience, the challenged statutes violate the Due Process Clause of the Fifth Amendment insofar as they require a female member to prove the dependency of her husband.

Reversed.

Justice Powell, with whom the Chief Justice and Justice Blackmun join, concurring in the judgment.

I agree that the challenged statutes constitute an unconstitutional discrimination against servicewomen in violation of the Due Process Clause of the Fifth Amendment, but I cannot join the opinion of [Justice] Brennan, which would hold that all classifications based upon sex, "like classifications based upon race, alienage, and national origin," are "inherently suspect and must therefore be subjected to close judicial scrutiny." It is unnecessary for the Court in this case to characterize sex as a suspect classification, with all of the far-reaching implications of such a holding. *Reed v. Reed* (1971) which abundantly supports our decision today, did not add sex to the narrowly limited group of classifications which are inherently suspect. In my view, we can and should decide this case on the authority of *Reed* and reserve for the future any expansion of its rationale.

There is another, and I find compelling, reason for deferring a general categorizing of sex classifications as invoking the strictest test of judicial scrutiny. The Equal Rights Amendment, which if adopted will resolve the substance of this precise question, has been approved by the Congress and submitted for ratification by the States. If this Amendment is duly adopted, it will represent the will of the people accomplished in the manner prescribed by the Constitution. By acting prematurely and unnecessarily, as I view it, the Court has assumed a decisional responsibility at the very time when state legislatures, functioning within the traditional democratic process, are debating the proposed Amendment. It seems to me that this reaching out to pre-empt by judicial action a major political decision which is currently in process of resolution does not reflect appropriate respect for duly prescribed legislative processes.

There are times when this Court, under our system, cannot avoid a constitutional decision on issues which normally should be resolved by the elected representatives of the people. But democratic institutions are weakened, and confidence in the restraint of the Court is impaired, when we appear unnecessarily to decide sensitive issues of broad social and political importance at the very time they are under consideration within the prescribed constitutional processes.

THE AFTERMATH AND SIGNIFICANCE OF *FRONTIERO V. RICHARDSON*

Frontiero was the closest the Court has ever come to elevating gender to strict scrutiny. While Justice Brennan's plurality opinion to that effect did not carry the day, the Court's overall 8–1 decision was nonetheless significant. For the first time in the history of the United States, the Court invalidated a federal law based on gender, and its precedential impact was immediately noted. Ruth Bader Ginsburg said at the time, "It is the most far-reaching and important ruling on sex discrimination to come out of the Supreme Court yet. It will spell the beginning of reforms in hundreds of statutes which do not give equal benefits to men and women."[38] For her part, Sharron Frontiero simply noted, "It was worth the fight . . . [and] gave a real life to the feminist movement. We like to think we've helped do something concrete rather than just talk."[39]

The Court's decision in *Frontiero* further underscored the argument that laws permitting gender discrimination deserved a higher level of "searching judicial inquiry" than that to which they had previously been subjected. Just three years later in *Craig v. Boren*, the Court did just what Joe Levin had argued in *Frontiero* and formally created a third level of equal protection review between rational basis and strict scrutiny.[40] This intermediate standard stipulated that, to be found constitutional, governmental actions that discriminate on the basis of gender "must serve important governmental objectives and must be substantially related to achievement of those objectives."[41] Twenty years later, with Ruth Bader Ginsburg (who by 1996 had become an associate justice on the Supreme Court) writing for the majority, the Court inched gender discrimination closer to strict scrutiny by appending to the intermediate standard a requirement that there must be an "exceedingly persuasive justification" for any gender-based action by the government.[42]

Sharron Frontiero fulfilled her four-year commitment to the US Air Force before the Court even heard her case, and she and Joseph left Alabama for New Hampshire, where they divorced. Joseph later moved to Charleston, South Carolina, where he died in February 2017 at the age of seventy. Sharron continued to work as a nurse and then later as a librarian and writer. Recounting the role she played in advancing the rights of all American women, Justice Ginsburg said of Sharron Frontiero, "[She] . . . is not someone you would choose from a crowd as a potential frontrunner. She is an everyday person, uncomfortable with publicity. But she knew she had been shortchanged and she had the courage to complain."[43]

7

ONE PERSON, ONE VOTE

Legislative Reapportionment and *Reynolds v. Sims* (1964)

THE MOST SIGNIFICANT CHALLENGE IN any republic is to ensure that the voice of its citizens is heard within the popularly elected branch of government. This has been met in the United States, in part, by removing obstacles that prevented women, racial minorities, and others from voting. Yet, even after the previously disenfranchised began to exercise their right to vote, inequalities in representation at the state level sometimes remained because certain localities had more power in the legislature than others. The voice of the people as a whole was thereby muted, often with grave consequences.

Allocating members of the legislature so that the more populous areas have a greater number of representatives is one way to avert such problems. The process of assigning the number of representatives to a given legislative district is called apportionment. This term is frequently aligned with the phrase "one person, one vote" to reflect the principle that no vote should be worth more than another, something that can only be accomplished when legislative districts represent roughly equal numbers of people.

The Supreme Court took the case of *Reynolds v. Sims* (1964) because Alabama had not reapportioned its legislature since 1901 despite state constitutional requirements that it be done every decade. By the time the Court considered the issue, many Alabamians were painfully underrepresented in the state legislature because population gains in places like Birmingham, Montgomery, and Mobile had not been accompanied by a commensurate increase in representatives from those areas. For more than sixty years, Alabama legislators relied on a variety of excuses to justify their failure to fulfill

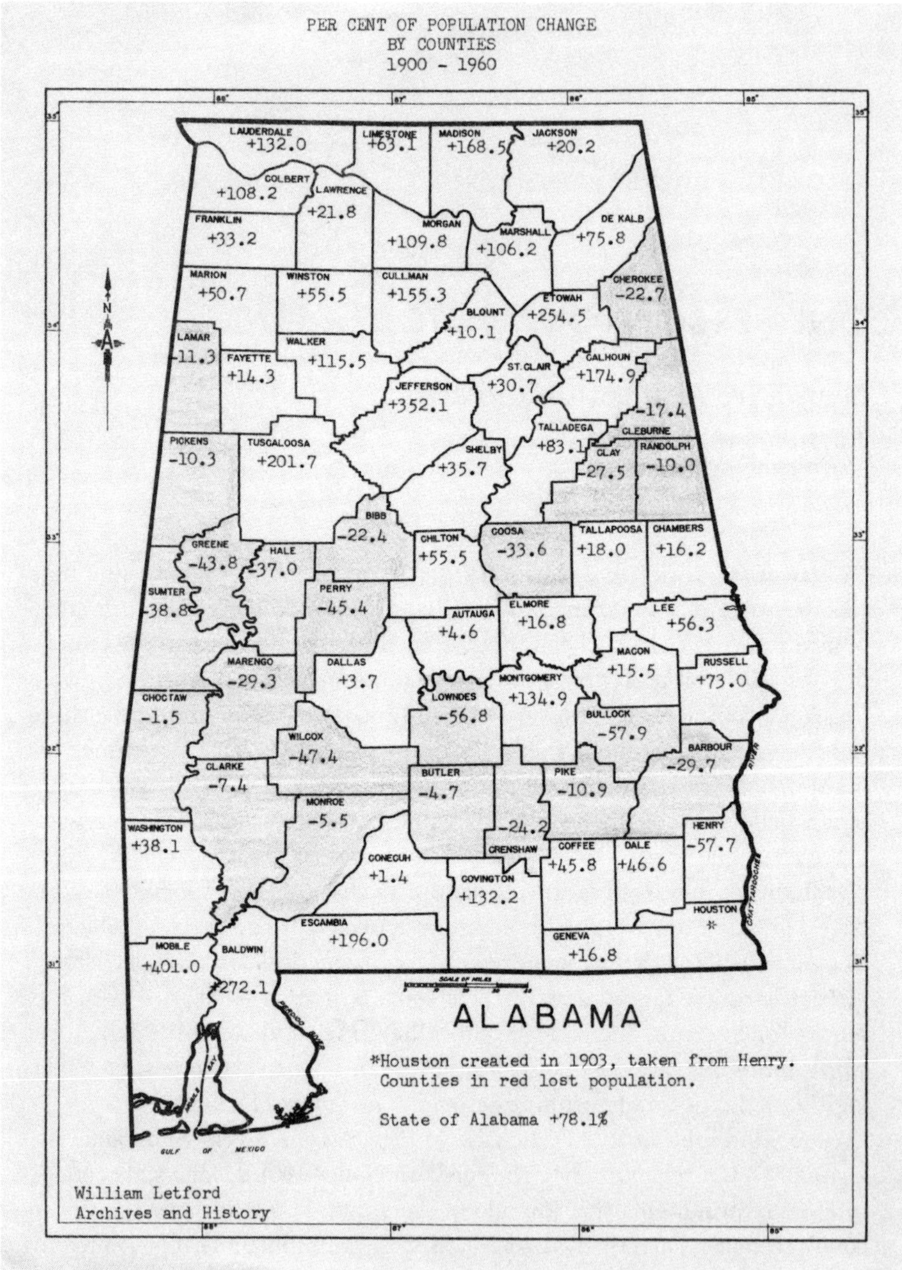

Figure 7. Percent of population change by county in Alabama, 1900–1960. Courtesy of the Alabama Department of Archives and History.

their constitutional duty to reapportion the statehouse, but they all ultimately arose from a single motive. As constitutional scholar Richard Cortner bluntly observed, "The apportionment of seats in a legislature is the apportionment of power within the community."[1] The Court's decision in *Reynolds* mandated that such power be dispersed throughout the state so that the voice of *all* the people could be heard.

THE STORY

The story behind *Reynolds v. Sims* is a simple one: Alabama's constitution requires the state legislature to reapportion legislative districts after each census, and for more than sixty years, a group of powerful legislators deliberately refused to do so.

Delegates to the 1901 Alabama Constitutional Convention understood the importance of reapportionment. For all of its considerable flaws, the 1901 Constitution left no room for misunderstanding either the role or the obligation of state legislators in this area. Article IX deals with representation in both houses of the legislature, with nearly every section therein mentioning apportionment. Sections 198 and 199, for example, assign one representative to each county with the remaining seats to be allocated by the legislature based on population as determined by the federal census every ten years. Section 200 requires legislators to meet after each census, establish the number of senators, and then divide the state into the same number of senatorial districts, "which districts shall be as nearly equal to each other in the number of inhabitants as may be."[2]

Convention delegates apparently thought enough of reapportionment that they added Section 201, which requires the legislature to conduct its *own* census of Alabama citizens, in the event a national census was not taken, so that "the apportionment of representatives and senators as provided for in this article" could be accomplished.[3] Finally, in setting forth the mode of amending the document, the very last article of the 1901 Constitution declares, "Representation in the legislature shall be based on population, and such basis of representation shall not be changed by constitutional amendments."[4]

Notwithstanding such constitutional mandates, a group of legislators successfully blocked any effort to reapportion for six decades. In general, the powerful interests they represented were associated with the "Big Mules" and "Black Belt" factions in Alabama, the social, economic, and political significance of which few outside the state understand. The Big Mules included leaders of the state's largest industries, financial institutions, utilities, and other wealthy interests in mostly urban areas, but particularly Birmingham, and the politicians who supported them.[5] The name of the Black Belt initially referred to the swath of rich, dark soil that cuts across the south-central part of Alabama (in contrast to the red clay that covers much of the rest of the state). That fertile farmland attracted thousands of would-be cotton magnates to the area in the early 1800s. At its peak, the area hosted 40 percent of Alabama's population, but that share began to decline even before the end of the 1800s. By the dawn of the twentieth century, large landowners in the Black Belt region along with timber and farming interests, as well as the politicians who supported them, pursued policies that entrenched their power and considerable wealth even as the majority population of African Americans in the area around them struggled against gripping poverty and racial discrimination.[6]

Alabama's much maligned 1901 Constitution was largely a product of the Big Mule–Black Belt political coalition, but even some of its admittedly egregious faults might have been overcome had the state legislature simply carried out its constitutional duty to reapportion representative districts.[7] However, this too was prevented by the Big Mule–Black Belt alliance. There is perhaps no better indicator of the utter dominance of this coalition than the fact that when other state legislators tried to heed the constitutional mandate to reapportion, nothing happened. Out of more than one thousand apportionment-related bills that were introduced in the Alabama legislature between 1901 and 1961, not a single one passed.[8]

Given Cortner's observation that reapportionment is really about the "apportionment of power," it is not difficult to understand the coalition's actions. The Black Belt region was overly represented in the legislature, so northern industrial interests curried the favor of its sizeable voting bloc to defeat measures that they viewed as detrimental to business, such as tax increases or pro-labor legislation. For their part, the south-central planter class and timber and agricultural industries looked to the Big Mules for assistance in keeping property taxes low on their land, a disproportionate share of state funds flowing to their area, and the preservation of segregation.[9] Both groups funneled money to candidates in each region to ensure that they retained control of the legislature. So long as legislative seats were not reapportioned, the Big Mule–Black Belt coalition could rule in perpetuity.

Over the course of the sixty years in which the legislature failed to reapportion, tremendous demographic shifts were taking place in Alabama. African Americans abandoned the state in droves, joining the six million other black southerners who, during the Great Migration, left the poverty and racism of the Deep South for equality and economic opportunities in the northern and western parts of the country. Within the state, the population of rural Alabama also declined dramatically as people left their farms for jobs in urban areas. The result of such population shifts was severe malapportionment in the Alabama legislature—that is, the distribution of representative seats in that body no longer accurately reflected the dispersion of population in the state.

In 1960, for example, the Black Belt's Lowndes County had one seat in the Alabama Senate for its 15,000 citizens, just as it had in 1900 when it had 35,000 people. A single senator had represented Jefferson County since 1900 as well, but the state's most populous county had more than 600,000 people living within its borders by 1960. Similar inequities existed in the Alabama House of Representatives. Bullock County's 13,000 citizens in the Black Belt sent two representatives to the House, just as they had in 1900 when the county could claim 31,000 people. Yet, Mobile County's 1960 population of 314,000 could only send three.[10] It was clear to anyone who was not part of the Big Mule–Black Belt coalition, as well as to every person living in Alabama's urban areas, that where representation was concerned, their votes just simply did not count as much. Indeed, the legislature was so malapportioned that a majority of legislators in both houses hailed from areas containing just 25 percent of the state's population.

On August 26, 1961, fourteen citizens of Jefferson County, including civil rights attorney Chuck Morgan, filed suit in US District Court against Bettye Frink, Alabama's secretary of state, all sixty-seven county probate judges, and several other government officials who oversaw elections.[11] Previous apportionment lawsuits had been filed in state courts, but each time, while acknowledging that the legislature had utterly failed in its constitutional duty to reapportion, the Alabama Supreme Court had concluded that the judiciary could not properly intrude on a matter that the state constitution had entrusted to the legislative branch.[12] The Birmingham plaintiffs claimed that Alabama's failure to reapportion its legislature debased their votes in violation of the Fourteenth Amendment's equal protection clause. They also argued that the legislature's abysmal history on the matter and the state supreme court's unwillingness to intervene left them with no choice but to turn to the federal courts for relief.[13]

Because the US Supreme Court had already calendared oral arguments on a similar apportionment dispute for the following October (the landmark case of *Baker v. Carr*), the three-judge panel in Montgomery that heard the Alabama reapportionment case chose to delay its consideration of the matter until after the Supreme Court ruled.[14]

THE CONSTITUTIONAL BACKGROUND

Since the founding era, discussions of voting and representation in America have largely focused on race, gender, and property. Those who did not qualify to vote based on these or other restrictions could legitimately argue that elected officials did not represent them. Nevertheless, even after constitutional and statutory changes at the national and state level expanded the voting franchise, many voters learned that they still were not fairly represented because of where they lived. Locality therefore became an important factor in the accrual of political power by public officials and the people who elected them. This might come as a surprise to modern Americans, but their political forebears in Great Britain and early America were well acquainted with both the custom and the corruption of disproportionate representation.

In his 1791 pamphlet, *Rights of Man,* Thomas Paine argued that those who valued individual liberty could learn much from France's National Assembly as it pieced together that country's first written constitution. He was particularly pleased with the new constitution's requirement that representation at any level of government be based on population. He challenged his readers, particularly government officials in England, to find anything amiss with this practice, as he knew that they were clearly aware that representation in the British Parliament was badly malapportioned. In an oft-quoted statement, Paine declared, "The county of Yorkshire, which contains near a million of souls, sends two county members [to Parliament]; and so does the county of Rutland, which contains not an hundredth part of that number. The town of old Sarum, which contains not three houses, sends two members; and the town of Manchester, which contains upwards of sixty thousand souls, is not admitted to send any. Is there any principle in these things?"[15]

Paine's reference to Old Sarum was a pointed reminder about the most notorious of the many so-called rotten boroughs in England. The term *rotten borough* described electoral districts where those who happened to own the property that had once been a thriving village or town essentially also held title to two seats in Parliament. In 1295, King Edward I summoned individuals from throughout his realm to meet with him in what would later be referred to as the Model Parliament because it was the first national assembly in England to include representatives from more than just the aristocracy and clergy. Without regard for existing variations in population, the king requested each county to send two knights, each borough or town like Old Sarum to send two burgesses, and each city to send two citizens. By the time of Paine's writing, Britain had become an empire, and the structure, responsibilities, and power of Parliament were vastly different, but nothing had changed with regard to Old Sarum's representation in that body. In fact, during the five hundred years that had transpired since the Model Parliament, Old Sarum as a town had essentially ceased to exist, and yet it still sent two representatives to Parliament as it always had.

Some members of Parliament from these boroughs had literally almost no one to represent, while others used their wealth and influence to manipulate a very small and decreasing populace for the seats still allotted to the area. By virtue of their holdings and influence, wealthy landowners assured themselves, their friends, and/or their descendants of two seats in Parliament.[16] Such representation was naturally controversial because of its resulting impact on Parliament itself. An 1831 publication arguing for reform estimated that of the 406 members of the British House of Commons elected from boroughs, more than half were elected from areas with fewer than one hundred voters, and nearly ninety were returned to Parliament by fewer than fifty voters![17] Other members represented cities and counties with hundreds of thousands and even millions of residents.

In advocating for the dissolution of rotten boroughs in the early nineteenth century, Lord John Russell asked his colleagues in Parliament to imagine the reaction of a foreign visitor when he learned that major industrial centers like the city of Manchester had no representatives in Great Britain's legislature because they did not exist when the Model Parliament was convened in 1295. Further, he questioned, with little exaggeration, "Would not such a foreigner [also] be much astonished if he were taken to a green mound, and informed that it sent two members to the British Parliament?—if he were shewn a stone wall, and told that it also sent two members to the British Parliament?"[18] The efforts of Russell and others brought about significant parliamentary reforms, and rotten boroughs were finally abolished in 1832.

Nothing in the American colonies or early states approached the level of England's rotten boroughs, but the lack of equality in representation was a common theme even beyond the familiar "taxation without representation" protests that accompanied the Stamp Act of 1765. For example, Thomas Jefferson used his *Summary View of the Rights of British America* (1774) to chastise King George III for instructing the royal governor of Virginia to cease creating new counties in the rapidly expanding colony until residents in the newly settled areas agreed to forego representation in the Virginia General Assembly. "[D]oes his majesty seriously wish," Jefferson asked incredulously, "and publish it to the world, that his subjects should give up the glorious right of representation?"[19] He would later use the Declaration of Independence to level the same charge against the king, asserting that the "the right of Representation in the Legislature [was] a right inestimable to [the people] and formidable to tyrants only."

Thirteen years later, Jefferson directed similar criticism at his fellow Virginians. Citing the fact that the state's constitution of 1776 "was formed when we were new and unexperienced in the science of government," he bluntly stated that "the majority of the men in the state, who pay and fight for its support, are unrepresented in the legislature."[20] Yet, even among those who *were* represented, inequalities existed because of malapportionment. "Thus the county of Warwick," he wrote, "with only one hundred fighting men, has an equal representation with the county of Loudon, which has 1746. So that every man in Warwick has as much influence in the government as seventeen men in Loudon."[21] In addition, Jefferson observed that a majority of the representatives in the General Assembly were primarily from the eastern portion of the commonwealth. The result was that the 19,000 voters they represented had greater political power in the legislature than the remaining 30,000 voters scattered about the rest of the state. In a classic understatement, Jefferson observed, "From the difference of their situation and circumstances, their interests will often be very different."[22]

During the 1800s, these different interests invariably clashed as laws governing representation were created and modified. As the nation pushed westward, newer states with fast-growing populations tended to be much more sympathetic to the idea of proportional representation, although many of the older states eventually embraced it as well. During the 1853 convention to revise the constitution of Massachusetts, for example, delegates debated ways to reform the manner in which state legislators were allocated. One of the delegates, author and diplomat Charles Francis Adams Sr., explained the consequences of inequitable representation—concerns that applied just as much to Old Sarum and Parliament a century before his time as to Alabama and its legislature a century later. He declared, "I maintain that the moment a majority in a republic assumes to draw a distinction with the intent that certain men shall be enabled to enjoy twice or thrice the amount of political power which an equal number of other men are to possess, that is the hour when tyranny begins."[23]

The Massachusetts convention ended without formal action on the topic, but the state implemented an apportionment plan based on population just a few years later. Half of the original thirteen states joined Massachusetts in amending their constitutions to embrace proportional representation. By 1900, the constitutions of nearly every state in the union required some variety of population-based representation in their state legislatures. In spite of this, a remarkable retreat from the principles of proportional representation was taking place in many of these same states at practically the same time.

Political power in the United States had once been strongest in rural areas, but massive demographic changes during the latter half of the nineteenth century began to shift that power to cities. The population of urban areas grew exponentially with the arrival of millions of European immigrants as well as hundreds of thousands of Americans who left their farms for jobs in the cities. They became not only part of a large labor class but also part of a significant voting bloc that, in several large cities in the Northeast and upper Midwest, was supported by urban political machines.

Loathing the corruption and excesses of urban political bosses, distrustful of immigrants, and fearful of the inevitable loss of power, politicians from rural areas and smaller communities were able to generate support for constitutional changes in several states that preserved rural political strength. For instance, some state constitutions were amended to require equal representation of towns in one house of their state legislature. Like Old Sarum in England, this led to a notable instance in Vermont just prior to the *Reynolds v. Sims* case where the twenty-four residents of Stratton had the same representation in the legislature as the 35,531 residents of Burlington, the state's most populous city.[24] California combined less populous counties into single senate districts to achieve the same effect, such that the 14,000 people in three rural counties had the same representation as the six million people who lived in Los Angeles County in 1960.

Other strategies included exploiting the requirements for representation already in their constitutions. In states whose constitutions required one representative from each county, for example, rural politicians were able to offset the power of growing population centers within the state by simply creating more counties. Using Kansas as an example, political scientist Gordon E. Baker, in his classic *Reapportionment Revolution*, described how state requirements of "minimum guarantees and maximum limits" of representation further strengthened rural power: "Kansas provided in its state constitution of 1861 that each county have at least one representative, with the remaining members distributed according to population. . . . But by the time the western part of the state became organized there were 106 counties and a constitutional maximum of 125 representatives."[25] Constitutional requirements of equal representation by county coupled with constitutional limits on the total number of legislators resulted in less than 20 percent of the total number of seats remaining to be allotted to urban areas and their large populations. Consequently, by 1960 the four counties that accounted for nearly 40 percent of Kansas's population had just 10 percent of the representation in the lower house of its legislature.

These and other actions were quite successful in preserving rural political strength. Yet, without question, the most effective approach to diluting the power of urban areas, as it had been since the days of Old Sarum, was simply for legislators to do nothing. State constitutions required regular reapportionment of legislative seats to ensure that representation followed the ebbs and flows of people moving into, out of, or within the state. During the time when most people in the United States lived in rural areas, reapportioning seats in the statehouse was rarely controversial, basically because the population was less mobile and generally already equally represented. As Americans moved to the cities, however, and rural interests were threatened by rapidly growing urban centers, legislators from less populous areas became far less willing to undertake their constitutional duty to reapportion legislative seats. So much so, that by the time the Court considered *Reynolds v. Sims*, almost every state in the union was guilty of having failed to reapportion its legislature fairly and regularly. By 1960, only Massachusetts, New Hampshire, West Virginia, and Wisconsin could claim that a majority of both houses of their legislatures represented more than 40 percent of their residents.[26] Conversely, in Alabama, Delaware, Florida, Georgia, and Maryland, a majority of state legislators represented just 25 percent or less of each state's total population.

Other states, using Congress as a model, adopted proportional representation in one house of their legislature with equal representation in the other—with predictable results.[27] Control of California's House of Representatives, which had been regularly apportioned, required 45 percent of the state's population. Yet, its state senate was so malapportioned that the largest senate district in California contained over six million people, more than four hundred times larger than the population of its smallest district. More importantly, majority control of the state senate turned on areas occupied by just 10 percent of California's population. Similarly, 11 percent of Vermont's population could win a majority of its state's house seats, and the representatives of just 8 percent of the people in Nevada could control its state senate.[28] Put another way, Democrats seeking to wrest control of the Nevada Senate from its Republican majority in 1960 would have needed the support of 92 percent of Nevada's population to do so.

Thus, by the time the Court considered *Reynolds v. Sims*, malapportionment was both well established in American political history and widespread throughout the country. Given the fraud, corruption, vote devaluation, and equal protection issues associated with it, it was not surprising that apportionment came before the Court. What was remarkable, was how long it took for the Court to finally address the issue.

As mentioned in the earlier chapter on *Gomillion v. Lightfoot,* the Court had historically been very reluctant to intervene in what it termed "political questions." Political questions were generally deemed to be matters that the judiciary was incapable of resolving and that were best left to the executive and legislative branches. Chief among these were issues related to the design and composition of legislative districts. The Court was loath to interfere because malapportionment was not simply an issue about population differences or rural versus urban interests, it was about control of the legislature and the significant power wielded by the party that held the majority.

In its 1946 decision in *Colegrove v. Green,* a narrow majority of the Court rejected the claim of several citizens of Illinois who argued that their votes were diluted because the state's congressional districts were not roughly equal in population.[29] Justice Frankfurter's opinion for the majority sympathized with their plight, but stated flatly, "[Reapportionment is] of a peculiarly political nature and therefore not meet for judicial determination."[30] The Court could scarcely conceive of reapportionment as anything other than "embroilment in politics, in the sense of party contests and party interests."[31] Into that jumble of politics, parties, and power, or what Justice Frankfurter referred to in *Colegrove* as the "political thicket," the Court simply refused to enter.[32]

For almost two decades, a majority of the justices rejected all attempts to draw the Court into issues dealing with malapportionment and redistricting. State and lower federal courts followed the Supreme Court's cautious tone in *Colegrove* and also refused to intervene. In 1960, the Court began to shift its stance on the issue when it confronted the Alabama legislature's redrawing of Tuskegee's boundaries from a simple square to a twenty-eight-sided figure that redistricted out nearly every black voter in the city. In *Gomillion v. Lightfoot,* the Court made it clear that where fundamental constitutional issues were at stake, it was prepared to intrude on the traditional legislative power of redistricting.[33] The denial of voting rights suffered by Tuskegee's black citizens, the Court ruled, violated the Fifteenth Amendment, which not only justified judicial action but also distinguished *Gomillion* from *Colegrove* where Illinois voters had claimed a dilution of their right to vote. Two years later, however, the Court announced that dilution itself was a type of deprivation of protected rights under the Fourteenth Amendment's equal protection clause.

In its seminal, though narrow, decision in *Baker v. Carr* (1962), the Supreme Court declared that redistricting and reapportionment schemes, such as the one from Tennessee challenged in that case, were not immune to judicial scrutiny.[34] Leaving the details to later decisions, Justice William Brennan's opinion for the Court asserted broadly that the federal courts "possessed jurisdiction of the subject matter" when there was substantial reason to believe that apportionment, or the lack thereof, violated the equal protection clause of the Fourteenth Amendment.[35] Within the next year, more than seventy-five apportionment-related lawsuits from around the country were filed in state and federal courts in response to the Court's decision. With its ruling in *Baker v. Carr*, as the legal scholar Robert Dixon once stated, the Court "not only entered the thicket, [it] proceeded to occupy it."[36]

A year after its decision in *Carr*, the Court struck down Georgia's county unit system of voting in primary elections because it gave greater weight to rural area voters.[37] It also issued the memorable phrase that would forever be linked to questions of apportionment. "The conception of political equality," the Court declared in *Gray v. Sanders*, "from the Declaration of Independence, to Lincoln's Gettysburg Address, to the Fifteenth, Seventeenth, and Nineteenth Amendments can mean only one thing—one person, one vote."[38]

THE LITIGATION

The Supreme Court handed down its decision in *Baker v. Carr* on March 26, 1962. Four days later and armed with the authority of that decision, the US district court panel in Montgomery stated that it would hold a hearing on the Alabama apportionment issue on July 16, 1962. It also indicated that it would render its decision quickly so that any action that might be necessary could be completed before the upcoming November elections.

Given the fact that the state had no experience in following the apportionment requirements of its 1901 Constitution, the district court expressed its desire that the Alabama legislature have a reasonable opportunity to perform its reapportioning duty prior to the July hearing. If it did so properly, the court pledged, the case would be dismissed. The court went on to warn legislators that if they failed to act or only went through the motions of reapportionment, the judges themselves would "be under a clear duty to take some action in time to take effect" before the election in November.[39]

Governor John Patterson convened a special session of the legislature on June 13, 1962, to deal with the district court's challenge. In his opening statement, Patterson pleaded with legislators to fulfill their constitutional duty to reapportion and gave them two important reasons for doing so. First, they all knew and had known for years, as he put it, that "representation in our Legislature no longer bears any reasonable relationship to population."[40] He added, "There exist grossly unfair variations in the number of people a legislator represents, and a large majority of the citizens of Alabama do not have a fair voice in the passage of the laws under which they live."[41] Patterson appealed to the legislators' conscience, patriotism, and sense of duty to finally address what their predecessors had ignored for sixty years.

His second reason for spurring them to action—the district court's threat to reapportion the legislature itself—was much more persuasive. Patterson told that legislature that he found the judges' mandate to be "dictatorial, unwarranted, . . . without any semblance of legal basis, . . . [and] meddling with matters that rightly are our business and nobody else's."[42] However, he also knew that the judges were serious and, empowered by the Supreme Court's decision in *Baker v. Carr*, unafraid to move forward under their own authority.

For the next thirty days, the legislature grappled with a variety of reapportionment and redistricting proposals, with several members ultimately resorting to race-based rhetoric in a desperate bid to win support. Representative Walter Perry introduced a measure to allot his home county of Jefferson seventeen seats in the House and seven in the Senate. The huge increase in representatives for his area was justified, he argued, not only because of the large population of Jefferson County but also to shift control of the legislature away from the Black Belt and the African American citizens who now constituted a majority there and who were registering to vote in ever-increasing numbers. He warned his fellow legislators what lay on the horizon: "The franchise to vote is going to be assured every citizen of Alabama regardless of race," he declared. "I don't mean 20 years from now, or even 10 years; we are talking about next week or the next."[43] Reapportioning seats away from those voters would therefore limit their influence.

Ironically, the steady increase in black voters was the very reason Black Belt legislators gave for opposing any measure that would lessen white representation from their region. Decrying the proposed combination of Macon and Bullock Counties into a single senatorial district, Montgomery County representative J. J. Pierce complained, "We are faced with the prospect of Negro representation in the House, . . . but why must we have Negro Senators?"[44] Covington County representative Fletcher Jones added this caution to those considering dramatic reapportionment changes: "[T]here are nine [proposed] senatorial districts with dangerous colored populations. You may bring about the election of nine colored senators."[45] Dallas County representative Val Hain called on his fellow legislators to reject such proposals. "It is a question of Anglo-Saxon blood calling upon Anglo-Saxon blood," he implored, "of white brothers calling upon white brothers."[46]

Nevertheless, on July 12, 1962, the legislature passed two reapportionment plans. The first proposed an amendment to the state constitution to allow for one senator per county and apportioned the house according to the requirements of the 1901 Constitution: one representative per county and the remainder of the seats apportioned by population. The second piece of legislation, known as the Crawford-Webb Act, was a standby law designed to take effect in 1966 in the event that voters rejected the constitutional amendment. It simply redrew all thirty-five senate districts, gave each county one representative in the house, and then apportioned the remainder of the house seats according to a population classification scheme. The plan did award more representatives to areas with greater population, but it could not explain why counties with fewer than 45,000 people received just one representative but those with 250,000 received four, or why counties with 300,000 and 600,000 people were each allotted the same number of six representatives.

Just two weeks after the end of the special session of the legislature, the district court panel held a hearing on the reapportionment plans and swiftly issued its opinion. The court was unimpressed with the legislature's efforts, stating bluntly that "each of the legislative acts, when considered as a whole, is . . . obviously discriminatory, arbitrary, and irrational."[47] Far from addressing the equal protection concerns that led to the court challenge in the first place, the district court pointed out that the constitutional amendment would actually make malapportionment in the state senate even worse. The judges were astonished to learn that the amendment would place control of the state senate in the hands of those elected by just 19 percent of the population, down from 25 percent under the sixty-year-old apportionment already in place! However, the court did look favorably on the amendment's population-based plan for allocating seats in the Alabama House of Representatives.

The court was also underwhelmed by the Crawford-Webb Act. In its entirety, the court found the law to be only "a slight improvement over the present system of representation."[48] It went on to characterize Crawford-Webb's illogical apportionment scheme for the house as "totally unacceptable," but did find some merit in the way the legislation reconfigured state senatorial districts.[49]

Dissatisfied with the legislature's overall efforts, but determined to keep its promise that Alabama's legislature would be reapportioned before the November 1962 election, the judicial panel combined the most promising features of the legislators' work (the constitutional amendment's plan for the house and the Crawford-Webb's proposal for the senate) with some additional modifications of its own. The result was the first reapportionment plan in American history to be ordered by a federal court. The judges acknowledged that their ruling could not serve as a permanent reapportionment measure, but, as a provisional matter, it could at least start, as they put it, "to break the strangle hold by the smaller counties on the Alabama Legislature."[50] The district court also announced that it would retain jurisdiction over the issue, carefully watching the implementation of its order while awaiting at some future date for legislators to complete "a true reapportionment of both Houses of the Alabama legislature."[51]

A number of probate judges in the Black Belt as well as other Alabama officials immediately appealed the ruling, claiming that the federal court had violated the principle of separation of powers and vastly overstepped its authority by directly inserting itself into the reapportionment process. Lawyers for the Jefferson County citizens, who had since been joined by like-minded people from Etowah and Mobile Counties, filed an appeal of their own. They appreciated the district court's action as a step in the right direction but complained that its remedy did not fully embrace proportional representation and thus failed to address the equal protection concerns that were at the heart of their grievance.

As mentioned earlier, *Baker v. Carr* had only acknowledged the justiciability of apportionment cases without setting forth any standards for how such matters should be settled. Within months of the Court's decision in that case, apportionment-related litigation had already commenced in thirty-four states, with several seeking additional guidance from the justices. In June 1963, the Court announced that it would hear oral arguments in the Alabama case as well as related challenges arising from five other states—which together represented the broad spectrum of malapportionment abuse.[52] The cases arising out of these six states "presented virtually every major variation of state apportionment arrangement" and were collectively known as the *Reapportionment Cases*.[53] The following November, the justices listened to five days of oral arguments on the issue, a modern record since the Court first imposed time limits in 1849. Their decision would forever alter the way legislatures apportion representatives.

During oral arguments on the Alabama case, W. McLean Pitts, representing state officials from the Black Belt in the suit, boldly challenged the district court's opinion as well as the rationale behind *Baker v. Carr*. He urged the Court to overturn that decision and return apportionment to the legislative branch where it belonged. In the event the Court refused to do so, he hoped that the judiciary's role would be limited to only reviewing the constitutionality of legislative action relative to apportionment rather than actually prescribing it. Pitts was especially critical of the district court's decision to strike down the constitutional amendment before the people of Alabama even had a chance to consider it. In short, he argued, the lower court simply went too far, and it was for legislators—not judges—to oversee statehouse reapportionment.

For their part, attorneys representing citizens in Jefferson, Mobile, and Etowah Counties told the justices that there was simply no other avenue to protect their vote than the judiciary. They went on to ridicule the notion that, free from judicial oversight, Alabama legislators would enact anything that would undercut their own power since they had refused to do just that for the previous six decades. They further implored the Court for guidelines that would help states reapportion their legislatures consistent with the equal protection clause of the Fourteenth Amendment, arguing that proportional representation in both houses was really the only way to accomplish that.

In February 1964, the Court drew heavily from the language of Article I of the Constitution, James Madison's notes on the 1789 Constitutional Convention, and extracts from *The Federalist Papers* to rule in *Wesberry v. Sanders* that the framers intended representatives in the US House to be drawn from districts that were generally equal in population.[54] That decision only pertained to federal election districts, and the founding generation had offered no further guidance for representation in state legislatures. Although it was a landmark reapportionment ruling where a single house of Congress was concerned, it was not clear to what extent *Wesberry* could serve as a precedent for apportioning seats in state legislative assemblies. On June 15, 1964, the Supreme Court announced its highly anticipated opinion on the matter.

THE DECISION

Reynolds v. Sims (8–1)
377 U.S. 533 (1964)

CHIEF JUSTICE WARREN delivered the opinion of the Court.

Undeniably the Constitution of the United States protects the right of all qualified citizens to vote, in state as well as in federal elections. . . . The right to vote freely for the candidate of one's choice is of the essence of a democratic society, and any restrictions on that right strike at the heart of representative government. And the right of suffrage can be denied by a debasement or dilution of the weight of a citizen's vote just as effectively as by wholly prohibiting the free exercise of the franchise. . . .

A predominant consideration in determining whether a State's legislative apportionment scheme constitutes an invidious discrimination violative of rights asserted under the Equal Protection Clause is that the rights allegedly impaired are individual and personal in nature. . . . While the result of a court decision in a state legislative apportionment controversy may be to require the restructuring of the geographical distribution of seats in a state legislature, the judicial focus must be concentrated upon ascertaining whether there has been any discrimination against certain of the State's citizens which constitutes an impermissible impairment of their constitutionally protected right to vote. . . . Undoubtedly, the right of suffrage is a fundamental matter in a free and democratic society. Especially since the right to exercise the franchise in a free and unimpaired manner is preservative of other basic civil and political rights, any alleged infringement of the right of citizens to vote must be carefully and meticulously scrutinized. . . .

Legislators represent people, not trees or acres. Legislators are elected by voters, not farms or cities or economic interests. As long as ours is a representative form of government, and our legislatures are those instruments of government elected directly by and directly representative of the people, the right to elect legislators in a free and unimpaired fashion is a bedrock of our political system. It could hardly be gainsaid that a constitutional claim had been asserted by an allegation that certain otherwise qualified voters had been entirely prohibited from voting for members of their state legislature. And, if a State should provide that the votes of citizens in one part of the State should be given two times, or five times, or 10 times the weight of votes of citizens in another part of the State, it could hardly be contended that the right to vote of those residing in the disfavored areas had not been effectively diluted. It would appear extraordinary to suggest that a State could be constitutionally permitted to enact a law providing that certain of the State's voters could vote two, five, or 10 times for their legislative representatives, while voters living elsewhere could vote only once. And it is inconceivable that a state law to the effect that, in counting votes for legislators, the votes of citizens in one part of the State would be multiplied by two, five, or 10, while the votes of persons in another area would be counted only at face value, could be constitutionally sustainable. Of course, the effect of state legislative districting schemes which give the same number of representatives to unequal numbers of constituents is identical. Overweighting and overvaluation of the votes of those living here has the certain effect of dilution and undervaluation of the votes of those living there. . . .

State legislatures are, historically, the fountainhead of representative government in this country. A number of them have their roots in colonial times, and substantially antedate the creation of our nation and our Federal Government. . . . But representative government is in essence self-government through the medium of elected representatives of the people, and each and every citizen has an inalienable right to full and effective participation in the political processes of his State's legislative bodies. . . . Full and effective participation by all citizens in state government requires, therefore, that each citizen have an equally effective voice in the election of members of his state legislature. . . .

Logically, in a society ostensibly grounded on representative government, it would seem reasonable that a majority of the people of a State could elect a majority of that State's legislators. To conclude differently, and to sanction minority control of state legislative bodies, would appear to deny majority rights in a way that far surpasses any possible denial of minority rights that might otherwise be thought to result. Since legislatures are responsible for enacting laws by which all citizens are to be governed, they should be bodies which are collectively responsive to the popular will. And the concept of equal protection has been traditionally viewed as requiring the uniform treatment of persons standing in the same relation to the governmental action questioned or challenged. With respect to the allocation of legislative representation, all voters, as citizens of a State, stand in the same relation regardless of where they live. Any suggested criteria for the differentiation of citizens are insufficient to justify any discrimination, as to the weight of their votes, unless relevant to the permissible purposes of legislative apportionment. Since the achieving of fair and effective representation for all citizens is concededly the basic aim of legislative apportionment, we conclude that the Equal Protection Clause guarantees the opportunity for equal participation by all voters in the election of state legislators. Diluting the weight of votes because of place of residence impairs basic constitutional rights under the Fourteenth Amendment. . . .

We are told that the matter of apportioning representation in a state legislature is a complex and many-faceted one. We are advised that States can rationally consider factors other than population in apportioning legislative representation. We are admonished not to restrict the power of the States to impose differing views as to political philosophy on their citizens. We are cautioned about the dangers of entering into political thickets and mathematical quagmires. Our answer is this: a denial of constitutionally protected rights demands judicial protection; our oath and our office require no less of us. . . .

To the extent that a citizen's right to vote is debased, he is that much less a citizen. The fact that an individual lives here or there is not a legitimate reason for overweighting or diluting the efficacy of his vote. The complexions of societies and civilizations change, often with amazing rapidity. A nation once primarily rural in character becomes predominantly urban. Representation schemes once fair and equitable become archaic and outdated. But the basic principle of representative government remains, and must remain, unchanged—the weight of a citizen's vote cannot be made to depend on where he lives. . . . The Equal Protection Clause demands no less than substantially equal state legislative representation for all citizens, of all places as well as of all races.

We hold that, as a basic constitutional standard, the Equal Protection Clause requires that the seats in both houses of a bicameral state legislature must be apportioned on a population basis. Simply stated, an individual's right to vote for state legislators is unconstitutionally impaired when its weight is in a substantial fashion diluted when compared with votes of citizens living in other parts of the State. . . .

By holding that as a federal constitutional requisite both houses of a state legislature must be apportioned on a population basis, we mean that the Equal Protection Clause requires that a State make an honest and good faith effort to construct districts, in both houses of its legislature, as nearly of equal population as is practicable. We realize that it is a practical impossibility to arrange legislative districts so that each one has an identical number of residents, or citizens, or voters. Mathematical exactness or precision is hardly a workable constitutional requirement.

In *Wesberry v. Sanders*, the Court stated that congressional representation must be based on population as nearly as is practicable. In implementing the basic constitutional principle of representative government as enunciated by the Court in *Wesberry*—equality of population among districts—some distinctions may well be made between congressional and state legislative representation. Since, almost invariably, there is a significantly larger number of seats in state legislative bodies to be distributed within a State than congressional seats, it may be feasible to use political subdivision lines to a greater extent in establishing state legislative districts than in congressional districting while still affording adequate representation to all parts of the State. To do so would be constitutionally valid, so long as the resulting apportionment was one based substantially on population and the equal-population principle was not diluted in any significant way. . . .

A State may legitimately desire to maintain the integrity of various political subdivisions, insofar as possible, and provide for compact districts of contiguous territory in designing a legislative apportionment scheme. Valid considerations may underlie such aims. Indiscriminate districting, without any regard for political subdivision or natural or historical boundary lines, may be little more than an open invitation to partisan gerrymandering. Single-member districts may be the rule in one State, while another State might desire to achieve some flexibility by creating multimember or floterial districts. Whatever the means of accomplishment, the overriding objective must be substantial equality of population among the various districts, so that the vote of any citizen is approximately equal in weight to that of any other citizen in the State. . . .

So long as the divergences from a strict population standard are based on legitimate considerations incident to the effectuation of a rational state policy, some deviations from the equal-population principle are constitutionally permissible with respect to the apportionment of seats in either or both of the two houses of a bicameral state legislature. But neither history alone, nor economic or other sorts of group interests, are permissible factors in attempting to justify disparities from population-based representation. Citizens, not history or economic interests, cast votes. Considerations of area alone provide an insufficient justification for deviations from the equal-population principle. Again, people, not land or trees or pastures, vote. Modern developments and improvements in transportation and communications make rather hollow, in the mid-1960's, most claims that deviations from population-based representation can validly be based solely on geographical considerations. Arguments for allowing such deviations in order to insure effective representation for sparsely settled areas and to prevent legislative districts from becoming so large that the availability of access of citizens to their representatives is impaired are today, for the most part, unconvincing.

A consideration that appears to be of more substance in justifying some deviations from population-based representation in state legislatures is that of insuring some voice to political subdivisions, as political subdivisions. Several factors make more than insubstantial claims that a State can rationally consider according political subdivisions some independent representation in at least one body of the state legislature, as long as the basic standard of equality of population among districts is maintained. Local governmental entities are frequently charged with various responsibilities incident to the operation of state government. In many States much of the legislature's activity involves the enactment of so-called local legislation, directed only to the concerns of particular political subdivisions. And a State may legitimately desire to construct districts along political subdivision lines to deter the possibilities of gerrymandering. However, permitting deviations from population-based representation does not mean that each local governmental unit or political subdivision can be given separate representation, regardless of population. Carried too far, a scheme of giving at least one seat in one house to each political subdivision (for example, to each county) could easily result, in many States, in a total subversion of the equal-population principle in that legislative body. This would be especially true in a State where the number of counties is large and many of them are sparsely populated, and the number of seats in the legislative body being apportioned does not significantly exceed the number of counties. Such a result, we conclude, would be constitutionally impermissible. And careful judicial scrutiny must of course be given, in evaluating state apportionment schemes, to the character as well as the degree of deviations from a strict population basis. But if, even as a result of a clearly rational state policy of according some legislative representation to political subdivisions, population is submerged as the controlling consideration in the apportionment of seats in the particular legislative body, then the right of all of the State's citizens to cast an effective and adequately weighted vote would be unconstitutionally impaired. . . .

We find, therefore, that the action taken by the District Court in this case, in ordering into effect a reapportionment of both houses of the Alabama Legislature for purposes of the 1962 primary and general elections, by using the best parts of the two proposed plans which it had found, as a whole, to be invalid, was an appropriate and well-considered exercise of judicial power. . . .

Affirmed and remanded.

Justice Harlan, dissenting.

The Court's elaboration of its new "constitutional" doctrine indicates how far—and how unwisely—it has strayed from the appropriate bounds of its authority. The consequence of today's decision is that in all but the handful of States which may already satisfy the new requirements the local District Court or, it may be, the state courts, are given blanket authority and the constitutional duty to supervise apportionment of the State Legislatures. It is difficult to imagine a more intolerable and inappropriate interference by the judiciary with the independent legislatures of the States. . . .

Generalities cannot obscure the cold truth that cases of this type are not amenable to the development of judicial standards. No set of standards can guide a court which has to decide how many legislative districts a State shall have, or what the shape of the districts shall be, or where to draw a particular district line. No judicially manageable standard can determine whether a

State should have single-member districts or multimember districts or some combination of both. No such standard can control the balance between keeping up with population shifts and having stable districts. . . .

Although the Court—necessarily, as I believe—provides only generalities in elaboration of its main thesis, its opinion nevertheless fully demonstrates how far removed these problems are from fields of judicial competence. Recognizing that 'indiscriminate districting' is an invitation to 'partisan gerrymandering,' the Court nevertheless excludes virtually every basis for the formation of electoral districts other than 'indiscriminate districting.' In one or another of today's opinions, the Court declares it unconstitutional for a State to give effective consideration to any of the following in establishing legislative districts:

(1) history;
(2) "economic or other sorts of group interests";
(3) area;
(4) geographical considerations;
(5) a desire "to insure effective representation for sparsely settled areas";
(6) "availability of access of citizens to their representatives";
(7) theories of bicameralism (except those approved by the Court);
(8) occupation;
(9) "an attempt to balance urban and rural power."
(10) the preference of a majority of voters in the State. . . .

I know of no principle of logic or practical or theoretical politics, still less any constitutional principle, which establishes all or any of these exclusions. Certain it is that the Court's opinion does not establish them. So far as the Court says anything at all on this score, it says only that "legislators represent people, not trees or acres"; that "citizens, not history or economic interests, cast votes"; that "people, not land or trees or pastures, vote," All this may be conceded. But it is surely equally obvious, and, in the context of elections, more meaningful to note that people are not ciphers and that legislators can represent their electors only by speaking for their interests—economic, social, political—many of which do reflect the place where the electors live. . . .

These decisions also cut deeply into the fabric of our federalism. What must follow from them may eventually appear to be the product of state legislatures. Nevertheless, no thinking person can fail to recognize that the aftermath of these cases, however desirable it may be thought in itself, will have been achieved at the cost of a radical alteration in the relationship between the States and the Federal Government, more particularly the Federal Judiciary. Only one who has an overbearing impatience with the federal system and its political processes will believe that that cost was not too high or was inevitable.

Finally, these decisions give support to a current mistaken view of the Constitution and the constitutional function of this Court. This view, in a nutshell, is that every major social ill in this country can find its cure in some constitutional "principle," and that this Court should "take the lead" in promoting reform when other branches of government fail to act. The Constitution is not a panacea for every blot upon the public welfare, nor should this Court, ordained as a judicial body, the thought of as a general haven for reform movements. The Constitution is an instrument of government, fundamental to which is the premise that in a diffusion of governmental authority lies the greatest promise that this Nation will realize liberty for all its citizens. This Court, limited in function in accordance with that premise, does not serve its high purpose when it exceeds its authority, even to satisfy justified impatience with the slow workings of the political process. For when, in the name of constitutional interpretation, the Court adds something to the Constitution that was deliberately excluded from it, the Court in reality substitutes its view of what should be so for the amending process.

THE AFTERMATH AND SIGNIFICANCE OF *REYNOLDS V. SIMS*

The impact and influence of the Court's decision in *Reynolds* was immediate. Although the Court considered several related apportionment cases during its 1963–64 term, it selected the Alabama case to be the vehicle for announcing that the "one person, one vote" principle applied to state-level reapportionment. The Court itself cited *Reynolds* as the leading precedent for the five other reapportionment cases that had been argued at the same time as the Alabama case and that were announced the same day. A week later, using *Reynolds* as its guide, the Court struck down the legislative apportionment schemes in nine other states from every region of the country. The Court's sweeping decision in *Reynolds* declaring that the equal protection clause required *both* houses of a legislature to be apportioned on the basis of population with roughly equal numbers of people affected in at least one house of nearly every state legislature. It also surprised reapportionment reformers. Given the long history of judicial reluctance to intrude on this area, many of them believed that the justices would take more time to nurse the principles announced just two years earlier in *Baker v. Carr*.

Not surprisingly, there was also opposition to the Court's decision. The newly elected Alabama governor, George Wallace, lambasted the ruling as "the most far-reaching decision every rendered."[55] "If the trend continues," he told a gathering of the state's county commissioners, "we won't have any state representatives except from three or four population centers. It could even extend to the national government, and the liberals and left-wingers could have a field day."[56] Others argued that it was inappropriate for the Court to step in when all state legislatures needed to do was simply "abide by their own constitutional provisions dealing with apportionment."[57] Daniel J. Elazar, a prominent political scientist specializing in federalism, declared that because of the Court's actions, "Our federal system is endangered, our system of separated powers is endangered, our very system of democratic decision-making is endangered."[58] He went on to warn, "It matters not that this danger stems from men acting with the best of intentions. It is no less a threat for that and may even be more of one because it is clothed in admirable motives and directed to admirable goals."[59]

Outraged members of Congress introduced a number of symbolic resolutions expressing their "indignation at the court's usurpation of the legislative power."[60] A wide array of bills were also filed in both the House and Senate. These included congressional authorization to delay implementation of the Court's order, a proposal to force the justices to retire at age seventy (Chief Justice Warren and Justice Hugo Black, two favorite targets, were both in their seventies at the time), and an effort to strip the federal judiciary of its ability to hear reapportionment cases, under Article III, Section 2 of the Constitution.[61] In addition, a constitutional amendment was advanced that would permit states with bicameral legislatures to apportion one house on a nonpopulation basis similar to Congress.

Senate Minority Leader Everett Dirksen of Illinois championed the constitutional amendment response to the *Reynolds* decision. However, in 1967, after his colleagues had twice voted against apportionment-related amendments, Dirksen resorted to a second method for amending the Constitution that does not require congressional approval. Article V of the Constitution authorizes a convention to consider amendments when state legislatures in two-thirds of the states call for one. Under that provision, delegates to that constitutional convention, rather than members of Congress, would determine which amendments would be sent on to the states for ratification.

Dirksen's proposal for a constitutional convention won quick approval from more than two dozen states, and by May 1969, he claimed to have thirty-three of the thirty-four states necessary to convene the assembly. Critics pointed out that several of the legislatures that supported a constitutional convention on apportionment had done so before they themselves were reapportioned in accordance with *Reynolds*, which should thereby negate their vote. In other states, recently elected legislators voted to rescind the decision of their predecessors who had voted in favor of the convention. The result was that neither constitutional scholars nor Dirksen himself knew for sure how many valid appeals for a constitutional convention existed. However counted, Dirksen's proposal ultimately failed to win the support of the necessary number of states. By the time he acknowledged defeat, forty-nine of the fifty state legislatures had already reapportioned, either on their own or by federal court order.

Critics were correct that the founders did not stipulate the absolute need for proportional representation in Congress, as evidenced by the composition of the United States Senate, and recognized that non-population-based factors such as geography, history, and others had long been accepted as viable guides in apportioning legislative seats. History also taught that legislators could and would entrench their power at the expense of the people whom they were to represent. As historian Alexander Keyssar explained, "Democracy indeed could be undone or circumvented through districting mechanisms as well as through disenfranchisement. . . . [T]hose who wielded disproportionate power in state governments were unlikely to surrender that power voluntarily."[62]

In giving citizens an equal voice and opportunity to challenge that power, *Reynolds* became the foundation for nearly every subsequent voting rights case and, coupled with the Voting Rights Act of 1965, fundamentally altered the country's political landscape. Yet, as one scholar bluntly observed, "*Reynolds v. Sims* promised more than it delivered."[63] The lofty goal of "fair and effective representation for all citizens" that the majority in *Reynolds* hoped to ensure by ending malapportionment quickly fell victim to the political gerrymander.[64] A determined majority in a statehouse could no longer rely on malapportionment to retain power, but it could manipulate voting district boundaries to achieve the same result.

In most states, the legislature redraws electoral district boundaries after each decade's census. Those districts, in keeping with *Reynolds*, must be roughly equal in population but can be drawn or gerrymandered in such a way that preserves majority party strength. The party that controls the statehouse after the census obviously has the advantage and can redraw districts that, barring major demographic shifts, essentially assure majority party dominance for the next decade.

For example, legislators might stretch and contort electoral districts to disperse the impact of a large bloc of voters from one party such that those voters would likely be in a minority within the new districts to which they are assigned. Conversely, legislators might crowd as many opposition party voters as they can into a handful of districts, leaving an overwhelming number of their own party's supporters to dominate in other districts. State and national political parties adopted these and related tactics in the early 1800s and continue to abuse their power to redraw districts by gerrymandering. Every Election Day, Democrats in overwhelmingly "red" districts and Republicans in "blue" electoral areas go to the polls to exercise their right to vote knowing that it is both a tremendous privilege but also, in their case, a meaningless exercise. Because of the way the districts are drawn, the weight of their vote counts for far less than that of those associated with the majority party.

Just four months before the Court handed down its opinion in *Reynolds*, it ruled that it would not intervene in political gerrymandering cases where sheer partisanship was the basis for the drawing of legislative districts.[65] Since that time, however, the Court has made occasional feints into this portion, the densest part, of the "political thicket," but has been unable to formulate a working standard for resolving equal protection claims.[66] When it finally does, the justices' decision will undoubtedly be based on the principles articulated by Chief Justice Earl Warren in *Reynolds v. Sims*: "Full and effective participation by all citizens . . . requires, therefore, that each citizen have an equally effective voice in the election of [representatives]."[67]

During his tenure on the Court from 1953 to 1969, Chief Justice Warren presided over a number of landmark cases that continue to influence every American. It was the Warren Court that banned racially segregated public schools, established the right of privacy, restricted public schools from mandating prayers and scripture readings, struck down miscegenation laws, expanded access to legal counsel for criminal defendants, and limited law enforcement's ability to coerce confessions. After he retired, and until his death in 1974, Earl Warren consistently maintained that for all the profound changes wrought by the Supreme Court during his years as its chief justice, the reapportionment cases like *Reynolds v. Sims* were the most significant. "If everyone in this country has an opportunity to participate in his government on equal terms with everyone else," he once said, "and can share in electing representatives of the entire community and not some special interest, then most of the problems that we are confronted with would be solved through the political process rather than through the courts."[68]

8

OLLIE'S BARBECUE

The Commerce Clause and *Katzenbach v. McClung* (1964)

THE DOCUMENT THAT EMERGED FROM the Constitutional Convention in September 1787 was unique in the way it guarded against the accrual of power. It provided for three branches of government: the executive, legislative, and judicial, and divided power further by allocating specific duties and responsibilities to the national government while reserving others to the states. Created on the premise that shared power among the institutions of government was the best defense for the rights and liberties of the American people, the Constitution was also ultimately ratified in the belief that the respective state governments would wield a much stronger influence over their citizens than the national government. So central were these ideas that Thomas Jefferson aptly referred to the division of powers and the system of federalism as "the foundation of the Constitution."[1]

Yet, questions about the parameters of state and national power arose almost immediately after ratification of the Constitution. Could Congress create a national bank? Could states nullify congressional acts they deemed unconstitutional? Could the national government sell lands and build roads and canals within states to encourage settlement? Were the states themselves to determine the issue of slavery? To these contentious issues was added the role of Congress in regulating commerce. The Constitution itself gave Congress authority over interstate commerce but failed to define exactly what that meant in relation to the states. In the 1960s, the owner of a small restaurant in Birmingham questioned the authority of Congress to regulate his business. Once known for his barbecue, Ollie

Figure 8. Ollie McClung Sr. in front of his famed restaurant. From the Birmingham News.

McClung is now remembered in every constitutional law casebook for lending his name to a Supreme Court case that vastly expanded the power of the national government.

THE STORY

The story of *Katzenbach v. McClung* actually began almost a century before the Court handed down its decision in that case. On March 1, 1875, President Ulysses S. Grant signed into law the most sweeping civil rights legislation in the history of the United States. It guaranteed to all citizens, regardless of their race and color, the "full and equal enjoyment of the accommodations, advantages, facilities, and privileges of inns, public conveyances on land or water, theaters, and other places of public amusement." Anyone denied access was entitled to monetary restitution by the federal government. Despite is promise, the legislation had little impact, particularly in the South, and eight years after its passage, the United States Supreme Court struck down the law. In *The Civil Rights Cases* (1883), the justices recognized that the Fourteenth Amendment gave Congress authority to prohibit racial discrimination by government action, but it was powerless, they declared, to regulate private race-based behavior.[2]

The practical effect of the Court's ruling was to provide constitutional protection to racism while essentially denying to Congress the authority to do anything about it. More than eight decades of discrimination, segregation, protests, and lawsuits followed. The Court rightly deserves credit for its opinions in the 1950s and 1960s to strike down segregation and extend the guarantees of equal protection to African Americans, but its ruling in *The Civil Rights Cases* was responsible for helping to create the social and legal environment that made those later decisions necessary.

In June 1963, against the backdrop of demonstrations a month earlier in which the country watched as fire hoses and police dogs were directed at teenage black protestors in Birmingham, President John F. Kennedy delivered a televised address to the nation to announce that he was sending a proposal to Congress to end racial discrimination in public accommodations. The debate that ensued both on and off Capitol Hill essentially pitted the president's civil rights initiative against the Supreme Court's pronouncement in *The Civil Rights Cases* that the Fourteenth Amendment gave Congress no authority to prohibit restaurant, hotel, theater, and other private business owners from deciding whom they would and would not serve.

Given that eighty-year-old precedent, congressional supporters of the new civil rights bill chose to deliberately avoid the Fourteenth Amendment and judicial interpretations about its application. Instead, they proposed that the legislation be grounded squarely in Congress's own authority over interstate commerce as granted to it by the Constitution.[3] Accordingly, Title II of the Civil Rights Act was carefully worded to prohibit places of public accommodation from discriminating or segregating on the basis of race. To extend congressional authority to this area, the bill defined a public accommodation, in part, as any business that affects commerce, serves interstate travelers, or offers food or other products that have moved in interstate commerce. Although the final vote in favor of the legislation was far from unanimous, the Civil Rights Act passed by comfortable margins in both the House and Senate.

After President Lyndon Johnson signed the bill into law on July 2, 1964, there were some demonstrations in the South, but civil rights leaders were surprised at the overall level of compliance. Several business organizations, however, maintained that Congress had exceeded its authority in passing the law. As the Civil Rights Act was rooted in the commerce clause, they believed that a constitutional challenge to its sweeping regulations might succeed if they could demonstrate that there was no substantial link between a given business and interstate commerce. With that argument in mind, members of the Birmingham Restaurant Association approached Ollie McClung.

The McClung family had operated their barbecue restaurant in the Southside area of Birmingham since 1926. It was located some eleven blocks from the interstate and even farther from railroad and bus stations and the airport. Ollie's Barbecue also did not engage in advertising, depending only on regular customers and their recommendation to others to attract new patrons. As one frequent visitor to Ollie's (Elizabeth S. Black, wife of Justice Hugo Black) reported to her husband, "They just have local people coming in for lunch. Nobody is a stranger in that place."[4] Together, these factors combined to make Ollie McClung the perfect party to challenge the Civil Rights Act since it was plain that his restaurant made no attempt to attract interstate travelers and because its location made it impractical for interstate visitors to Birmingham to visit.

Despite the above circumstances that suggested that McClung had a real chance to win the case, he had reservations about filing the lawsuit. He was not an ardent segregationist like many of those who opposed the civil rights movement. He denied inside seating to African Americans like proprietors of other eating establishments throughout the South, but he provided take-out service for anyone regardless of race. In addition, as Doris Bonner, an African American waitress who worked at Ollie's Barbecue for forty years, later recalled, McClung gave his employees food discounts, which black employees—with his full knowledge—used at rallies in black churches in the area and to help feed civil rights workers.[5]

McClung was also a lay minister with Cumberland Presbyterian Church and had traveled the country preaching in a variety of settings, including in many black churches. His religious beliefs played a central role in his life, causing him to sell bibles along with his barbecue, close his restaurant on Sundays, refuse to sell beer or liquor, and reportedly donate 10 percent of the restaurant's gross revenue to a local church. Those beliefs also taught him to respect and obey the law, which he found difficult to do relative to the Civil Rights Act.

McClung was convinced that if he seated and served black and white customers inside, the latter would refuse to patronize the restaurant. The result, he feared, was that he would lose his business. As Congress debated the Civil Rights Act, he met with his thirty-six employees, twenty-six of whom were African American, to discuss how Ollie's Barbecue should proceed if the law passed. His employees received no set wages for their work but rather a percentage of all profits, and when McClung told them that he thought the restaurant should maintain its practice of segregation to avoid a possible closure, his employees unanimously agreed.[6]

The day after President Johnson signed the Civil Rights Act into law, Ollie's Barbecue deliberately violated it by turning away black customers seeking service inside. Shortly thereafter, attorneys with the Birmingham Restaurant Association met with McClung and, again with the approval of his employees, he agreed to challenge the legislation. On July 31, 1964, McClung filed a lawsuit in US District Court in Birmingham seeking an injunction against the Department of Justice to stop it from enforcing the Civil Rights Act.

THE CONSTITUTIONAL BACKGROUND

Ollie McClung was concerned primarily about his restaurant, so it is unlikely that there were any other guiding constitutional or governmental theories motivating him to challenge the Civil Rights Act. However, his question about government's role in the "business of business" is older than the Constitution itself. Indeed, it was the primary reason for the assembling of state delegates in Philadelphia for the Constitutional Convention of 1787. Until the end of the Revolutionary War in 1783, the colonies that declared their independence from Great Britain were not fully aware of how the necessities of that conflict shrouded them from some very real domestic problems. Upon the war's conclusion, however, and "flushed with the enjoyment of independent and sovereign power," as James Madison later recalled, "[the states engaged] in omissions and measures incompatible with their relations . . . among themselves."[7] The area in which relationships between the states were the most "incompatible" and strained was interstate commerce.

Removed from the oversight of British rule and extending few powers to the new national authority established by the Articles of Confederation that loosely governed them, each of the thirteen states, according to Alexander Hamilton, "pursue[d] a system of commercial policy peculiar to itself."[8] They coined their own money, tussled over navigation rights to shared waterways, protected in-state industries and generated revenue by placing tariffs on out-of-state products, and, for those with major ports, levied taxes on surrounding states who imported or exported through those ports.

States already possessing advantageous infrastructure and economic resources readily dominated their less fortunate neighbors. Madison wrote of the latter's situation in the years leading up to the Constitutional Convention: "New Jersey, placed between Philadelphia and New York, was likened to a cask tapped at both ends; and North Carolina, between Virginia and South Carolina to a patient bleeding at both arms."[9] The result, as constitutional historian Max Farrand observed, was that individual state "interference with the arteries of commerce was cutting off the very life-blood of the nation, and something needed to be done."[10]

Delegates to the Constitutional Convention directly addressed the issue, giving Congress sole authority to "regulate commerce with foreign nations, and among the several states."[11] However, because the Constitution is not self-defining, it fell to the Supreme Court to determine exactly what such words as "commerce" and "among the several states" really meant with regard to governmental regulation.

It took almost four decades after the convention, but when the Court finally addressed the commerce clause, it did so in a major way. In 1824, the Court considered a case in which a steamboat company with a monopoly license from the New York legislature to conduct operations on the state's waterways, confronted another steamboat, licensed by Congress, plying its trade in the same waters. When the Court was asked to decide whose licensing power should prevail, it responded that it was for Congress to "prescribe the rules by which commerce is to be governed."[12] Defining commerce in *Gibbons v. Ogden* as commercial activity that affects more than one state, the Court held that only a national authority could avoid the problems that occurred under the Articles of Confederation. The unanimous ruling went on to assert that congressional authority over commerce "is complete in itself, may be exercised to its utmost extent, and acknowledges no limitations, other than are prescribed in the Constitution."[13]

Despite this sweeping declaration, the Court acknowledged in *Gibbons* that the states did not surrender all of their commerce-regulating authority. Those commercial activities that "are completely within a particular State," it explained, "which do not affect other States, and with which it is not necessary to interfere for the purpose of executing some of the general powers of the government" could not be regulated by Congress.[14] In short, "the completely internal commerce of a State, . . . may be considered as reserved for the State itself."[15] That simple statement, however, was very difficult to implement in practice.

The justices generally did not have to worry about the tension between the national and state governments created by their decision in *Gibbons* because commerce did not become a significant issue on the Supreme Court's docket until the latter part of the nineteenth century. By that time, vast industrial expansion was taking place, and small intrastate businesses were becoming interstate corporations. The infamous oil and steel barons created large monopolies that dominated the national economy. Industrial combines that controlled the railroads also, in effect, controlled agriculture and other interests that relied on the interstate railroad system to transport their goods to market. Commercial growth during this period brought great success and wealth to some, but there were negative costs for much of this business activity as well, including unsafe working conditions, child labor, excessively long work hours, and low wages. In light of such developments, Congress began to assert its authority to regulate commerce and many of its attendant issues. When these congressional actions were challenged, however, the Court found itself struggling to follow *Gibbons* as it tried to determine which commerce was interstate—to be properly regulated by Congress—and which was intrastate and protected against federal regulation.

The Court thus created a variety of legal definitions and rules to try and keep the commerce powers of Congress and the states separate. For example in 1895, the Supreme Court held that the antimonopoly regulations of the Sherman Antitrust Act did not apply to E. C. Knight, the nation's largest sugar-refining business.[16] Even though that company controlled 98 percent of all sugar refining in the United States, the Court ruled that it operations were primarily focused on production and manufacturing, which were under the complete regulatory authority of the states. The Court conceded that there was a role for congressional regulation too, but only insofar as the actual distribution and transportation of a product across state lines was concerned.

The Court's recognition that states alone could regulate production and manufacturing led to some surprising and even extreme outcomes. After the census of 1900 revealed that two million American children were employed on farms and in factories and mines, reform groups pressed for the national regulation of child labor. In 1916, using its authority under the interstate commerce clause, Congress passed the Keating-Owen Child Labor Act. This law forbade the shipment of any goods produced by businesses that either employed children under the age of fourteen or employed children between the ages of fourteen and sixteen for more than eight hours a day or more than six days a week. Two years later, however, the Supreme Court struck down the law in *Hammer v. Dagenhart* (1918), holding that child labor involved only in the manufacturing of goods, but not their transportation, was governed by the authority of the states and could not be regulated by Congress.[17]

The Court later stipulated that Congress lacked the power to pass legislation regulating business activities that had no connection to or effect on interstate commerce. The direct or indirect effect on interstate commerce thus became another way for the justices to determine the constitutionality of congressional regulations and was an approach the Court used as late as the mid-1930s to strike down several early New Deal programs.[18]

Some interstate commerce doctrines developed by the Court, however, did permit federal regulation of businesses. In 1905, for example, the Court considered the claims of Chicago stockyard owners who argued that Congress lacked the power to regulate them. The Court, in turn, formulated a "stream of commerce" test that questioned, in this case, where the cattle came from and where were they going? The fact that cattle in those stockyards neither originated nor remained in Illinois created enough of a connection with interstate commerce, the Court ruled, to allow Congress to regulate in this area.[19]

Later decisions would see the Court hold that where intrastate and interstate commerce were so intermingled that it was difficult to determine which level of government possessed actual regulatory authority, the power of Congress would prevail.[20] Similarly, the Court ruled that where state and federal regulations coexist on a certain issue, such as in a 1914 case dealing with railroad shipping fees between Shreveport, Louisiana, and Texas levied by both the Texas Railroad Commission and the federal Interstate Commerce Commission, the state regulation must yield to the federal order.[21]

With the election of President Franklin Roosevelt in 1932 and his subsequent eight appointments to the Court (beginning with the senior US senator from Alabama, Hugo Black, in 1937), the Court began to reconsider its hodgepodge of interstate commerce doctrines and substantially expand congressional authority over commerce. In 1941, the Court overturned its child labor decision in *Dagenhart* and upheld the constitutionality of the Fair Labor Standards Act. The Court recognized Congress's authority under the commerce clause to ban the interstate shipment of goods to reach other social goals such as child labor, minimum wages, and maximum weekly employment hours.[22]

A year later, the justices decided a case that serves as the best illustration of the Court's newfound approval of congressional authority under the commerce clause during the mid-1900s. One of the Court's most controversial decisions, *Wickard v. Filburn* (1942) involved the Agricultural Adjustment Act of 1938 and the national quotas it set on grain production in an attempt to stabilize prices.[23] When government authorities learned that an Ohio dairy farmer named Roscoe Filburn had exceeded his quota by planting winter wheat to feed his own chickens and small herd of cattle, he was found in violation of the law and fined. Filburn challenged the law believing the Congress lacked the authority to regulate wheat that he had grown for his own use and never intended to sell at market.

However, the Court upheld the fine and the regulation as a valid exercise of congressional power, ruling that Filburn took himself out of the market when he grew his own wheat. According to the Court, Filburn's reasoning that he was protected against congressional regulation because he did not sell wheat grown for his own purposes was actually an argument for the legislation. That is, his effort to stay out of the market actually affected the market, and if every American farmer did the same, the wheat market would be devastated. The Court used *Wickard* to announce that its variety of previous standards for distinguishing state and national government spheres for the regulation of commerce were never particularly helpful and were no longer to be relied on. Instead, it declared that the realities of a vibrant and growing national economy would guide the justices in their future commerce clause decisions.

THE LITIGATION

McClung's challenge to the Civil Rights Act coincided with a similar lawsuit filed by an Atlanta motel owner just hours after Lyndon Johnson signed the legislation. Unlike other downtown Atlanta businesses that had ended their discriminatory practices, Moreton Rolliston's 216-room Heart of Atlanta Motel steadfastly refused to accommodate African American patrons. In fact, even though his motel's own restaurant, which was leased by another company, welcomed all customers regardless of race, Rolliston resisted every effort to change his lodging policy. Rolliston's lawsuit contended that the law was unconstitutional because it sought to regulate his motel, which was not involved in interstate commerce. His attorneys argued that because people are literally sleeping at a motel, they are no longer a part of interstate commerce as they would be when awake and traveling or buying food and other products that have moved in commerce.

On July 22, 1964, the panel of US district court judges convened to hear the dispute unanimously rejected Heart of Atlanta's challenge to the law.[24] The court denied Rolliston's contention that the motel was outside the stream of interstate commerce, in part, by relying on another federal court ruling against him just two weeks earlier. In that decision, a federal judge held that actions taken by Rolliston and other Atlanta hotel and motel owners (who, together, already controlled half of all hotel beds downtown) to prevent the Marriott company from establishing a hotel in the area essentially constituted a monopoly that affected interstate commerce in violation of the Sherman Antitrust Act. The district court panel sitting on the discrimination case reasoned that congressional authority to pass the Civil Rights Act must "be at least as broad as that which it exercised in the adoption of the Sherman Act."[25] Further, if there was enough of a connection between the motel and interstate commerce to invoke federal antitrust law, there was enough to uphold the application of the Civil Rights Act. The district court dismissed Heart of Atlanta's suit and ordered it to accept all people seeking lodging regardless of race.

The three-judge panel in the Ollie's Barbecue case came to a very different conclusion. During the one-day hearing on the matter, McClung's attorneys stressed that because his restaurant was located so far away from the highway and airport and so much of the food it served was purchased locally, it simply was not a part of interstate commerce. Further, McClung himself testified that he stood to lose as much as 90 percent of his business if the Civil Rights Act forced him to integrate, a denial, he believed, of his Fifth Amendment right to not be deprived of his property by the government without due process of law.

In their subsequent opinion, the district judges acknowledged the vast expansion of Congress's commerce power since the 1930s, but they also noted that previous commerce clause legislation upheld by the Supreme Court had been accompanied by clear congressional findings that such regulations were necessary. However, "the Civil Rights Act of 1964," the court observed, "contains no legislative findings."[26]

It declared further that it was unaware of any case that gave Congress the "power to control the conduct of people on the local level because they happen to trade sporadically with persons who may be traveling in interstate commerce."[27] It went on to chastise Congress for essentially focusing on a desired outcome (ending discriminatory practices) and then creating legislation (public accommodations and interstate commerce) completely unrelated to that outcome to bring it about. To permit the national government to do that, the court explained, was a much bigger issue than about who was or was not served barbecue. "If Congress has the naked power to do what it has attempted in Title II of [the Civil Rights] act," it warned, "there is no facet of human behavior which it may not control by mere legislative *ipse dixit* that conduct 'affects commerce' when in fact it does not do so at all, and rights of the individual to liberty and property are in dire peril."[28] The district court concluded that the Civil Rights Act exceeded Congress's authority at least as it applied to Ollie's Barbecue and issued an injunction that prevented the Department of Justice from enforcing the law against the restaurant. Nicholas Katzenbach, the attorney general of the United States, immediately appealed the decision to the Supreme Court.

The Court agreed to hear both cases and, given the similar questions raised by each, calendared *Heart of Atlanta v. U.S.* and *Katzenbach v. McClung* for back-to-back oral arguments on October 5, the first day of the Court's 1964 term. That date was fewer than three weeks after the district court rendered its opinion in *McClung*, and the abbreviated preparation schedule challenged both parties.

At oral arguments, Archibald Cox, the US solicitor general who defended the law, stressed three main points. First, he emphatically argued that McClung's initial complaint should have been dismissed entirely by the lower court because the Department of Justice had no knowledge of Ollie's Barbecue and had done nothing to enforce the Civil Rights Act against it. Fear of being prosecuted under the law, he reminded the Court, was grounds for neither a lawsuit nor a legal judgment. Beyond that jurisdictional matter, he also argued that racial discrimination in business was an issue of national magnitude that burdened interstate commerce. He told the justices that the ripple effect of denying service to African Americans and the consequent boycotts, sit-ins, and demonstrations all affected and disrupted businesses locally and throughout the state, region, and nation.

Finally, Cox reiterated that the Court's own precedents recognized the Civil Rights Act as a valid exercise of congressional power to regulate interstate commerce. He freely acknowledged that some restaurants that practiced segregation like Ollie's Barbecue had little to no connection with interstate commerce, but that, he added, was irrelevant. "This particular establishment is tied to its trickle of goods that will be coming in the future," Cox explained, and, much like the wheat farmer in *Wickard v. Filburn*, "this trickle is representative of thousands, hundreds of thousands of similar trickles and that together they are a great [economic] stream" that cannot be exempt from Congress's interstate commerce authority.[29]

McClung's lawyer, Robert McDavid Smith, repeated the key points of his successful argument in the lower federal court: that there was no close and substantial relationship between Ollie's Barbecue and interstate commerce, and that the loss of business resulting from integration would violate the Fifth Amendment. He paid special attention, however, to the fact that the purpose of the Civil Rights Act was not clearly tied to interstate commerce. Unlike other similar laws, he argued, Congress had submitted no findings whatsoever that discrimination in restaurant service affected interstate commerce. When questioned by Justices William Brennan and Byron White why that was an issue, Smith responded that without specific findings it appeared that Congress had simply "cast about, to find some constitutional basis for [the Civil Rights Act]," eventually deciding to ground it in the commerce clause.[30] If Congress can use the commerce clause to delve into and regulate anything that it finds amiss in American society, without finding a specific connection with interstate commerce, Smith questioned, where does its power end? In short, he concluded, the law "was not enacted in the usual manner at all."[31]

Two months later, a unanimous Supreme Court announced its decision in both cases.

THE DECISION

Katzenbach v. McClung (9–0)
379 U.S. 294 (1964)

JUSTICE CLARK delivered the opinion of the Court.

This case was argued with . . . *Heart of Atlanta Motel v. United States*, decided this date, in which we upheld the constitutional validity of Title II of the Civil Rights Act of 1964 against an attack by hotels, motels, and like establishments. This complaint for injunctive relief against appellants attacks the constitutionality of the Act as applied to a restaurant. The case was heard by a three-judge United States District Court and an injunction was issued restraining appellants from enforcing the Act against the restaurant. . . . We now reverse the judgment.

Ollie's Barbecue is a family-owned restaurant in Birmingham, Alabama, specializing in barbecued meats and homemade pies, with a seating capacity of 220 customers. It is located on a state highway 11 blocks from an interstate and a somewhat greater distance from railroad and bus stations. The restaurant caters to a family and white-collar trade with a take-out service for Negroes. It employs 36 persons, two-thirds of whom are Negroes.

In the 12 months preceding the passage of the Act, the restaurant purchased locally approximately $150,000 worth of food, $69,683 or 46% of which was meat that it bought from a local supplier who had procured it from outside the State. The District Court expressly found that a substantial portion of the food served in the restaurant had moved in interstate commerce. The restaurant has refused to serve Negroes in its dining accommodations since its original opening in 1927, and since July 2, 1964, it has been operating in violation of the Act. The court below concluded that if it were required to serve Negroes it would lose a substantial amount of business.

On the merits, the District Court held that the Act could not be applied under the Fourteenth Amendment because it was conceded that the State of Alabama was not involved in the refusal of the restaurant to serve Negroes. It was also admitted that the Thirteenth Amendment was authority neither for validating nor for invalidating the Act. As to the Commerce Clause, the court found that it was "an express grant of power to Congress to regulate interstate commerce, which consists of the movement of persons, goods or information from one state to another"; and it found that the clause was also a grant of power "to regulate intrastate activities, but only to the extent that action on its part is necessary or appropriate to the effective execution of its expressly granted power to regulate interstate commerce." There must be, it said, a close and substantial relation between local activities and interstate commerce which requires control of the former in the protection of the latter. The court concluded, however, that the Congress, rather than finding facts sufficient to meet this rule, had legislated a conclusive presumption that a restaurant affects interstate commerce if it serves or offers to serve interstate travelers or if a substantial portion of the food which it serves has moved in commerce. This, the court held, it could not do because there was no demonstrable connection between food purchased in interstate commerce and sold in a restaurant and the conclusion of Congress that discrimination in the restaurant would affect that commerce.

The basic holding in *Heart of Atlanta Motel*, answers many of the contentions made by the appellees. There we outlined the overall purpose and operational plan of Title II and found it a valid exercise of the power to regulate interstate commerce insofar as it requires hotels and motels to serve transients without regard to their race or color. In this case we consider its application to restaurants which serve food a substantial portion of which has moved in commerce.

Section 201 (a) of Title II commands that all persons shall be entitled to the full and equal enjoyment of the goods and services of any place of public accommodation without discrimination or segregation on the ground of race, color, religion, or national origin; and 201 (b) defines establishments as places of public accommodation if their operations affect commerce or segregation by them is supported by state action. Sections 201 (b) (2) and (c) place any "restaurant . . . principally engaged in selling food for consumption on the premises" under the Act "if . . . it serves or offers to serve interstate travelers or a substantial portion of the food which it serves . . . has moved in commerce."

Ollie's Barbecue admits that it is covered by these provisions of the Act. The Government makes no contention that the discrimination at the restaurant was supported by the State of Alabama. There is no claim that interstate travelers frequented the restaurant. The sole question, therefore, narrows down to whether Title II, as applied to a restaurant annually receiving about $70,000 worth of food which has moved in commerce, is a valid exercise of the power of Congress. The Government has contended that Congress had ample basis upon which to find that racial discrimination at restaurants which receive from out of state a substantial portion of the food served does, in fact, impose commercial burdens of national magnitude upon interstate commerce. The appellees' major argument is directed to this premise. They urge that no such basis existed. It is to that question that we now turn.

As we noted in *Heart of Atlanta Motel* both Houses of Congress conducted prolonged hearings on the Act. And, as we said there, while no formal findings were made, which of course are not necessary, it is well that we make mention of the testimony at these hearings the better to understand the problem before Congress and determine whether the Act is a reasonable and appropriate means toward its solution. The record is replete with testimony of the burdens placed on interstate commerce by racial discrimination in restaurants. A comparison of per capita spending by Negroes in restaurants, theaters, and like establishments indicated less spending, after discounting income differences, in areas where discrimination is widely practiced. This condition, which was especially aggravated in the South, was attributed in the testimony of the Under Secretary of Commerce to racial segregation. This diminutive spending springing from a refusal to serve Negroes and their total loss as customers has, regardless of the absence of direct evidence, a close connection to interstate commerce. The fewer customers a restaurant enjoys the less food it sells and consequently the less it buys. In addition, the Attorney General testified that this type of discrimination imposed "an artificial restriction on the market" and interfered with the flow of merchandise. In addition, there were many references to discriminatory situations causing wide unrest and having a depressant effect on general business conditions in the respective communities.

Moreover there was an impressive array of testimony that discrimination in restaurants had a direct and highly restrictive effect upon interstate travel by Negroes. This resulted, it was said, because discriminatory practices prevent Negroes from buying prepared food served on the premises while on a trip, except in isolated and unkempt restaurants and under most unsatisfactory and often unpleasant conditions. This obviously discourages travel and obstructs interstate commerce for one can hardly travel without eating. Likewise, it was said, that discrimination deterred professional, as well as skilled, people from moving into areas where such practices occurred and thereby caused industry to be reluctant to establish there.

We believe that this testimony afforded ample basis for the conclusion that established restaurants in such areas sold less interstate goods because of the discrimination, that interstate travel was obstructed directly by it, that business in general suffered and that many new businesses refrained from establishing there as a result of it. Hence the District Court was in error in concluding that there was no connection between discrimination and the movement of interstate commerce. The court's conclusion that such a connection is outside "common experience" flies in the face of stubborn fact.

It goes without saying that, viewed in isolation, the volume of food purchased by Ollie's Barbecue from sources supplied from out of state was insignificant when compared with the total foodstuffs moving in commerce. But, as [Justice] Jackson said for the Court in *Wickard v. Filburn* (1942):

> That appellee's own contribution to the demand for wheat may be trivial by itself is not enough to remove him from the scope of federal regulation where, as here, his contribution, taken together with that of many others similarly situated, is far from trivial.

We noted in *Heart of Atlanta Motel* that a number of witnesses attested to the fact that racial discrimination was not merely a state or regional problem but was one of nationwide scope. Against this background, we must conclude that while the focus of the legislation was on the individual restaurant's relation to interstate commerce, Congress appropriately considered the importance of that connection with the knowledge that the discrimination was but "representative of many others throughout the country, the total incidence of which if left unchecked may well become far-reaching in its harm to commerce."...

Article I . . . confers upon Congress the power "to regulate Commerce . . . among the several States" and Clause 18 of the same Article grants it the power "to make all Laws which shall be necessary and proper for carrying into Execution the foregoing Powers. . . ." This grant, as we have pointed out in *Heart of Atlanta Motel* "extends to those activities intrastate which so affect interstate commerce, or the exertion of the power of Congress over it, as to make regulation of them appropriate means to the attainment of a legitimate end, the effective execution of the granted power to regulate interstate commerce." Much is said about a restaurant business being local but "even if appellee's activity be local and though it may not be regarded as commerce, it may still, whatever its nature, be reached by Congress if it exerts a substantial economic effect on interstate commerce. . . ." The activities that are beyond the reach of Congress are "those which are completely within a particular State, which do not affect other States, and with which it is not necessary to interfere, for the purpose of executing some of the general powers of the government." This rule is as good today as it was when Chief Justice Marshall laid it down almost a century and a half ago.

This Court has held time and again that this power extends to activities of retail establishments, including restaurants, which directly or indirectly burden or obstruct interstate commerce. We have detailed the cases in *Heart of Atlanta Motel*, and will not repeat them here.

Nor are the cases holding that interstate commerce ends when goods come to rest in the State of destination apposite here. That line of cases has been applied with reference to state taxation or regulation but not in the field of federal regulation.

The appellees contend that Congress has arbitrarily created a conclusive presumption that all restaurants meeting the criteria set out in the Act "affect commerce." Stated another way, they object to the omission of a provision for a case-by-case determination—judicial or administrative—that racial discrimination in a particular restaurant affects commerce.

But Congress' action in framing this Act was not unprecedented. In *United States v. Darby* (1941), this Court held constitutional the Fair Labor Standards Act of 1938. There Congress determined that the payment of substandard wages to employees engaged in the production of goods for commerce, while not itself commerce, so inhibited it as to be subject to federal regulation. The appellees in that case argued, as do the appellees here, that the Act was invalid because it included no provision for an independent inquiry regarding the effect on commerce of substandard wages in a particular business. But the Court rejected the argument, observing that:

> Sometimes Congress itself has said that a particular activity affects the commerce, as it did in the present Act, the Safety Appliance Act and the Railway Labor Act. In passing on the validity of legislation of the class last mentioned the only function of courts is to determine whether the particular activity regulated or prohibited is within the reach of the federal power.

Here, as there, Congress has determined for itself that refusals of service to Negroes have imposed burdens both upon the interstate flow of food and upon the movement of products generally. Of course, the mere fact that Congress has said when particular activity shall be deemed to affect commerce does not preclude further examination by this Court. But where we find that the legislators, in light of the facts and testimony before them, have a rational basis for finding a chosen regulatory scheme necessary to the protection of commerce, our investigation is at an end. The only remaining question—one answered in the affirmative by the court below—is whether the particular restaurant either serves or offers to serve interstate travelers or serves food a substantial portion of which has moved in interstate commerce.

The appellees urge that Congress, in passing the Fair Labor Standards Act and the National Labor Relations Act, made specific findings which were embodied in those statutes. Here, of course, Congress has included no formal findings. But their absence is not fatal to the validity of the statute, for the evidence presented at the hearings fully indicated the nature and effect of the burdens on commerce which Congress meant to alleviate.

Confronted as we are with the facts laid before Congress, we must conclude that it had a rational basis for finding that racial discrimination in restaurants had a direct and adverse effect on the free flow of interstate commerce. Insofar as the sections of the Act here relevant are concerned, 201 (b) (2) and (c), Congress prohibited discrimination only in those establishments having a close tie to interstate commerce, i.e., those, like the McClungs', serving food that has come from out of the State. We think in so doing that Congress acted well within its power to protect and foster commerce in extending the coverage of Title II only to those restaurants offering to serve interstate travelers or serving food, a substantial portion of which has moved in interstate commerce.

The absence of direct evidence connecting discriminatory restaurant service with the flow of interstate food, a factor on which the appellees place much reliance, is not, given the evidence as to the effect of such practices on other aspects of commerce, a crucial matter.

The power of Congress in this field is broad and sweeping; where it keeps within its sphere and violates no express constitutional limitation it has been the rule of this Court, going back almost to the founding days of the Republic, not to interfere. The Civil Rights Act of 1964, as here applied, we find to be plainly appropriate in the resolution of what the Congress found to be a national commercial problem of the first magnitude. We find it in no violation of any express limitations of the Constitution and we therefore declare it valid.

The judgment is therefore reversed.

THE AFTERMATH AND SIGNIFICANCE OF *KATZENBACH V. MCCLUNG*

Two days after the Court announced its decision, Ollie McClung held a press conference to publicly declare his intention to comply. He also used the occasion to express his worry about the scope of the ruling, which, he believed, "gives the federal government control over the life and behavior of every American."[32] The following day, the *Anniston Star* reported that "five Negroes entered the restaurant, were seated and served without incident."[33]

True to his word, McClung accommodated all customers at Ollie's Barbecue regardless of their race from that point on. That included, incidentally, thousands of interstate travelers who, after McClung relocated his restaurant next to Interstate 65 in 1968, saw his large sign proclaiming "Ollie's—World's Best Bar-B-Q" from the highway as they traveled through Birmingham. A landmark among Alabama restaurants and US Supreme Court decisions, Ollie's Barbecue relocated to Hoover, Alabama, in 1998, but was unable to duplicate its previous success. It served its last customer on September 10, 2001, and closed its doors.

Because it forbade racial discrimination by private individuals whose businesses purport to serve the public, the Civil Rights Act of 1964 was transformative, and its legacy on other types of nonracial discrimination far-reaching. The Court's decision in *McClung* to uphold that law, however, was also the high-water mark of congressional authority under the commerce clause. The Supreme Court had long been criticized for its role in the tremendous growth of national government power since the New Deal era. While *McClung* dealt with racial matters, the Court's decision suggested that there may be no activity, however local in nature, that was completely free of federal government regulation if a plausible connection could be made between that local activity (multiplied across the nation) and interstate commerce. Yet, personnel shifts on the bench in later decades caused even the Court to reevaluate the power its decisions had given to the national government.

In the mid-1990s, in only the second Supreme Court case of the previous sixty years to reject congressional authority to regulate under the commerce clause, the justices struck down a federal law that made it a crime to possess a firearm within one thousand feet of a school.[34] While recognizing that *Darby*, *Wickard*, *McClung*, and other cases had extended the reach of the national government, the Court boldly affirmed in *U.S. v. Lopez* (1995) that congressional authority under the commerce clause was still "subject to outer limits."[35] In establishing those boundaries, Chief Justice William Rehnquist announced a new test for determining the constitutionality of congressional regulations under the commerce clause. Congress, he declared, could regulate the channels of interstate commerce (such as roads and rivers); the instrumentalities of interstate commerce (such as railroads, buses, trucks, and boats) as well as the things and people involved in interstate commerce; and those activities that have a substantial relation to or effect on interstate commerce. The Court held that the federal Gun-Free School Zone Act, which was the subject of the *Lopez* case, did not fit into any of these categories and was thus unconstitutional.

Five years later, the Court subjected the federal Violence Against Women Act to the *Lopez* test. While sympathetic to the motivations behind the legislation, a narrow majority of justices in *U.S. v. Morrison* (2000) was unable to see a connection between violence against women and any of the points of the *Lopez* test.[36] The Court ruled that Congress had again exceeded its interstate commerce authority with the legislation. Finally, in 2012, the Court ruled that President Barack Obama's signature legislative feat, the Affordable Care Act, could not be justified under the commerce clause power of Congress.[37] The Court did, however, uphold key sections of that law under Congress's constitutional authority to tax.

For more than eighty years, the Court's commerce clause decisions have been castigated for first expanding and then contracting the power of Congress. Partisans on both sides of these decisions have had plenty to criticize during that time, including the Court's ruling in *McClung*. However, that decision and the unique circumstances behind it may have been more in keeping with the intent of at least some of the founders than is typically acknowledged.

In a February 1829 letter to Virginia politician Joseph C. Cabell, James Madison explained the purpose of the Constitution's interstate commerce clause. It was, as noted earlier, a product of how the early states had treated one another, particularly "the abuse of the power by the importing states in taxing the non-importing."[38] "[R]ather than as a power to be used for the positive purposes of the [national] government," Madison confirmed, Congress's authority over interstate commerce was intended to be "a negative and preventative provision against injustice among the states themselves."[39] In other words, the commerce clause was not to be used to pursue some national government objective at the expense of the states, but rather to protect the states from one another.

Perhaps it is not stretching Madison's words too much to suggest that "injustice among the states themselves" could also include the very situation that *McClung* addressed. After all, even Madison understood that no state actually bore the injustice of the tariffs and taxes imposed by surrounding states. The costs of these and other types of commercial abuse were shouldered by individual citizens.

Similarly, Alabama and other southern states suffered nothing when black customers had to look elsewhere after Ollie's Barbecue and other restaurants denied them service. Black travelers to the segregated South who were unfamiliar with the region had to spend much more time trying to find establishments that would serve them. Other African Americans from outside of the South but familiar with social conventions there might find them such a deterrent as to alter their travel plans completely. All of these, the Court held, were examples of how discrimination against individuals even in a local restaurant tucked away in a Birmingham neighborhood could affect the commerce of a nation.

9

REVERED AND REVILED

The Supreme Court Legacies of John McKinley, John Archibald Campbell, and Hugo Black

Any consideration of Alabama's contributions to American constitutional law would be incomplete without reference to the three Supreme Court justices appointed from the state. Two of the three joined the Court at significant moments in its history. In 1837, John McKinley was the first to occupy the ninth seat on the bench after Congress expanded the membership of the Supreme Court from seven to nine. One hundred years later, Hugo Black became the first of Franklin Roosevelt's eight appointees, ushering in a period of sweeping constitutional change. John Archibald Campbell served between them, and though his appointment to and resignation from the Court were both historic events in their own right, his greatest impact actually occurred after he returned to private practice. In addition to the fact that these men were appointed from the state of Alabama, they also shared the common experience of being heralded and vilified as associate justices of the Supreme Court. Critics scrutinized and disparaged both their judicial decisions and personal lives. Their contributions differed, of course, mirroring the demands and opportunities that the Court of their day permitted, but each left a legacy.

John McKinley's tenure on the Supreme Court is best characterized by his responsibilities far from Washington as he labored to complete his tasks as a circuit court judge. For him, the Court was an obligation to be fulfilled. John Archibald Campbell succeeded McKinley but resigned from the Court after just eight years. He later advanced an argument before his former colleagues that envisioned the Court as a guardian of fundamental rights, be they enumerated in the Constitution or not. Hugo Black played an important role in many of the cases in this book, but he also saw the Court as an opportunity to take Campbell's foundational argument and build on it by insisting that the protections of the Bill of Rights applied against local, state, and national governments. Over the span of 130 years, these three Supreme Court justices from Alabama helped transform the Court, the Constitution, and the country. What follows is a brief review of their lives and singular contributions.[1]

JOHN MCKINLEY: THE COURT AS AN OBLIGATION

John McKinley was born on May 1, 1780, in Culpeper County, Virginia, and moved to what is now Kentucky when he was very young.[2] He apprenticed as a carpenter but later read for the law and passed the Kentucky bar in 1800. He soon acquired property and wealth in Lexington as well as a reputation as a very accomplished lawyer, all of which were factors that brought McKinley to the attention of local political leaders. Given prominent family

Figure 9. John McKinley. Portrait by Matthew Jouett, circa 1817–18. Courtesy of the Collection of the Supreme Court of the United States.

connections in the state on his mother's side, McKinley likely would have become a renowned legal and political figure in Kentucky had he chosen to remain there. However, Andrew Jackson's crushing defeat of the Creek Indians at Horseshoe Bend in 1814 and their subsequent cession of some twenty million acres of land to the US government caused McKinley to turn his attention to Alabama.

The Creek lands became the site of an unprecedented land rush. Rumors spread throughout the Eastern Seaboard and even overseas of a climate so favorable and soil so fertile that one could grow twelve-foot-high cotton plants with bolls as big as a man's fist. The contagion to own land there became known as the "Alabama Fever," and McKinley, like tens of thousands of others, contracted it.[3] So many people flooded into the area that the land that had belonged to the Creeks in 1814 became a territory of the United States in 1817 and then the twenty-second state in the union just two years later.

McKinley set up a lucrative law practice in Huntsville and was reported "to be the first lawyer in the three states [of Tennessee, Alabama, and Mississippi]."[4] He quickly established himself as a man of influence. He played a key role in the formation of the Cypress Land Company, a land speculation firm that purchased thousands of acres of public land that it then resold to settlers eager to relocate to northern Alabama. As an original member of Cypress, McKinley helped to establish the city of Florence, Alabama, in 1818, and through his association with the company, he was also able to obtain extensive land holdings in Lauderdale, Lawrence, Limestone, and Madison Counties. In 1821, the state legislature appointed McKinley to the University of Alabama's first board of trustees, which was tasked with recommending a site for the campus, overseeing construction of its buildings and developing a curriculum. In 1822, McKinley donated a tract of land to the citizens of Athens on the condition that they use it to "establish a respectable Female Academy."[5] That school for young women went on to become the Athens Female Academy and later Athens State University, the oldest operating institution of higher learning in Alabama.

McKinley served in the first Alabama legislature after statehood was granted in 1819 and was elected to several other terms. He was twice elected to the US Senate and once to the US House of Representatives. His political prominence in Alabama was such that he probably would have been elected governor had he chosen to run, but he declined the invitation to do so at least twice. McKinley's reputation led an 1826 Rhode Island newspaper to observe that he "is associated with the best interests of Alabama, and he has done more than any other individual . . . [for] the inhabitants of that

State."[6] Andrew Jackson would refer to McKinley as "the most prominent man in allabama."[7]

On Jackson's last full day in office as president, Congress passed the Judiciary Act of 1837, which expanded the number of seats on the Supreme Court from seven to nine. James K. Polk, who was then serving as the Speaker of the House of Representatives, notified Jackson of the successful passage of the legislation and also recommended two men from the newer states in the union to fill the open slots. The first was John Catron, who, like Polk and Jackson, was from Tennessee. The other was Jackson and Polk's mutual friend from Alabama, John McKinley. Jackson followed Polk's advice with respect to Catron, but nominated William Smith, a lifelong associate and former senator from South Carolina then residing in Alabama, instead of McKinley. The Senate confirmed both men five days later, but Smith refused the appointment.

Upon his inauguration, the new president, Martin Van Buren, followed up on Polk's recommendation and immediately nominated fifty-six-year-old John McKinley to fill the new ninth seat on the Supreme Court. Since Congress was out of session when Van Buren submitted the nomination, the Senate was unable to confirm McKinley until the following September. At that time, McKinley became the first Alabamian to take a seat on the United States Supreme Court. He also became the first of just four justices in American history to have served in both houses of Congress before joining the Court.[8]

McKinley's appointment as an associate justice should have been the capstone to a long life of public service. He was a successful lawyer and wealthy landowner in northern Alabama and was closely associated with the legal, social, and educational affairs of the state. He had been deeply involved in both state and national politics, praised throughout the country for his political skills, and he had enjoyed the respect and public approbation of Jackson, Polk, Van Buren, and other notable government figures. Yet, his tenure on the Court did not follow the successful pattern of the rest of his life. In fact, he could not possibly have anticipated how his position on the Supreme Court would negatively affect his wealth, health, and reputation, all of which began to decline almost immediately on his appointment.

Just two weeks after Van Buren announced his nomination of McKinley, the Panic of 1837 began. This nationwide financial crisis was brought about, in part, by widespread speculation, particularly in the East and South. Taking out millions of dollars in loans, investors sank their money and credit "into unproductive, uncultivated lands of the West; . . . into imaginary steamboat and river-dredging companies; into unmarketable supplies of cotton and woolen goods; into urban real estate, and rural highways and wilderness canals."[9] The depression left very few Americans untouched, but southerners like McKinley were hit especially hard because of plummeting cotton prices, which remained low for much of the next decade. He was unable to make the necessary adjustments to protect his own investments because his responsibilities on the Supreme Court left him with little time at home. His considerable wealth, so much of which derived from land and cotton, declined precipitously during the nearly seven-year depression.

McKinley's reputation and work ethic were also called into question once he joined the Court. Within months of his appointment, members of Congress from Arkansas, Mississippi, and Louisiana charged McKinley with ignoring his judicial responsibilities for their constituents. From the time these states joined the union as territories, each had a single US district judge assigned to oversee litigation. However, those judges were utterly incapable of dealing with the thousands of legal claims—primarily related to disputed land titles—that accumulated. The creation of the Ninth Circuit (to which each of these states and Alabama belonged) was supposed to alleviate this situation, as Justice McKinley and the district judges could now work together to resolve these cases.

Progress was slow but not because McKinley failed to perform his duties, as his congressional critics alleged. The sheer number of lawsuits itself was a problem. Indeed, of approximately six thousand cases on the justices' *cumulative* circuit dockets during his first year on the bench, McKinley's new Ninth Circuit alone accounted for 4,700 of that total. In addition to this mass of litigation, there were also several other significant and inherent challenges to the Ninth Circuit that severely limited McKinley's ability to effectively carry out his judicial duties at circuit.

Circuit riding was the single most arduous task of the early Supreme Court justices and comprised the bulk of their business. The first Supreme Court consisted of six members appointed by George Washington who were assigned in pairs to attend to judicial business in the northern, middle, and southern circuits, each consisting of a grouping of states along the Eastern Seaboard. The justices left for their circuit assignments at the conclusion of their short three- or four-month term in Washington. At circuit, the justices served as both trial and appellate judges and were required to hold court at specific sites and according to a particular timetable designated by Congress.

The combined responsibilities of holding two Supreme Court sessions in Washington in addition to their semiannual circuit court duties was a huge burden on the early justices, and all of them complained about their circuit-riding duties. They were not only away from home for extended periods, they also had to cope with less than ideal traveling conditions and lodging. As the nation expanded to include Kentucky, Tennessee, and Ohio (which necessitated the creation of another circuit and a seventh seat on the Supreme Court in 1807), the traveling demands on the justices increased, as did their complaints. The subsequent addition of several new and much larger states in virtually every direction (Alabama, Illinois, Indiana, Louisiana, Maine, Mississippi, and Missouri, all by 1821) only exacerbated the problem.[10]

By the time Congress expanded the seven seats on the Supreme Court to nine in March 1837, it had restructured the Court's circuit duties such that each justice presided over a single circuit, which they traversed twice a year, and attended a single session of the Supreme Court in Washington. While these accommodations provided some benefit, they did little to ease the practical burdens of circuit riding. The duties of the circuit were truly onerous for many of the early justices and were inconvenient for all. John McKinley's Ninth Circuit responsibilities, however, were impossible to fulfill, and they would exact a particularly harsh toll on him during his fifteen years on the Court.

McKinley's first and most obvious problem with his Ninth Circuit assignment was financial in nature. At the time of his appointment, each of the associate justices received a $4,500 salary, while the chief justice received $5,000. Congress set that pay scale in 1819 and did not adjust it again until 1856, despite the huge increase in the justices' workload during the intervening four decades.[11] To compound matters (and unlike the stipend its own members received), Congress had yet to authorize a travel allowance for the members of the Supreme Court. Such costs were far from negligible for any of the justices, but they clearly weighed more heavily on those assigned to the larger circuits or who had longer distances to travel to reach Washington for the Court's term there.

McKinley lived the farthest from Washington of all the justices. He traveled nearly one thousand miles one way from his home in Florence to attend the Court's term. When it adjourned, the justices headed to their circuits. McKinley's Ninth was by far the biggest, encompassing Alabama, Arkansas, Louisiana, and Mississippi, all of which were among the top ten largest states in the union at the time. The size of his circuit and the distance between his home and Washington, DC, meant that McKinley would pay a far larger proportion of out-of-pocket expenses to carry out his judicial duties than any other member of the Court. Before he was even confirmed, McKinley estimated that travel costs alone would require at least a third of his associate justice salary.[12] This was a significant challenge for him particularly during the economic depression that began with the Panic of 1837.

In addition to the financial costs, the new Ninth Circuit's unusual cultural, commercial, and economic diversity created its own set of problems for McKinley. For example, in 1840, New Orleans was over 120 years old, the cultural and commercial center of the South, and, with some one hundred thousand residents, one of the nation's largest and wealthiest cities. Little Rock, Arkansas, on the other hand, was home to fewer than two thousand people and would not even have a real hotel in the city for another year. On the edge of the frontier, Little Rock was a young and violent town awash with land speculators, settlers, and squatters. The differences in these circuit court sites led to a vast spectrum of legal disputes that would have challenged the abilities of any Supreme Court justice.

The inclusion of Louisiana was itself problematic because of the unique status of Spanish and French civil law there. Like nearly every lawyer from outside of that state (including all of the members of the Supreme Court), McKinley had trained in the English common law tradition and thus was initially ill-prepared to consider disputes arising out of Louisiana's civil law heritage. Judicial proceedings at New Orleans were further complicated and protracted by the ongoing use of the French language by many of the parties, which required additional time for translation.

The third and most demanding aspect of McKinley's Ninth Circuit was the travel. While each of the circuits undoubtedly had its own unique transportation challenges, the Ninth was arguably the most grueling because, with the exception of New Orleans and Mobile, there simply was no convenient way for McKinley to get to the courts within the 206,000 square miles of his circuit. Congress appeared to have organized the Ninth Circuit with little regard for the actual means of reaching the population centers there. As a result, transportation difficulties in the largely unsettled area together with the congressionally mandated court schedule requiring him to crisscross his way across the circuit took a terrible toll on McKinley's health.

Before he had even completed his first term, McKinley petitioned both President Van Buren and his former colleagues in Congress to divide the vast Ninth Circuit so that he could spend less time traveling and more time adjudicating disputes, a plea he would issue repeatedly over the next several years. Contemporary judicial scholars have often noted that McKinley's lasting fame, such as it is, lies mostly in his frequent complaints regarding the difficulties of his circuit. Such characterizations are unfair and ignore the fact that McKinley was from the Ninth Circuit himself and, given his business interests and the national political offices he had held, frequently traveled to, from, and throughout the area. His were not the concerns of some East Coast urban dweller unacquainted with life and travel on the American frontier. He was very familiar with the transportation challenges of his region long before he was appointed to the Court, and thus his concerns and complaints should not be casually dismissed.

It is important to remember also that Americans were far less mobile then, and thus few people, comparatively speaking, traveled great distances on a regular basis as he was required to twice a year while riding his circuit. The nature of Justice McKinley's responsibilities, as well as the size of his circuit, demanded that he spend a considerable amount of time each year traveling by stagecoach and steamboat and finding accommodations along the way as best as he could.

As if the financial costs, the size and unique characteristics of his jurisdiction, and the difficulties of travel within the Ninth Circuit were not enough, McKinley also had to deal with a congressionally mandated court schedule that was impossible to meet. He and the other justices were expected to be in Washington when the Supreme Court's term began on the second Monday in January (later to be moved to the first Monday in December). When the term ended, typically in March, the justices would then embark on their circuit duties. Of course, because there was no set date for ending the Supreme Court's Washington term, sessions that lasted longer than expected forced the justices to choose between leaving the Court early in order to attend to their circuit duties or remaining in DC until the Court finished its business at the risk of missing the early round of circuit courts.

McKinley had to leave Washington immediately, because he was due at the annual session of circuit court in Little Rock, which began on the fourth Monday in March. He was expected to conclude his business there in time to arrive at Mobile by the second Monday in April. He then returned north to attend court in Jackson, Mississippi, on the first Monday in May and, two weeks later, journeyed back south to New Orleans where circuit court opened on the third Monday in May. His route would conclude with a trip to northern Alabama for Huntsville's circuit court on the second Monday in June.

The legislation creating the Eighth and Ninth Circuits stipulated that circuit court be convened twice a year in some locations and annually in others. McKinley's fall session of circuit court required him to leave Florence in time to return to Mobile by the second Monday in October. He would then head north to Jackson by the first Monday in November, and back south to New Orleans two weeks later. From there, he would return to

Washington, DC, to await the beginning of the Supreme Court's term.[13] A more grueling route than this congressionally mandated zigzagged path is hard to imagine. His circuit route not only made no sense in terms of efficiency, it also appeared that no one in Congress had actually traversed the route laid out for McKinley within the required time frame. In the words of two eminent judicial scholars, the Ninth Circuit's route was not only "unworkable, [but also] bizarre."[14]

In an 1839 report commissioned by Congress as it considered ways to equalize the justices' circuit duties, McKinley estimated that, using available transportation modes and routes, he traveled some ten thousand miles annually in attending court sessions at circuit and in Washington, DC. That was nearly three times as much as the next most-traveled justice. McKinley also reported that his Supreme Court responsibilities kept him away from his family and home for almost ten months of the year.

A related complication for the justices was that Congress had only mandated the *start* dates for circuit court. They were left to decide on their own whether to leave some matters unfinished in order to adhere to the circuit schedule or devote as much time as possible to clearing their docket knowing that in so doing they would be late to their next assignment. Between his large dockets, travel difficulties within the circuit, and the large area he was forced to cover, McKinley was routinely late in arriving at both his circuit court and Supreme Court sessions, for which he was harshly criticized at circuit as well as in Washington. In August 1842, having long ignored McKinley's claims that the Ninth Circuit was too large and its circuit court schedule too compressed, Congress finally reorganized the circuits. Mississippi and Arkansas remained in the Ninth Circuit, while Alabama and Louisiana occupied a newly reconstituted Fifth Circuit.[15]

As Chief Justice Roger Taney would not assign justices to the reorganized circuits until the Court's term in Washington that winter, McKinley made plans to attend circuit court one more time according to the schedule he had followed since his appointment. In November 1842, however, Mississippi newspapers reported that the sixty-two-year-old McKinley had fallen ill on his way to Jackson and would not attend circuit court. It is not clear what brought on the malady, but his age, his years spent in fulfilling his demanding circuit duties, and the recent loss of his eldest daughter and all of her children (four of his five grandchildren) to a diphtheria epidemic have all been cited as factors. Later newspaper announcements stated that the justice was partially paralyzed and not expected to live.

McKinley survived, but never regained his full health or mobility. A special rule was adopted within his Ninth Circuit to permit the clerks at the various court sites to endorse rulings and other legal documents on McKinley's behalf because he could no longer sign his name. He also moved to Louisville, Kentucky, to be closer to water routes that would take him to DC and to circuit court more efficiently. For ten more years, even while partially paralyzed, he served faithfully on the Supreme Court while struggling to fulfill his circuit-riding duties. On July 19, 1852, "an enduring but exhausted"[16] John McKinley died in Louisville. He was buried beside the two young grandsons, who had preceded him in death, in Louisville's Cave Hill Cemetery.

Just fifty years later, in his celebrated history of the Supreme Court, Hampton L. Carson referred to McKinley—the man once reported to be the best attorney in three states, the former United States senator and representative, and the first ninth justice—as "little known, even to the profession."[17] McKinley's subsequent and almost complete disappearance from public memory compelled a later Court observer to declare with little exaggeration, "Who was John McKinley? You will search all the compendiums of universal knowledge in your libraries in vain to find any answer to this question. His name will not be mentioned therein."[18] For the first century after his death, that was true wherever one sought information about McKinley, including in Alabama.

There are several reasons why John McKinley is worth remembering, however, but the most important may be the circuit changes that he helped bring about.[19] For the Court's first fifty years, Congress did nothing to relieve the justices' burdens at circuit but eventually enacted exactly what McKinley had repeatedly requested: smaller, more equitable circuits and attendance at only one circuit court session annually. Congress reduced the Court's circuit-riding duties even further in the late 1800s and in 1911, after more than a century of protests from presidents and justices alike, abolished them entirely.

The justices themselves sacrificed the most during the continuance of this practice, and none paid a greater price than John McKinley, the first and only justice to oversee the original Ninth Circuit. Well did Chief Justice Roger Taney memorialize him as "a sound lawyer, faithful and assiduous in the discharge of his duties while his health was sufficient to undergo the labor. . . . And no man could be more free from guile, or more honestly endeavor to fulfill the obligations which his office imposed on him."[20]

JOHN ARCHIBALD CAMPBELL: THE COURT AS A GUARDIAN

On February 3, 1873, the United States Supreme Court prepared to hear oral arguments in the *Slaughterhouse Cases*.[21] While all of the justices were

Figure 10. John Archibald Campbell. Photograph by W. W. Washburn. Courtesy of the Collection of the Supreme Court of the United States.

familiar with the famed John Archibald Campbell who stood before them as an attorney in the case, only one, Nathan Clifford, had been present in 1861 when that same lawyer, then Associate Justice Campbell, had resigned from the Supreme Court.[22]

Campbell was born in Wilkes County, Georgia, on June 24, 1811. He was something of a child prodigy, entering Franklin College (now the University of Georgia) at age eleven and graduating at the head of his class three years later. His father was a trustee of the college, a member of the state legislature, and a very successful attorney, but the younger Campbell professed little interest in the law, intending to become a career officer in the military instead. To that end and with the assistance of Senator John C. Calhoun (who was a close family friend), Campbell received an appointment to the United States Military Academy at West Point in 1826. Just two years later, however, his father died, leaving his family, to the great surprise of all who knew him, in disastrous financial circumstances. Campbell resigned from West Point to assist his mother after the family lost their home and nearly all they possessed in settling their financial affairs. He also began to read law under the guidance of his uncle, John Clark, who had been governor of Georgia from 1819 to 1823.

Campbell became a member of the Georgia bar in 1829, but only after a special act of the legislature permitted him to do so because he was only eighteen years old at the time. He then left for Alabama, was admitted to its state bar in March 1830, and immediately embarked on an enormously successful legal practice—first in Montgomery and later in Mobile, where he became very wealthy. He also dabbled in politics, representing both cities in the Alabama legislature. Campbell established himself as the leading attorney in the state; he had a particular talent for land title disputes, which were a constant source of litigation in Alabama and other Gulf states. He frequently argued before the Alabama Supreme Court and before Justice John McKinley when the latter presided at the federal circuit court in Mobile. Witnessing one of his performances in the courtroom, a newspaper breathlessly declared, "[Campbell's] name . . . is heard on every side, and appears to be in the mouths of everyone. His wondrous argument . . . has all but immortalized him, so lucid, forcible, and convincing was it."[23] He reportedly possessed the largest personal collection of law books in the country, and his intellect, legal ability, and courtroom skills became so well known that he began to take cases from outside of Alabama.

Campbell presented his first US Supreme Court case in 1849 and would argue before that bench many more times in the future.[24] In fact, during John McKinley's last term, Campbell appeared before the Court as counsel in six different cases. The justices thus became very well acquainted with his abilities, and the fact that he lost several of those Supreme Court arguments did nothing to dampen their respect for him.

When McKinley died in July 1852, President Millard Fillmore attempted to fill the vacant Supreme Court seat, ultimately nominating three different men for the open slot. With the 1852 presidential election looming, the Democrats who controlled the Senate refused to confirm any of his nominees because Fillmore belonged to the Whig Party.[25] Franklin Pierce, a Democrat, won the presidential election that November and immediately began to field recommendations from advisors, Democratic senators, and others regarding candidates for the judicial vacancy. Perhaps the most unusual and surely the most influential recommendation Pierce received, however, came from the Supreme Court itself.

On behalf of their fellow justices, Justices John Catron and Benjamin Curtis hand delivered letters to the president in which they collectively recommended that he appoint forty-one-year-old John Archibald Campbell to fill the Supreme Court seat that had lain vacant for eight months.[26] Although it is likely that individual justices who were personally acquainted with previous presidents had offered similar recommendations when such vacancies arose, this was the first (and presumably the only) time when the Supreme Court as a body made a recommendation as to who should join its ranks.

On March 21, 1853, President Pierce nominated Campbell as an associate justice of the Supreme Court, and the Senate unanimously confirmed him. That there were no dissenting votes, including from the Whig senators who believed that Democrats had stolen the Supreme Court seat by refusing to confirm Fillmore's nominees, says much about Campbell's national reputation. In fact, despite Campbell's status as a Southern Democrat who had previously owned slaves, even some northern Whig abolitionist newspapers heralded his appointment. The *New York Tribune*, for example, deemed Campbell "the ablest man connected with the ultra State-Rights organization anywhere. That is, he is chock full of talent, genius, industry and energy. . . . [A]s a jurist and a man[, he] commands the respect and confidence of everyone."[27]

Given his age, intellect, and abilities, Campbell was expected to have a long and influential tenure on the Court. He compared favorably with the great Justice Joseph Story, and Chief Justice Roger Taney himself believed Campbell to be "the man best fitted to succeed him as Chief Justice."[28] Like the man he replaced, however, Campbell never lived up to his potential on the Court. For McKinley, it was his duties at circuit that prevented him from fulfilling his promise as a member of the Supreme Court. For Campbell, it was war.

During his eight short years on the Supreme Court, Campbell and his fellow justices considered a variety of legal disputes, many of which, during this still formative period in the country's history, raised questions about the relationship between the national and state governments. For his part, Campbell fully recognized the constitutional role and authority of the national government, but where that government, including its courts, began to step beyond what Campbell believed were its constitutional limits, he consistently voted to protect the states against such encroachment.

For instance, he argued that federal court recognition of corporations as citizens and the legal rights that followed undermined state authority to regulate businesses.[29] In other cases, typically in dissents, Campbell could barely disguise his contempt for banks, railroads, insurance companies, and other corporations, which, having once been granted tax exemptions by their states, convinced federal judges that the Constitution's contract clause shielded them from subsequent changes in state tax law that might have negatively affected them.[30] Campbell's articulation of and efforts to protect the states' authority to regulate corporate interests within their borders earned him accolades on both sides of the Mason-Dixon Line. Of course, northerners were admittedly apprehensive about the application of this same protective stance for states' rights as slavery loomed larger and larger on the Court's docket.

The justices had inched their way into slavery-related disputes in the decade prior to Campbell's appointment, but they would eventually be consumed by the issue along with the rest of the country. Landmark rulings in *U.S. v. Amistad* (1841), *Prigg v. Pennsylvania* (1842), and *Jones v. Van Zandt* (1847) deeply angered both supporters and opponents of slavery and focused the nation's attention on the Court.[31] However, the impact of these cases paled in comparison to that of the Supreme Court's 1857 decision in *Dred Scott v. Sandford*.[32]

Chief Justice Taney wrote the majority opinion in *Dred Scott*, which held that black persons, free or enslaved, were not citizens and thus could not sue in federal court. Taney might have simply stopped there and dismissed the case, but instead he went on to consider the central question of Dred Scott's appeal. Scott had been born into slavery in Virginia, coming to Alabama in 1818 when the family that owned him moved to the Huntsville area during the Alabama Fever land rush. The family and their slaves relocated to St. Louis in the early 1830s, and Scott was sold to John Emerson, a doctor in the US Army. Emerson's assignments took him and Scott to military installations in the upper Midwest where slavery was not permitted because of the Missouri Compromise of 1820. The two returned to Missouri, a slave state, where Emerson died. Scott attempted to purchase his freedom from Emerson's widow, but when she refused, he filed suit against her, arguing that because of his time on free soil, he was no longer a slave.[33]

The Court held that the time Scott spent in states and territories where the Missouri Compromise banned slavery did not change his status as a slave. It went on to rule that the Fifth Amendment's defense against government deprivation of "life, liberty or property without due process of law" also protected slaveholders. In other words, Congress violated the Fifth Amendment when it passed the Missouri Compromise, denying citizens the right to transport their property, including slaves, to whatever area of the United States that they wanted. The law, therefore, was unconstitutional. Campbell wrote a concurring opinion, consistent with his views about the reach of the national government into the internal affairs of the states. Congress had the power to regulate slavery in interstate commerce, he noted, and even abolish the slave trade outright. However, the national government lacked the authority to define property or regulate it within the borders of a given territory or state.

The *Dred Scott* decision created a firestorm of controversy, sharpened already strident public opinion for and against slavery, tarnished Chief Justice Taney's name forever, and so undermined the stature of the Court that it would take decades to recover. Northern newspapers that had once praised Campbell castigated him and the other justices in the majority. The country was already deeply divided over the issue of slavery, but the *Dred Scott* decision in no small measure contributed to the onset of the Civil War.

Campbell was always an advocate for states' rights, but he also recognized that each of the individual states was part of a larger whole. He argued for the preservation of the Union long before he joined the Court at a time when others in Alabama and elsewhere in the South were issuing early calls to secede. With Abraham Lincoln's election in November 1860, that threat of secession became reality. South Carolina seceded that December, followed by Mississippi and Florida in early January 1861. On the eve of Alabama following suit, Campbell wrote a letter addressed to delegates of his state's secession convention that was reprinted in newspapers throughout the country. He argued that Lincoln's election alone was not sufficient reason to dissolve the Union. More importantly, he saw secession as a final course of action to be taken once all other options had been exhausted. To secede before other measures were tried first, he warned, "will result in the discredit and defeat of every measure for reparation and security."[34] The letter had little impact, and on January 11, 1861, Alabama seceded from the United States, with seven more southern states to follow.

Campbell met with the outgoing president, James Buchanan; sought the help of former president Franklin Pierce; and later worked with Lincoln's secretary of state, William Seward, all in an attempt to preserve a dialogue with the seceding states. He and Justice Samuel Nelson of New York also worked with the Lincoln administration and commissioners from the new Confederate government to defuse the standoff that was unfolding at Fort Sumter, South Carolina. Those efforts were ultimately unsuccessful, however, and on April 25, 1861, just two weeks after Confederate forces fired on Fort Sumter and Lincoln called for 75,000 men to put down the rebellion, John Archibald Campbell sent a one-sentence letter to the president announcing his resignation from the Supreme Court.

He returned to Mobile and was shocked to find that the animosity that Northerners directed toward him over *Dred Scott* and other rulings was very nearly matched by his fellow Alabamians when some of his private letters became public. Campbell had denounced secession in these letters to his friends and family and was bitterly criticized for it by the southern press. In addition, his delay in resigning from the Court instead of immediately doing so when Alabama seceded and even his attempts at mediating the dispute at Fort Sumter caused many to question his loyalty to the southern cause. Campbell later recalled to former Justice Benjamin Curtis that when he returned to Alabama in 1861, "it was to receive coldness, aversion, or contumely from the secession population. I did not agree to recant what I had said, or to explain what I had done; and, thus, instead of appeasing my opponents, I aggravated my offense."[35]

These circumstances resulted in the former Supreme Court justice and most prominent attorney in the South being unable to reestablish his law practice in Mobile. Believing he would find a more hospitable climate elsewhere, Campbell and his family moved to New Orleans after spending just two months in Alabama. However, the strategic importance of that city to both Federal and Confederate control of the lower Mississippi caused him to worry for his family's safety, so he again moved in October 1861, this time to Richmond. There, Campbell was offered several positions with the Confederate government, but he ultimately accepted appointment only as assistant secretary of war, which, despite the title, involved little more than clerical functions. Leaders in both the North and South still held him in high regard, however, and Lincoln himself met with Campbell and two other Confederate representatives at Hampton Roads, Virginia, on February 3, 1865, in an unsuccessful attempt to negotiate an end to the war. Campbell was imprisoned after the war along with several other notable Confederate officials, but he won his freedom after five months when Justice Samuel Nelson and former Justice Benjamin Curtis intervened with President Andrew Johnson on his behalf.

Campbell returned to New Orleans to practice law and quickly reestablished his reputation as one of the best attorneys in the country. He remained active in state and federal court for nearly all of the remaining twenty-four years of his life, devoting himself almost solely to Supreme Court litigation by the mid-1870s. Most judicial scholars acknowledge that John Archibald Campbell would have been one of the greatest Supreme Court justices in American history had he remained on the Court. Yet, even as an attorney in private practice, he arguably made a greater impact on American constitutional law than most of the men and women who have served on the Supreme Court—and he did so, ironically, in a losing cause.

The Butchers' Benevolent Association hired Campbell to challenge an 1869 Louisiana law that authorized the creation of the Crescent City Live-Stock Landing and Slaughter-House Company and tasked it with overseeing the slaughtering of all livestock in New Orleans and surrounding areas. The legislation also granted the company a twenty-five-year monopoly over slaughtering operations. Proponents defended the monopoly as the only possible remedy to the city's serious public health concerns. More than 300,000 animals were slaughtered annually in and around New Orleans. Butchers disposed of carcasses and offal wherever it was convenient, which resulted in mountains of animal waste and stomach-churning smells throughout the city, as well as contaminated water and the disease and death that accompanied it.

While state authorities believed that the creation of a single, centrally located slaughterhouse would eliminate the public health problems, the Butchers' Benevolent Association was more concerned about the practical effect of the legislation. In granting the slaughterhouse a monopoly, the law also mandated the closure of all other butchering facilities, putting some one thousand independent butchers out of work.[36] The Butchers' Benevolent Association saw this action as an unconstitutional deprivation of both the butchers' property rights and their right to pursue the livelihood of their choice.

As an associate justice of the Supreme Court, John Archibald Campbell was a consistent defender of the right of states to be generally free from the encroaching power of the national government. As a private attorney in the *Slaughterhouse Cases* (1873), however, Campbell argued that the relationship between the states and the national government was radically different from that which existed in pre–Civil War America and that the far-reaching authority of the federal government was essential to protect citizens from actions taken by their own states.

While Campbell claimed that the Louisiana law violated the Thirteenth Amendment's ban on "involuntary servitude" because it forced the independent butchers to use the Crescent City facility, he grounded his strongest arguments in Section One of the Fourteenth Amendment. Drafted and ratified in response to the Supreme Court's *Dred Scott* ruling, the Fourteenth Amendment imposed clear limitations on the states with regard to the treatment of African Americans: "All persons born or naturalized in the United States and subject to the jurisdiction thereof, are citizens of the United States and of the State wherein they reside. No State shall make or enforce any law which shall abridge the privileges and immunities of citizens of the United States; nor shall any State deprive any person of life, liberty, or property, without due process of law; nor deny to any person within its jurisdiction the equal protection of the laws."[37]

Only five years had passed since the ratification of the Fourteenth Amendment in 1868, and *Slaughterhouse* would be the Court's first opportunity to consider its meaning and reach. Campbell challenged the justices to adopt an expansive interpretation, one that recognized that the amendment's protections applied to more than just newly freed slaves. He argued that the amendment had a larger purpose that guaranteed to all Americans freedom from arbitrary, oppressive, and unfair state regulation. The Fourteenth Amendment, he wrote in his brief to the Court, "is not confined to any class or race. It comprehends all within the scope of its provisions. The vast number of laborers in mines, manufactories, commerce as well as the laborers on the plantations are defended against the unequal legislation of the States. . . . The mandate is universal in its application to persons of every class and condition of persons."[38]

During the two-day oral argument, Campbell repeatedly declared that the Fourteenth Amendment was a shield against state government infringement. He stressed that the right of citizens, like the butchers whom he represented, to pursue their labors, in whatever lawful manner they chose and free from state interference, was a protected right under the privileges and immunities clause of the Fourteenth Amendment. In words that were completely at odds with what he had expressed as a member of the Supreme Court, he also contended that the Constitution established a unique relationship between the national government and its citizens that could not be breached by the states. "The Constitution," he argued, "by declaring that every member in the empire is its citizen, every person born with its jurisdiction derives his state and condition from its authority, and at the same time stating to those States that this citizen of ours must not be disturbed in his privileges or immunities, or in his life, liberty, or property, brings the government into immediate contact with every person, and gives to every citizen a claim upon its protecting power."

The significance of Campbell's argument was twofold: First, despite his consistent stance previously about limiting the power of the federal government, *Slaughterhouse* saw him invite the nation's highest court to intervene in a state regulatory matter and overturn the Louisiana law.[39] Second, the right he sought the Court to protect—the pursuit of a lawful vocation of one's choice—is nowhere to be found in the Fourteenth Amendment. But Campbell insisted that fundamental rights, whether enumerated in the Constitution or not, were under the guardianship of the national government and particularly the Supreme Court.

By a narrow 5–4 decision, the Supreme Court rejected Campbell's arguments in the *Slaughterhouse Cases*. The majority held that while there may be constitutional provisions limiting the national government's ability to infringe on the right to engage in the occupation of one's choice, such protections simply did not extend to state action, outside of the specific prohibitions outlined to protect newly freed slaves. So thoroughly did Justice

Samuel Miller repudiate Campbell's contention that the Fourteenth Amendment's privileges and immunities clause protected the butchers' right to work that that clause, as a source of protection for fundamental rights, has never recovered. The four dissenting justices questioned the majority's refusal to recognize that there were others whom state governments had deprived of life, liberty, and property besides the newly freed slaves.

Although Campbell lost the case, he lived long enough to see the Court embrace his view. Within a decade of its *Slaughterhouse* decision, the Court began to acknowledge that the Fourteenth Amendment did indeed protect all Americans. It was still unable or unwilling to find any protections in the privileges and immunities clause for individuals against state action, but it adopted Campbell's expansive interpretative approach using the Fourteenth's due process clause instead. For a forty-year period ending in 1937, the Court recognized economic liberty (or the liberty of contract, as it was known), as a right embedded in the Fourteenth Amendment's due process clause. Such recognition largely shielded businesses and employers during this time from government regulations.[40] During this time, the Court came under heavy criticism from those who believed the justices were interjecting their own laissez-faire economic views into their decisions.

President Franklin D. Roosevelt was so incensed at the notion of an unenumerated liberty of contract (which a narrow majority of the justices used to repeatedly strike down his early New Deal programs) that he proposed that the Supreme Court be expanded to fifteen seats so that he could appoint justices who would rule otherwise. That drastic action became unnecessary when, in March 1937, Justice Owen Roberts—who had previously voted against government regulation of businesses and the economy—began to vote in favor of such laws. Roberts's actions, combined with Roosevelt's appointment later that year of a trusted ally to the Supreme Court, Alabama senator Hugo Black, led to a repudiation of both Supreme Court precedent and John Archibald Campbell. It appeared that the Court had reverted back to its position in *Slaughterhouse*, laying to rest the notion of unenumerated rights.

For thirty years the justices resisted the temptation to read rights into the Fourteenth Amendment. In 1965, however, the Court announced a constitutional right to privacy in *Griswold v. Connecticut*.[41] Writing for the majority, Justice William Douglas found this right in the penumbras or shadows of the First, Third, Fourth, Fifth, and Ninth Amendments and made it applicable against the states by way of the Fourteenth Amendment's due process clause. When the Court later based its controversial and landmark abortion decision *Roe v. Wade* (1973) on this same inferred right of privacy, it ensured that Campbell's constitutional contributions would never be forgotten.

In recent decades, the Court has been reluctant to further expand "substantive due process" or the recognition of substantive, albeit unenumerated, rights within the due process clause of the Fourteenth Amendment. Chief Justice William Rehnquist explained why the Court rightly exercises caution with regard to rights that are not expressly designated in the Constitution: "By extending constitutional protection to an asserted right or liberty interest," he wrote in *Washington v. Glucksburg* (1997), "we, to a great extent, place the matter outside the arena of public debate and legislative action."[42] He continued, "We must therefore exercise the utmost care whenever we are asked to break new ground in this field, lest the liberty protected by the Due Process Clause be subtly transformed into the policy preferences of the Members of this Court."[43]

Campbell's *Slaughterhouse* arguments foresaw that the Fourteenth Amendment and the Court would loom ever larger in the lives of Americans in protecting them against government infringement on their rights. "Every act of [a state] legislature that affects any individual member of its population," he declared, "by abridging [his] privileges and immunities . . . , which affects his life, liberty, or property arbitrarily, or which denies him an equal protection of his laws, all these become subject to the . . . revisory power of this Court."[44] More than six decades would pass after Campbell's *Slaughterhouse* arguments before the Court began to assume the guardian power he had envisioned that it possessed to strike down state laws infringing on other basic rights. The justices would do so only cautiously at first, but later with confidence after the persistent urging of Hugo Black.

In the 1870s, John Archibald Campbell moved from New Orleans to Baltimore to be closer to his daughters and grandchildren who lived there. He also continued to argue several cases a year before the Court until 1886. As the oldest living former justice when the Supreme Court celebrated its centennial in January 1889, Campbell disappointed his many friends and admirers when his poor health prevented his attendance at the gala event in Washington. He sent his regrets with this short note appended: "Tell the Court that I join daily in the prayer, 'God Save the United States and its Honorable Court.'"[45] He died two months later at the age of seventy-seven and is buried in Baltimore's Green Mount Cemetery.

HUGO L. BLACK: THE COURT AS AN OPPORTUNITY

That Campbell's losing argument in one specific case would have such a lasting impact on the Court and the nation was, perhaps, not altogether surprising given his intellect, legal talents, experience, and reputation both

Figure 11. Hugo L. Black. Courtesy of the Collection of the Supreme Court of the United States.

before and after his service on the Court. What was unexpected, however, was the appointment of a fellow Alabamian who lacked the training, understanding, and status of Campbell, but who would rely on his arguments in *Slaughterhouse* to expand the protections of the Bill of Rights to exert an even greater influence on all Americans.[46]

When legal historians and scholars rank the justices of the Supreme Court in order of greatness, they invariably place Hugo Black near the top of the list.[47] The highest ranked group typically includes such names as Chief Justices John Marshall, Charles Evan Hughes, and Earl Warren, and Associate Justices Joseph Story and Benjamin Cardozo. They were indeed great justices, but they were also eminent politicians and jurists before joining the Court, and their appointments came as no surprise. It is very difficult to imagine any other circumstances, other than those that actually occurred, in which a man from rural Alabama with little judicial experience could be appointed as an associate justice and have the type of lasting influence that Black did. His tenure coincided with tremendous personnel changes on the Court, and while other justices joined him in the effort, it was Hugo Black who saw and seized the opportunity to produce a judicial revolution.

Hugo LaFayette Black was born in Clay County, Alabama, on February 27, 1886, the youngest of eight children. He was interested in legal matters from a young age, spending a considerable amount of time observing the courthouse proceedings in Ashland, the Clay County seat, where his family moved when he was four years old. The fact that one of his brothers, Pelham, was a practicing attorney also spurred his love for the law.[48] However, with Pelham's accidental death in 1902 at the age of twenty-two, Black was persuaded by his mother and another brother, Orlando, who was an outstanding young physician, to go to medical school.

At the age of seventeen Black enrolled in the Birmingham Medical College and completed two years' worth of credit in a single year. He was a voracious reader and had always been a good student, but his accelerated progress in medical school was not due to his intellect alone. As Black's son later recalled, he tried to hurry through medical school because "he did not like dismembering corpses and he could not stand the sight of blood."[49]

Abandoning medicine, Black tried to enroll in the University of Alabama's liberal arts college, trusting that his two years of medical school credit would count for something toward a four-year degree. He sought entrance as a sophomore but university officials refused to admit him until he took an exam to determine his placement status. Black refused to take the placement test and turned to the University of Alabama's law school instead, since it admitted students without examination. In 1906, twenty-year-old Hugo Black and forty of his classmates graduated with their Bachelor of Law degrees, and Black returned to Ashland to open his practice.

He had very little business in his hometown, however, and the following year the grocery store beneath his law office caught on fire and the entire building burned to the ground. When Black was unable to salvage anything from the debris, he sought a fresh start elsewhere. He reestablished his law practice in Birmingham and there became a leading personal injury attorney. He also began to cultivate friends and relationships by joining the First Baptist Church and fraternal organizations including the Masons, Odd Fellows, Knights of Pythias, and others. Black served for eighteen months as an appointed police court judge in Birmingham (his only judicial experience before joining the Supreme Court) and later as Jefferson County's elected prosecuting attorney. He held the prosecuting attorney position until 1917, when he joined the United States Army for the duration of World War I. Black later ran for and won an open seat in the United States Senate in 1926, and after Franklin Roosevelt's election in 1932 became a fiery defender of the president's policies.

It was his loyalty to Roosevelt more than any other factor that led to

Black's appointment to the Supreme Court. As mentioned earlier, a majority of the justices had consistently voted to strike down Roosevelt's New Deal programs during his first term. Reelected in 1936, with no change of personnel on the Court, Roosevelt announced a proposal to enlarge the Court from nine seats to fifteen. It was a blatant attempt at Court-packing, which met with little enthusiasm even among some of the president's strongest supporters. Nevertheless, Black vigorously defended the plan in the Senate and in public. Roosevelt's need to pack the Court became less critical, however, when Justice Roberts voted in favor of Oregon's minimum wage law in March 1937, and then became completely unnecessary two months later when Justice Willis Van Devanter announced his retirement from the Court after twenty-six years of service.[50]

Roosevelt planned to fill Van Devanter's seat with Joseph Robinson, the Senate Majority Leader from Arkansas, who had used his office, personality, and legislative skills to champion every aspect of the New Deal. Robinson's fatal heart attack in the summer of 1937, however, forced Roosevelt to consider several other potential nominees before settling on Hugo Black. He knew that Black's lack of substantive judicial experience would draw criticism, but he also believed it was worth having such a staunch defender of his policies as his first appointment to the Supreme Court. In addition, he realized that even if questions about Black's qualifications arose, it was very unlikely that the senators would fail to confirm one of their own. Roosevelt nominated Black on August 12, 1937, and the Senate confirmed him as an associate justice a week later, along a mostly party-line vote of 63–16.

Immediately after Black's nomination became public though, rumors began to circulate that he was, or at least had been, a member of the Ku Klux Klan in Birmingham. The claims did not derail his confirmation, but in September 1937, the *Pittsburgh Post-Gazette* published a series of articles about Black's relationship with the KKK, which led to a flurry of negative press and calls for Black to step down from the Court.

He addressed his past with the KKK in a short nationwide radio address on October 1, 1937, just three days before the start of the Court's 1937–38 term. He admitted that he had once belonged to the group but had resigned his membership before running for the Senate in 1926.[51] He further disavowed the racial and religious intolerance associated with the KKK and reminded listeners of his civil rights record in the Senate. His statement satisfied some of his critics, but many thought it left much to be desired and continued to demand his resignation. The *Newark Ledger* bitingly observed, "[Black] resigned from the Klan to maintain an appearance of decency. He should resign from the Supreme Court to attain the substance of decency."[52] Even in Alabama, he was criticized for having created the entire mess by failing to reveal his relationship with the KKK in private discussions with President Roosevelt and during his confirmation hearings.[53]

His statement did nothing to appease those who already opposed Roosevelt and who thought Black was unqualified, on multiple levels, for the Court. The *Montgomery Advertiser* warned those critics that their focus on his lack of judicial experience and past Klan membership just might have blinded them to his real potential. "What a joke it would be on Hugo's impassioned detractors," the paper mused, "if he should now turn out to be a very great justice of the Supreme Court!"[54]

Black served on the Supreme Court for thirty-four years and did indeed become "a very great justice." Yet his greatness is not rooted in the manner in which he defended Roosevelt's programs and policies on the Court. Any of the president's seven other appointees would have worked just as hard as Black to propel the New Deal through the impasse at the Supreme Court. Nor is Black's impact due to his generally consistent stance on civil rights. He never became the caricature anticipated by his detractors in 1937 who were horrified by the thought of a former Klansman on the Court, but he was also far from the only justice who sought racial equality. No member of the Supreme Court, however, received more abuse for the Court's desegregation and civil rights rulings than Black did.

His support of *Brown v. Board of Education,* which declared that segregated public schools violated the Fourteenth Amendment's equal protection clause, brought scathing denunciations throughout the South and especially in Alabama.[55] Newspaper editorials bitterly rebuked him for betraying the South and tearing down its customs. Vile statements about Black and his family caused his children to move out of state, and he purposely stayed away from Alabama for several years. In 1956, he was banned from attending his fifty-year reunion at the University of Alabama Law School, and three years later the Alabama Senate passed a resolution stating that, on his death, Black was not to be buried within the state.

Black lived more than a decade after that resolution and, by that time, was widely recognized, including in Alabama, for his lasting constitutional influence as a member of the Supreme Court. Those contributions included his attempts to interpret the Constitution as literally as possible, leading to an absolutist approach to the First Amendment that vastly expanded the protection of the speech and press clauses. Quoting the opening lines of that amendment, he often said, "'Congress shall make no law' means Congress shall make no law."[56] He was thus skeptical of government efforts to regulate sexually explicit material, subversive speech, slander and libel, and, during the McCarthy era congressional hearings, to demand people reveal their past association with Communist organizations.[57] "My view is," he would later write, "without deviation, without exception, without any ifs, buts, or whereases, that freedom of speech means that government shall not do anything to [the] people . . . [because of] the views they have or the views they express or the words they speak or write."[58]

As important as Black's contributions were to the Court's First Amendment jurisprudence, his greatest legacy and the one that touches all Americans was his constant and consistent position on incorporation or the nationalization of the Bill of Rights. Incorporation refers to the process of applying the guarantees of the Bill of Rights against state and local government action. As mentioned in earlier chapters, the purpose for ratifying the Bill of Rights in 1791 was to protect citizens against the considerable power of the new national government that emerged from the 1787 Constitutional Convention. State and local government infringement on fundamental rights was constrained only insofar as their own state bills of rights limited their powers. Between 1789 and 1937, the Supreme Court largely remained true to Chief Justice John Marshall's 1833 pronouncement that the Bill of Rights contains "no expression indicating an intention to apply them to the state governments. This court cannot so apply them."[59]

The ratification of the Fourteenth Amendment in 1868, however, raised new questions about constitutional limits on state and local government action, as John Archibald Campbell later argued in the *Slaughterhouse Cases.* If the proscription in that amendment held that "no state shall make or enforce any law which shall abridge the privileges or immunities of citizens of the United States," could states still infringe on one's free exercise of religion and freedom of speech and press? Were state and local government actors limited in how they conducted searches or seizures, compelled suspects to testify against themselves, or imposed cruel and unusual punishment? For the next several decades, and despite repeated attempts by some of their colleagues to convince them to rule otherwise, a majority of justices on the Court refused to subject state action to the guarantees of the Bill of Rights.

Finally in 1937, and just a few months before Black joined the Court, the justices formally announced in *Palko v. Connecticut* that "the due process clause of the Fourteenth Amendment may make it unlawful for a state [or local government]" to infringe on certain rights.[60] Writing for an 8–1 majority, Justice Benjamin Cardozo stated that such rights, protected by the Bill of Rights against national government infringement and now against the states by way of the Fourteenth Amendment's due process clause, included those "implicit in the concept of ordered liberty."[61] He then identified those rights without which no free society could exist: the entire First Amendment; the Fifth Amendment's principle of eminent domain; and, because of *Powell v. Alabama* and the Scottsboro Boys, the Sixth Amendment's right to counsel. Cardozo's approach became known as "selective incorporation" because it isolated certain protections in the Bill of Rights and made those alone applicable to state and local governments.

As rendered by Cardozo, the *Palko* decision gained instant legitimacy. Cardozo, a longtime New York state judge, was nationally known for his influential lectures and legal writings and had been widely expected to join the Court at some point. In fact, the only surprise about his elevation to the Supreme Court in 1932 was that it occurred across party lines: President Herbert Hoover, a Republican, appointed Cardozo, who was a Democrat. But even this was viewed as only further testament to Cardozo's well-respected ability and reputation. When he died suddenly in 1938, no one could have predicted that Hugo Black, the controversial junior member of the Court at the time, would far surpass Cardozo as a champion for incorporation.

For the remainder of his life, Black pressed for a "total incorporation" approach to the Bill of Rights. He could not conceive how an action deemed unconstitutional if undertaken by the national government was somehow permissible when performed by state and local governments instead. He set forth his views in detail in the 1947 case of *Adamson v. California*.[62] While the majority opinion in *Adamson* was not particularly significant, the case provided a forum for Black, in dissent, to lay the groundwork for the tremendous constitutional changes that he would later oversee.

Hugo Black played an important role in the constitutional revolution of criminal procedure by the Warren Court (1953–69), extended the boundaries of the free speech clause further than they had ever been, and, with the other justices of his era, gave life to the Fourteenth Amendment's equal protection clause to protect racial minorities. His tenure on the Court coincided with some of the most momentous cases in American legal history, and yet Black had surprisingly little difficulty in choosing the case he thought was the most significant during his long career. When asked that question in a 1967 radio interview, Black replied without hesitation: "*Adamson v. California*. That's the case where I asserted at full length for the first time my belief that the passage of the Fourteenth Amendment made the Bill of Rights applicable to the states."[63]

The case concerned a man named Admiral Dewey Adamson who challenged his first-degree burglary and murder convictions because of an odd circumstance at his trial that he believed violated his Fifth Amendment right against self-incrimination. Adamson had amassed a lengthy criminal record long before he broke into the apartment of an elderly Los Angeles woman and killed her. At his trial, he refused to testify in his own defense believing that if he did, prosecutors would ask questions about his criminal record and then use his prior convictions for larceny, burglary, and robbery to impeach his testimony.

At the time, California law permitted prosecutors to infer guilt by commenting on the unwillingness of defendants to take the stand. During Adamson's trial, the state's attorney referred to his refusal to testify several times, concluding with this declaration to the jury: "I am going to just make this one statement to you: Counsel asked you to find this defendant not guilty. But does the defendant get on the stand and say, under oath, 'I am not guilty?' Not one word from him, and not one word from a single witness. I leave the case in your hands."[64] The jury convicted Adamson on both counts and sentenced him to death.

On appeal, Adamson argued that the Fifth Amendment protected both his words and silence from being used by prosecutors as "a witness against himself." Writing for the majority in *Adamson v. California*, Justice Stanley Reed acknowledged that the Fifth Amendment would have shielded Adamson had his trial taken place in the federal courts. His was a state offense, however, and the Court's precedents, including the *Palko* decision of a decade earlier, had made it clear that the Fourteenth Amendment's due process clause protected only certain rights against state action. Reed stressed that "*Palko* held that such provisions of the Bill of Rights as were 'implicit in the concept of ordered liberty' became secure from state interference by the clause. But it held nothing more."[65] In other words, there were indeed some rights special or sacred enough to limit government at every level, but the right against self-incrimination was not one of them. Adamson was executed in California's gas chamber two years later.

Black responded to the majority opinion in *Adamson* with a blistering dissent in which he chastised his Supreme Court brethren, past and present, for presuming that they were "endowed by the Constitution with boundless power . . . periodically to expand and contract constitutional safeguards."[66] He acknowledged that the Bill of Rights had been ratified to guard against the national government and that the Court had properly refused to extend those guarantees against the states during its early history. Nevertheless, Black believed the Fourteenth Amendment had changed everything.

He appended thirty-two pages to his dissent in which he marshalled a raft of historical evidence, including excerpts from the 1866 congressional floor debates on the Fourteenth Amendment as well as selected opinions from previous Supreme Court justices who were familiar with the amendment's original purpose. Black cited the Court's failure in *Slaughterhouse* to consider any of the congressional proceedings relative to the Fourteenth Amendment that, he believed, would have altered the outcome of that case. From his review of the Fourteenth Amendment's history, Black concluded that "the expressions of those who sponsored and favored, as well as those who opposed, its submission and passage persuades me that one of [its] chief objects . . . was to make the Bill of Rights, applicable to the states."[67]

Black also addressed the Court's decision in *Palko*, whose canon of rights the *Adamson* majority apparently considered closed. While *Palko* was the creation of the great Justice Cardozo, Black was not above gently scorning the consequences of that decision. He wrote, "Nothing in the *Palko* opinion requires that when the Court decides that a Bill of Rights' provision is to be applied to the States, it is to be applied piecemeal. Nothing in the *Palko* opinion recommends that the Court apply part of an amendment's established meaning and discard that part which does not suit the current style of fundamentals."[68] He concluded that while the selective incorporation approach of *Palko* was better than nothing at all, he hoped the Court would one day "extend to all the people of the nation the complete protection of the Bill of Rights."[69]

As noted, Black considered *Adamson* his most significant opinion. That was not because he was on the winning side (he wrote in dissent) or that his historical analysis of the Fourteenth Amendment was undisputed (historians and legal scholars have assembled alternative narratives to the one Black presented). It was his most important because it set the stage for the greatest extension of rights and liberties to the American people since the ratification of the Bill of Rights itself in 1791.

Black was never able to convince a majority of his colleagues to adopt his total incorporation argument. Yet, the following year, the Court incorporated the Sixth Amendment's right to a public trial, making it applicable against the states.[70] It did the same thing in 1949 with the Fourth Amendment's protection against unreasonable searches and seizures.[71] Over the next twenty years, in case after case, the Court incorporated nearly all of the provisions of the Bill of Rights, one clause at a time. Although there are still those who believe the Fourteenth Amendment was never intended to be used for such a purpose, Hugo Black's legacy of incorporation lives on. Its most recent expression came in February 2019, over seven decades after Black authored his dissent in *Adamson*, when the Roberts Court made the Eighth Amendment's ban on excessive fines applicable against the states.[72]

Of the standard that guided Black's persistent efforts to expand incorporation, the *New York Times* later wrote, "The Bill of Rights was his holy writ, a set of 'absolutes' erected by the framers to shield and nurture individual freedom."[73] Black agreed, stating "Our Constitution, with its absolute guarantee of individual rights, is the best hope for the aspirations of freedom which men share everywhere."[74]

In 1968, the Columbia University School of Law invited Black to address its students as part of its prestigious Carpentier Lecture series. Black later revised the three lectures he presented and had them published in a small volume titled *Constitutional Faith*. Its final passage not only concludes that book but also offers a pithy summation of Hugo Black's Supreme Court career and jurisprudence. "My experiences with and for our government have filled my heart with gratitude and devotion to the Constitution which made my public life possible. . . . [I]ts plan of our government is my plan and its destiny my destiny. I cherish every word of it, from the first to the last."[75]

Black was extremely ill when, after thirty-four years on the Supreme Court, he announced his retirement on September 17, 1971, which, fittingly, was the 184th anniversary of the signing of the Constitution. He died a week later. Hundreds of people attended funeral services at the National Cathedral before his body was interred at Arlington National Cemetery, but close friends were invited to pay their respects at a funeral home in Washington. There, as constitutional scholar Henry Abraham recalled, "[o]n a desk bearing a book for visitors' signatures was a pile of small paperbound copies of the document Black so often referred to as 'my legal bible'—a copy of which he always carried in his suit pocket."[76] Visitors to the funeral home left with their own copy of the Constitution, which served as dual reminder of Hugo Black and the incalculable importance of his efforts to extend the protections of the Bill of Rights to them.

At the times of their deaths, McKinley, Campbell, and Black had long since moved elsewhere and, consequently, none of them are buried in Alabama. The passage of years since their Supreme Court service has further dimmed the memory of each of their lives and contributions. Fortunately, however, due to the efforts of their fellow Alabamians, they have not been forgotten.

After more than a century of neglect, recent decades have seen an increase in attention to John McKinley as Alabama and especially the city of Florence has come to appreciate and honor its first Supreme Court justice. In 1974, the Alabama Historical Commission erected a marker in McKinley's honor near where his three-story brick mansion once stood in Florence. Fifteen years later, President Bill Clinton signed a bill changing the name of the U.S. Post Office and Courthouse in Florence to the Justice John McKinley Federal Building. The city later created a memorial to McKinley and fifteen other notable people from the area within its River Heritage Park. The Alabama State Bar inducted McKinley into the 2011 class of its Alabama Lawyers Hall of Fame, and a commemorative plaque about the honor is on display at the Alabama Judicial Building in Montgomery.

In Mobile, the former federal courthouse was renamed the John Archibald Campbell United States Courthouse in 1981. It served as the home of the US District Court for the Southern District of Alabama until 2018 when a new $90 million federal courthouse was constructed. After extensive renovations, the ninety-year-old Campbell Courthouse will house the US Bankruptcy Court and other federal offices. Outstanding students at the University of Alabama School of Law are reminded of the justice when they participate in the John A. Campbell Moot Court competition that is named in his honor. He was inducted into the Alabama Lawyers Hall of Fame in 2007.

Justice Black's name has been attached to countless symposia and lectures, but the more enduring memorials to his life include the postage stamp issued by the US Postal Service in 1986 on the one hundredth anniversary of his birth. A memorial park in his hometown of Ashland is named for him as is the Hugo L. Black United States Courthouse in Birmingham. The University of Alabama School of Law has a particularly interesting remembrance: The Bounds Law Library houses the Hugo Black Study, which is a replica of Black's office. Complete with Black's writing desk and other furniture, as well as such items as his tennis rackets, golf clubs, and antique globes, it is near perfect reproduction of the justice's own study in his Alexandria, Virginia, home. Its focal point is the more than one thousand volumes from Black's personal library that reflect the enormous breadth of interests of this extraordinary Alabamian. He was inducted into the Alabama Lawyers Hall of Fame in 2005.

NOTES

Chapter 1

1. The words the schoolchildren recited are from Matthew 6:9–13 (King James Version): "Our Father, which art in heaven, Hallowed by thy name. Thy kingdom come. Thy will be done in earth, as it is in heaven. Give us this day our daily bread. And forgive us our debts, as we forgive our debtors. And lead us not into temptation, but deliver us from evil: For thine is the kingdom, and the power, and the glory forever. Amen." Luke 11:2–4 offers a slightly different version of the prayer.

2. Rod Griffith, "A Self-Proclaimed Agnostic Who Was Once a Street Preacher" UPI, November 16, 1982, accessed May 22, 2017, https://www.upi.com/Archives/1982/11/16/A-self-proclaimed-agnostic-who-was-once-a-street-preacher/7398406270800/.

3. Quoted in Peter Irons, *The Courage of Their Convictions* (New York: Free Press, 1988), 363.

4. Alabama Code, §16-1-20 (1978).

5. Alabama Code, §16-1-20.1 (1981).

6. Quoted in Burt Rieff, "Conflicting Rights and Religious Liberty: The School-Prayer Controversy in Alabama, 1962–1985," *Alabama Review* 54 (July 2001): 187.

7. Quoted in *Journal of the Senate of the State of Alabama, Regular Session of 1982*, vol. 1 (Montgomery, AL: Brown Printing, 1981), 921.

8. Quoted in *Journal of the Senate of the State of Alabama, Second Extraordinary Session of 1982* (Montgomery, AL: Brown Printing, 1982), 3.

9. Alabama Code, §16-1-20.2 (1982).

10. Alabama Code, §16-1-20.2 (1982). Interestingly, out of concerns about its close affiliation with Christianity, the legislature rejected an amendment that would have allowed the recitation of the Lord's Prayer instead. That caused one Alabama political observer to quip that legislators had thereby "rejected a prayer written by the Son of God in favor of one drafted by the Son of Fob." See Mike Sherman, "Surely...thou are a politician, and thy speech agreeth thereto," *Montgomery (AL) Advertiser*, July 4, 1982, 13.

11. Sam Duvall, "Governor Signs Prayer Bill into Law," *Montgomery (AL) Advertiser*, July 13, 1982, 1.

12. Jaffree v. James, 544 F.Supp. 727, 729 (1982).

13. Anne Shutt, "Prayer Issue Heats up in Alabama," *Christian Science Monitor* (Boston, MA), August 4, 1982, 2.

14. Joanne Omang, "Alabama Governor Tries for an End Run on Son's School Prayer," *Washington Post*, September 16, 1982, accessed May 22, 2017, https://www.washingtonpost.com/archive/politics/1982/09/16/alabama-governor-tries-for-an-end-run-on-sons-school-prayer/5cb40e8a-71f5–4986–90c4–60cdc69de987/?utm_term=.b6bb666cc101.

15. Omang, "Alabama Governor Tries for an End Run on Son's School Prayer." Reporters at the news conference asked James how his declaration differed from that of Governor George Wallace's public stand against Supreme-Court-ordered school integration. James testily replied that school prayer was a jurisdictional issue between the Supreme Court and the states, while due process governed integration and the rights of African Americans. "There is not one scintilla, one iota of similarity between myself—philosophically, politically and operationally—and my predecessor," he retorted. See Omang, "Alabama Governor Tries for an End Run on Son's School Prayer."

16. See Terrett v. Taylor, 13 U.S. 43 (1815), and Town of Pawlet v. Clark, 13 U.S. 292 (1815).

17. J. Gordon Hylton, "Virginia and the Ratification of the Bill of Rights, 1789–1791," *University of Richmond Law Review* 25 (1991): 439. Religion was the subject of the last of the twenty amendments Marshall's convention committee forwarded to Congress along with the ratification vote. The amendment stated, "That religion, or the duty which we owe to our Creator, and the manner of discharging it, can be directed only by reason and conviction, not by force or violence; and therefore all men have an equal, natural, and unalienable right to the free exercise of religion, according to the dictates of conscience, and that no particular religious sect or society ought to be favored or established, by law, in preference to others." See Philip B. Kurland and Ralph Lerner, eds., *The Founders' Constitution*, vol. 5 (Indianapolis: Liberty Fund, 2001), 89.

18. Barron v. Mayor and City Council of Baltimore, 32 U.S. 243 (1833).

19. The Twenty-Seventh Amendment was also submitted to the states in 1789 at the same time as the other proposals that became the Bill of Rights, but it was not ratified until 1992.

20. *Barron*, 250.

21. *Barron*, 250.

22. Even in one of the few early cases in which the Court dealt specifically with religion, the justices affirmed that the "Constitution makes no provision for protecting the citizens of the respective states in their religious liberties; this is left to the state constitutions and laws: nor is there any inhibition imposed by the Constitution of the United States in this respect on the states." See Permoli v. New Orleans, 44 U.S. 589, 609 (1845).

23. Near v. Minnesota, 283 U.S. 697, 707 (1931).

24. Everson v. Board of Education of the Township of Ewing, 330 U.S. 1 (1947).

25. *Everson*, 15–16.

26. *Everson*, 16. Roger Williams first used the phrase in 1644 when he referenced a "wall of separation, between the garden of the Church and the wilderness of the world." Thomas Jefferson later referred to it in his famous letter to the Danbury Baptist Association in 1802. The Court itself first used the metaphor in the Free Exercise case of Reynolds v. United States, 98 U.S. 145, 164 (1879).

27. Engel v. Vitale, 370 U.S. 421 (1962). The regents' prayer read as follows: "Almighty God, we acknowledge our dependence upon Thee, and we beg Thy blessings upon us, our parents, our teachers and our country."

28. *Engel*, 435.

29. Although they arose out of separate disputes, the Court considered the Pennsylvania and Maryland laws together and rendered a single opinion. See School District of Abington Township v. Schempp and Murray v. Curlett, 374 U.S. 203 (1963).

30. These rulings were immediately denounced across the country and have been criticized ever since. Indeed, some evangelical Christian groups hold judicial decisions taking "God out of schools" responsible for everything from increases in teenage pregnancies and violent crime to decreases in SAT scores. See David Barton, *Original Intent: The Courts, the Constitution, and Religion* (Aledo, TX: Wallbuilder Press, 1996), 241–45.

31. Lemon v. Kurtzman, 403 U.S. 602, 613 (1971).

32. The opinion in *Kurtzman* also applied to two companion cases: *Earley v. DiCenso* and *Robinson v. DiCenso.*

33. See, for example, the endorsement test in Justice O'Connor's concurring opinion in Lynch v. Donnelly, 465 U.S. 668 (1984) and Justice Kennedy's coercion test in Lee v. Weisman, 505 U.S. 577 (1992).

34. Jaffree v. James, 544 F.Supp. 727, 731 (1982).

35. Jaffree v. James, 732.

36. Jaffree v. Board of School Commissioners of Mobile County, 554 F.Supp. 1104, 1122 (1983).

37. Jaffree v. Board of School Commissioners of Mobile County, 1118.

38. Jaffree v. Board of School Commissioners of Mobile County, 1128.

39. Jaffree v. Board of School Commissioners of Mobile County, 1128.

40. Jaffree v. James, 554 F.Supp. 1130 (1983).

41. Jaffree v. Board of Commissioners of Mobile County, 459 U.S. 1314 (1983).

42. Jaffree v. Wallace, 705 F.2d 1526, 1532 (1983).

43. Jaffree v. Wallace, 1532.

44. Jaffree v. Wallace, 1533.

45. Jaffree v. Wallace, 1535–36.

46. Oral argument quotes taken from audio of Wallace v. Jaffree, accessed September 17, 2018, https://www.oyez.org/cases/1984/83–812.

47. Oral argument, Wallace v. Jaffree.

48. Oral argument, Wallace v. Jaffree.

49. Oral argument, Wallace v. Jaffree.

50. Lynch v. Donnelly, 465 U.S. 668 (1984).

51. *Lynch*, 688.

52. *Lynch*, 692.

53. Lee v. Weisman, 505 U.S. 577 (1992).

54. See Steven P. Brown, *Trumping Religion: The New Christian Right, the Free Speech Clause, and the Courts* (Tuscaloosa: University of Alabama Press, 2002).

55. The case became a candidate for Supreme Court trivia when a rare wording change was made to the Court's already published decision. Justice John Paul Stevens had used the now obsolete word "Mohammedism" in his original opinion for the majority. But after Arab-American groups responded that they found the term offensive, the Court replaced it with "Islam." See "Court Makes Word Switch after Arab Complaint," *Washington Post*, October 26, 1985, A8.

56. Memo from John Roberts to Fred Fielding (June 4, 1985) (available in Reagan Library Collection, Roberts Box 48). Conference notes taken by the justices in *Wallace v. Jaffree* reveal that the amended Alabama law permitting prayer never had the support of five members of the Court. See Del Dickson, ed., *The Supreme Court in Conference (1940–1985)* (New York: Oxford University Press, 2001), 427–29.

57. Wallace v. Jaffree, 472 U.S. 38, 59 (1985).

58. Jesse Merriam, "Courts Not Silent on Moments of Silence," Pew Research Center: Religion and Public Life, April 24, 2008, accessed on June 30, 2017, http://www.pewforum.org/2008/04/24/courts-not-silent-on-moments-of-silence/.

59. Robert M. Hutchins, "The Future of the Wall," in *The Wall between Church and State*, ed. Dallin H. Oaks (Chicago: University of Chicago Press, 1963), 19.

60. Brown v. Gilmore, 258 F.3d 265, 272 (2001).

61. *Brown*, 271.

62. *Brown*, 277.

Chapter 2

1. Alexis de Tocqueville, *Democracy in America*, trans. George Lawrence (New York: Harper and Row, 1988), 193.

2. Wayne Powell, "Air of Tension Spreads over University Campus," *Montgomery (AL) Advertiser*, February 5, 1956, 1.

3. "Negro Student Barred from Capstone Classes," *Montgomery (AL) Advertiser*, February 7, 1956, 10.

4. "Alabama's Race Problem," *Anniston (AL) Star*, February 7, 1956, 4.

5. "Alabama's Race Problem," *Anniston (AL) Star*, 4.

6. Brown v. Board of Education of Topeka, 347 U.S. 483 (1954).

7. US Constitution, Article III.

8. Fred D. Gray, *Bus Ride to Justice: Changing the System by the System; The Life and Works of Fred D. Gray, Preacher, Attorney, Politician*, 2nd ed. (Montgomery, AL: New South Books, 2013).

9. Gene Howard, *Patterson for Alabama: The Life and Career of John Patterson* (Tuscaloosa: University of Alabama Press, 2008), 76.

10. Walter B. Jones, "I Speak For the White Race," *Montgomery (AL) Advertiser*, March 4, 1957, 4.

11. Jones, "I Speak For the White Race."

12. "Attorney General Sets Action in Montgomery, *Anniston (AL) Star*, June 1, 1956, 1.

13. Tocqueville, *Democracy in America*, 509.

14. See Bureau of Democracy, Human Rights, and Labor, "Country Reports on Human Rights Practices," 2015, accessed March 15, 2018, https://www.state.gov/j/drl/rls/hrrpt/humanrightsreport/index.htm#wrapper.

15. Waugh v. Board of Trustees of the University of Mississippi, 237 U.S. 589, 597 (1915).

16. New York ex rel. Bryant v. Zimmerman, 278 U.S. 63, 75 (1928).

17. DeJonge v. Oregon, 299 U.S. 353 (1937).

18. *DeJonge*, 365.

19. *DeJonge*, 365.

20. Gerende v. Election Board, 341 U.S. 56, 57 (1951).

21. See Garner v. Los Angeles Board, 341 U.S. 716 (1951), and Adler v. Board of Education, 342 U.S. 485 (1952).

22. Watkins v. U.S., 354 U.S. 178, 199 (1957). The Court held that similarly invasive investigatory practices by state legislatures or their designees to ferret out "subversive persons" and the groups with which they were affiliated also violated the freedom of association. See Sweezy v. New Hampshire, 354 U.S. 234 (1957).

23. *Sweezy*, 197.

24. *Sweezy*, 197.

25. Ex parte NAACP, 265 Ala. 349, 353 (1956).

26. *Ex parte NAACP*, 352.

27. *Ex parte NAACP*, 354.

28. "Transcript of Oral Arguments, *NAACP v. Alabama*, No. 91. (1958)," in Phillip B. Kurland and Gerhard Casper, *Landmark Briefs and Arguments of the Supreme Court of the United States* (Arlington, VA: University Publications of America, 1975), 54: 507.

29. "Transcript of Oral Arguments, *NAACP v. Alabama*," 521.

30. "Transcript of Oral Arguments, *NAACP v. Alabama*," 521.

31. "Transcript of Oral Arguments, *NAACP v. Alabama*," 521.

32. "Transcript of Oral Arguments, *NAACP v. Alabama*," 521.

33. Ex parte NAACP, 268 Ala. 531, 532 (1959).

34. *Ex parte NAACP*, 532

35. NAACP v. Alabama, 360 U.S. 240, 243 (1959).

36. *NAACP v. Alabama*, 245.

37. *Ex parte NAACP*, 271 Ala. 33, 34 (1960).

38. Quoted in NAACP v. Gaillion, 290 F.2d 337, 340 (1961).

39. NAACP v. Flowers, 377 U.S. 288, 309 (1964).

40. *NAACP v. Flowers*, 310.

41. Quoted in Warren Trest, *Nobody but the People: The Life and Times of Alabama's Youngest Governor* (Montgomery, AL: New South Books, 2008), 205.

42. Roberts v. United States Jaycees, 468 U.S. 609 (1984).

43. See Harvard's student newspaper account: Angela N. Fu and Lucy Wang,

"Faculty Vote to Include Sanctions in Handbook," March 7, 2018, accessed April 5, 2018, http://www.thecrimson.com/article/2018/3/7/faculty-sanctions-handbook/.

44. "Civil Liberties," Gallup, accessed April 5, 2018, http://news.gallup.com/poll/5263/civil-liberties.aspx.

45. "Civil Liberties."

46. Barenblatt v. U.S., 360 U.S. 109 (1959)

47. *Barenblatt*, 134.

48. *Barenblatt*, 144.

49. *Barenblatt*, 144.

50. *Barenblatt*, 144.

51. David Fellman, *The Constitutional Right of Association* (Chicago: University of Chicago Press, 1963), 104.

52. Fellman, *Constitutional Right of Association*, 105.

Chapter 3

1. Brown v. Board of Education of Topeka, 347 U.S. 483 (1954).

2. Data from Proquest Historical Newspapers.

3. "Amendment XV," *New York Times*, March 19, 1960, 20.

4. Kermit L. Hall and Melvin I. Urofsky, *"New York Times v. Sullivan": Civil Rights, Libel Law, and the Free Press* (Lawrence: University Press of Kansas, 2011), 21.

5. In fact, three years previously he had represented other Montgomery officials in a $750,000 libel suit against a New York–based magazine that claimed the city was rife with prostitution, drugs, and gambling. The magazine eventually settled out of court for a much smaller amount and a public apology.

6. Quoted in Hall and Urofsky, *"New York Times v. Sullivan": Civil Rights, Libel Law, and the Free Press*, 27.

7. Some of the ad's inaccuracies, including the padlocking reference, apparently came from a statement made by one of the expelled students. Speaking at a rally attended by more than nine hundred Alabama State students on behalf of their dismissed colleagues, Bernard Lee urged his peers "not to register . . . let 'em put locks on the doors of the college." See Bob Ingram, "900 Negroes Shout Pledge of Protest," *Montgomery (AL) Advertiser*, March 5, 1960, 7.

8. "Brief for Respondent in Opposition, *New York Times v. Sullivan*," in Phillip B. Kurland and Gerhard Casper, *Landmark Briefs and Arguments of the Supreme Court of the United States* (Arlington, VA: University Publications of America, 1975), 58: 353.

9. Although also unnamed in the ad, the paper did publish a retraction for Governor John Patterson who also complained about how the described events in Alabama reflected on him.

10. Kermit L. Hall, "'Lies, Lies, Lies': The Origins of New York Times v. Sullivan," *Communication Law and Policy* 9 (Autumn 2004): 420.

11. Exodus 20:16; 22:28, and 23:1, respectively.

12. Peter F. Carter-Ruck, *Libel and Slander* (London: Faber and Faber, 1972), 36.

13. Carter-Ruck, *Libel and Slander*, 37.

14. Carter-Ruck, *Libel and Slander*, 37–38.

15. Quoted in Carter-Ruck, *Libel and Slander*, 42.

16. Hall and Urofsky, *"New York Times v. Sullivan": Civil Rights, Libel Law, and the Free Press*, 34.

17. Roger Williams provides an early example of how English libel law was applied in British America. Arriving in Boston in 1631, he quickly upset Massachusetts Bay authorities with his unorthodox views on religion, local politics, and Native Americans. Completely exasperated with him by October 1635, authorities charged Williams with undermining governmental authority with his "lies of defamation, both of the magistrates and churches here" and sentenced him to be deported to England. He fled the colony, purchased land from the Wampanoag Indians, and established the colony of Rhode Island and Providence Plantations.

18. Transcript of Alien and Sedition Acts, 1798, accessed August 30, 2019, https://www.ourdocuments.gov/doc.php?flash=false&doc=16.

19. United States v. Hudson and Goodwin, 11 U.S. 32 (1812).

20. White v. Nicholls, 44 U.S. 266 (1845).

21. *White*, 290.

22. *White*, 290.

23. Ex parte Vallandigham, 68 U.S. 243 (1864). In 1863, a military commission sentenced Representative Clement Vallandigham of Ohio to prison for the duration of the war because of his critical statements about Abraham Lincoln. Lincoln ordered him deported to the Confederate States instead. See generally Geoffrey R. Stone, "Abraham Lincoln's First Amendment," *New York University Law Review* 78 (April 2003).

24. Near v. Minnesota ex rel Olson, 283 U.S. 697 (1931).

25. Chaplinsky v. New Hampshire, 315 U.S. 568, 572 (1942).

26. Beauharnais v. Illinois, 343 U.S. 250, 266 (1952).

27. Roth v. United States, 354 U.S. 476, 483 (1957).

28. Bruce Weber, "M. Roland Nachman, Lawyer in Times v. Sullivan Libel Case, Dies at 91," *New York Times*, December 6, 2015, A20.

29. None of the twenty black ministers from the South consented to the use of their names, but as each was a member of the Southern Christian Leadership Conference, which Martin Luther King headed, *Times* personnel did not think it necessary to get their permission.

30. "Brief for Respondent in Opposition," in Kurland and Casper, *Landmark Briefs and Arguments of the Supreme Court*, 58: 354.

31. "Brief for Respondent in Opposition," in Kurland and Casper, *Landmark Briefs and Arguments of the Supreme Court*, 58: 354.

32. Arthur Osgoode, "$500,000 Damages Awarded Sullivan by Times Suit Jury," *Montgomery (AL) Advertiser*, November 4, 1960, A1.

33. New York Times v. Sullivan, 273 Ala. 656, 676 (1962).

34. *Sullivan*, 687.

35. *Sullivan*, 686.

36. *Sullivan*, 686.

37. *Sullivan*, 686.

38. "Petition for a Writ of Certiorari," in Kurland and Casper, *Landmark Briefs and Arguments of the Supreme Court*, 58: 321.

39. "Petitioner's Brief," in Kurland and Casper, *Landmark Briefs and Arguments of the Supreme Court*, 58: 58: 447.

40. "Petition for a Writ of Certiorari," in Kurland and Casper, *Landmark Briefs and Arguments of the Supreme Court*, 58: 321.

41. "Brief for Respondent in Opposition," in Kurland and Casper, *Landmark Briefs and Arguments of the Supreme Court*, 58: 352.

42. "Brief for Respondent in Opposition," in Kurland and Casper, *Landmark Briefs and Arguments of the Supreme Court*, 58: 352.

43. Justices Black, Douglas, and Goldberg filed concurring opinions in which they expressed their belief that the First Amendment protects all speech pertaining to the government and its officials, defamatory or not.

44. Although common law cases had previously used the "actual malice" phrase, the Court's opinion changed its definition. Common law actual malice referred to malicious intent or ill will on the part of a publisher toward another, which resulted in the defamatory publication. The *New York Times* version of actual malice completely ignores the intent and, despite the phrase, maliciousness of the publisher. It is only concerned with whether the publisher knew the material in question to be false or completely disregarded whether it was true or false and published it anyway. See W. Wat Hopkins, *Actual Malice: Twenty-Five Years after "Times v. Sullivan"* (New York: Praeger, 1989, 68.

45. Curtis Publishing Company v. Butts, 388 U.S. 130 (1967). This case, incidentally, had an Alabama connection of its own. It dealt with allegations by the *Saturday Evening Post* that Wallace Butts, the University of Georgia's head football coach, had conspired with Coach Paul "Bear" Bryant of the University of Alabama to throw a game in the Crimson Tide's favor. Butts's libel suit against the publication formed the basis for this case.

46. Gertz v. Welch, 418 U.S. 323 (1974).

47. Susan D. Ross and R. Kenton Bird, "The Ad That Changed Libel Law: Judicial Realism and Social Activism in *New York Times v. Sullivan*," *Communication Law and Policy* 9 (Autumn 2004): 521.

48. "The Uninhibited Press, 50 Years Later," editorial, *New York Times*, March 9, 2014, SR10.

49. Quoted in Judith S. Koffler and Bennett L. Gershman, "New Seditious Libel," *Cornell Law Review* 69 (April 1984): 870.

50. New York Times v. Sullivan, 376 U.S. 254, 270.

51. James Madison, *The Writings of James Madison*, ed. Gaillard Hunt, 9 vols. (New York: G. P. Putnam's Sons, 1910), 6: 336.

52. Madison, *Writings of James Madison*, 6: 336.

Chapter 4

1. Quoted in James Goodman, *Stories of Scottsboro* (New York: Vintage Books, 1995), 3.

2. Quoted in Goodman, *Stories of Scottsboro*, 3.

3. Quoted in Kwando M. Kinshasa, *The Man from Scottsboro: Clarence Norris and the Infamous 1931 Alabama Rape Trial, in His Own Words* (Jefferson, NC: McFarland, 1997), 34.

4. "Nine Negroes held; Girls on Train Attacked," *Weekly Town Talk* (Alexandria, LA), March 28, 1931, 8.

5. Quoted in Kinshasa, *Man from Scottsboro*, 34.

6. Dan T. Carter, *Scottsboro: A Tragedy of the American South* (New York: Oxford University Press, 1971), 7.

7. Quoted in Kinshasa, *Man from Scottsboro*, 37.

8. Quoted in Kinshasa, *Man from Scottsboro*, 37. Wann was murdered a year later while attempting to arrest a man. See "Sheriff Wann of Jackson Shot to Death on Tuesday," *Cullman (AL) Democrat*, May 5, 1932, 1. While known to everyone in Scottsboro, the shooter, Harry Hambrick, was never apprehended or brought to trial, fueling speculation that the murder was ordered by the Ku Klux Klan in retaliation for Wann's actions on the night of the Scottsboro Boys' arrest.

9. Quoted in Kinshasa, *Man from Scottsboro*, 38.

10. When the case was appealed to the US Supreme Court, lawyers for the Scottsboro Boys pointed out that Hawkins's "appointment" of the entire Scottsboro bar actually violated Alabama law. Section 5567 of the Alabama Code of 1928 reads: "If the defendant is indicted for a capital offense, and is unable to employ counsel, the court must appoint counsel for him, not exceeding two." Quoted in "Petition and Brief in Support of Application for Certiorari, *Powell, et al. v. Alabama*, Nos. 98, 99, and 100 (1931)," in Philip B. Kurland and Gerhard Casper, *Landmark Briefs and Arguments of the Supreme Court of the United States* (Arlington, VA: University Publications of America, 1975), 27: 275.

11. Quoted in Carter, *Scottsboro: A Tragedy of the American South*, 18.

12. "Petition and Brief in Support of Application for Certiorari," Kurland and Casper, *Landmark Briefs and Arguments of the Supreme Court of the United States*, 224.

13. "Troops Guard 9 Negroes Facing Trial for Rape," *Chicago (IL) Daily Tribune*, April 7, 1931, 16.

14. "Troops Guard 9 Negroes Facing Trial for Rape," *Chicago (IL) Daily Tribune*.

15. Powell v. Alabama, 287 U.S. 45, 53 (1932).

16. *Powell*, 53.

17. *Powell*, 54.

18. *Powell*, 55.

19. *Powell*, 55.

20. *Powell*, 55. Clarence Norris recalled, "The first lawyer we had in Scottsboro was some little white guy out of Tennessee. . . . We had never seen him until the day we were supposed to go on trial. He got us all in a side room in the courthouse and told us that some little group in Tennessee sent him down to Alabama to defend us. He added, 'It was possible to save some of your lives if you plead guilty to all the charges!' Now, what kind of . . . lawyer is that? We told him we wasn't going to plead guilty to anything which we didn't do." Quoted in Kinshasa, *Man from Scottsboro*, 40.

21. In a scathing April 1931 NAACP report about the trial, Roddy was described as "a drunkard recently released from an asylum where he was treated for mental disorders brought on by excessive drinking and 'fast living.'" Quoted in Kwando M. Kinshasa, ed., *The Scottsboro Boys in Their Own Words: Selected Letters, 1931–1950* (Jefferson, NC: McFarland, 2014), 25. A more restrained view was offered a month later by Walter White, the NAACP's general secretary, after interviewing Roddy: "[He] is a heavy drinker, and impressed me as not being diligent or well trained. . . . On the other hand Roddy was the only lawyer who had the courage to go down there and defend the boys." Kinshasa, *Scottsboro Boys in Their Own Words*, 28. Roddy died three years later at the age of forty-four.

22. Carter, *Scottsboro: A Tragedy of the American South*, 22.

23. However, Clarence Norris also recalled in his 1979 autobiography that when Roddy met with them he "had liquor on his breath and he was as scared as we were." Clarence Norris and Sybil D. Washington, *The Last of the Scottsboro Boys* (New York: Putnam, 1979), 22.

24. Biased newspaper accounts reimagined the doddering Milo Moody and Stephen Roddy, a real estate attorney from Tennessee, as established and well-respected defense lawyers. When the case went up for appeal, the editor of the *Jackson County Sentinel* was quoted in northern newspapers as follows: "The Negroes were given a fair trial in every respect. They were represented not only by the ablest criminal lawyers in this county, but the defense was led by Stephen Roddy of Chattanooga, one of the best known criminal lawyers in the South." Quoted in "Mr. Black Says Negroes There Had a Fair Trial," *Hartford (CT) Courant*, August 16, 1931, 12.

25. Just a few weeks later, Norris confessed that neither he nor any of the boys had done anything to the young women. He claimed that he had been beaten while held in the Scottsboro jail and told to accuse the others. "When I testified in my trial at Scottsboro," he said, "I was afraid for my life and did not there testify to the true facts." Quoted in Kinshasa, *Scottsboro Boys in Their Own Words*, 40.

26. Quoted in Carter, *Scottsboro: A Tragedy of the American South*, 35.

27. Quoted in Carter, *Scottsboro: A Tragedy of the American South*, 43.

28. "Petition and Brief in Support of Application for Certiorari," Kurland and Casper, *Landmark Briefs and Arguments of the Supreme Court of the United States*, 229.

29. "8 Negro Attackers Sentenced to Chair," *Atlanta Constitution*, April 10, 1931, 11.

30. "Deny Negroes' Trial Is Legal Lynching," *New York Times*, April 9, 1931, 31.

31. Quoted in Philip B. Kurland and Ralph Lerner, eds., *The Founders Constitution* (Chicago: University of Chicago Press, 1987; reprint, Indianapolis: Liberty Fund, 2000), 246 (page references are to reprint edition).

32. Kurland and Lerner, *Founders Constitution*, 259.

33. The NAACP also tried to intervene, arguing that the renowned attorney Clarence Darrow (whom it had retained for the case) would be their best advocate on appeal. However, when representatives of that organization contacted the boys in jail, they were told they were welcome to assist, but the ILD would continue to be lead counsel. See Arthur Garfield Hays, *Trial by Prejudice* (New York:

Covici-Friede, 1933; reprint, New York: Da Capo Press, 1970), 87 (page references are to reprint edition).

34. "Negro Pastors Assail Labor Defense Body," *New York Times,* May 24, 1931, N6.

35. Files Crenshaw Jr. and Kenneth A. Miller, *Scottsboro: The Firebrand of Communism* (Montgomery, AL: Brown Printing, 1936), 9–10. On the day the Supreme Court announced its decision in *Powell v. Alabama,* the Ku Klux Klan issued a statement to African Americans and Communists gathered to protest in Birmingham. Some two thousand flyers were dropped from tall buildings onto the protestors. Each flyer bore this message: "Negroes of Birmingham, the Ku Klux Klan is watching you. Tell the Communists to get out of town. They mean only trouble for you, for Alabama is a good place for good Negroes and a bad place for Negroes who believe in racial equality. Report Communist activities to the Ku Klux Klan, Box 661, Birmingham." Quoted in "New Trial Ordered by Supreme Court in Scottsboro Case," *New York Times,* November 8, 1932, 1.

36. Walter T. Howard, ed., *Black Communists Speak on Scottsboro: A Documentary History* (Philadelphia: Temple University Press, 2007), 9.

37. Hays, *Trial by Prejudice,* 90.

38. Powell v. State, 224 Ala 540 (1932), and Weems v. State, 224 Ala 524 (1932).

39. *Powell,* 554.

40. *Powell,* 555.

41. *Powell,* 555.

42. *Powell,* 555.

43. *Powell,* 555.

44. The name of this landmark case, *Powell v. Alabama,* was the result of the Court consolidating the three cases on appeal that were officially known separately as *Ozie Powell, Willie Roberson, Andy Wright, and Olen Montgomery v. Alabama; Haywood Patterson v. Same;* and *Charlie Weems and Clarence Norris v. Same.*

45. Douglas O. Linder, "The Trials of 'The Scottsboro Boys': An Account," Famous Trials, accessed August 31, 2017, http://famous-trials.com/scottsboroboys/1531-home.

46. Barron v. Mayor and City Council of Baltimore, 32 U.S. 243, 247 (1833).

47. Chicago, Burlington, & Quincy Railroad Company Co. v. Chicago, 166 U.S. 226, 241 (1897).

48. Twining v. New Jersey, 211 U.S. 78, 99 (1908).

49. Gitlow v. New York, 268 U.S. 652, 666 (1925).

50. See, for example, Fiske v. Kansas, 274 U.S. 380 (1927); Stromberg v. California, 283 U.S. 359 (1931); and Near v. Minnesota, 283 U.S. 697 (1931).

51. Palko v. Connecticut, 302 U.S. 319, 325 (1937).

52. *Palko,* 325.

53. *Palko,* 326, footnote 4.

54. Betts v. Brady, 316 U.S. 455 (1942). In light of the Court's surprising ruling in *Betts,* forty-five states passed laws to require appointed counsel for those too poor to retain an attorney on their own.

55. Gideon v. Wainright, 372 U.S. 335 (1963).

56. Argersinger v. Hamlin, 407 U.S. 25 (1972).

57. Eugene Williams and Roy Wright were determined to be juveniles, and their cases were sent to juvenile court.

58. Quoted in Hays, *Trial by Prejudice*, 128.

59. Quoted in Hays, *Trial by Prejudice*, 108.

60. Linder, http://famous-trials.com/scottsboroboys/1578-hortonsinstruct, accessed August 31, 2017.

61. The jury returned its verdict after twelve hours. However, it reached a guilty verdict "in just under five minutes. It had taken the rest of the time to reason with one of the jurors who had held out for life imprisonment." See Mark S. Weiner, *Black Trials: Citizenship from the Beginnings of Slavery to the End of Caste* (New York: Alfred A. Knopf, 2004), 267.

62. Quoted in Kinshasa, *Man from Scottsboro*, 196.

63. Quoted in Kinshasa, *Man from Scottsboro*, 208.

64. Norris v. Alabama, 294 U.S. 587, 588 (1935). See also Patterson v. Alabama, 294 U.S. 600 (1935).

65. "Four Negros Go Free; Five Face Penalty," *Escanaba (MI) Daily Press*, July, 25, 1937, 2.

66. "Scottsboro Boy Leaves Prisons," *Tampa Bay (Saint Petersburg, FL) Times*, November 19, 1943, 18.

67. "Scottsboro Boy in Trouble Once More," *Troy (NY) Record*, November 15, 1954, 7.

68. Clyde H. Reid, "'Scottsboro Boy' Tells Tragedy of Rediscovery 28 Year Later," *New York Age*, August 29, 1959, 2.

69. "'Scottsboro Boy' Flies South for Pardon," *Los Angeles Times*, November 30, 1976, 4.

Chapter 5

1. *Journal of the Proceedings of the Constitutional Convention of the State of Alabama* (Montgomery, AL: Brown Printing, 1901), 8.

2. *Journal of the Proceedings of the Constitutional Convention of the State of Alabama*, 9.

3. *Journal of the Proceedings of the Constitutional Convention of the State of Alabama*, 9.

4. *Journal of the Proceedings of the Constitutional Convention of the State of Alabama*, 12.

5. *Journal of the Proceedings of the Constitutional Convention of the State of Alabama*, 12.

6. Until December 20, 1902, the 1901 Constitution extended the vote to any veteran of any war, to any descendent of a veteran, or to "all persons who are of good character and who understand the duties and obligations of citizenship under a republican form of government." The property requirement that applied in January 1903 was subsequently dropped and replaced with the "good character" test. Five years later, the legislature added an additional requirement that potential voters

must complete a written questionnaire to the satisfaction of the registrar without any assistance.

7. United States v. Alabama, 252 F.Supp. 95, 99 (1966).

8. Schnell v. Davis, 336 U.S. 933 (1949).

9. William A. Ellwood, "An Interview with Charles G. Gomillion," *Callaloo* 40 (Summer 1989): 585. Thus registered, he was still unable to vote until he had paid the poll tax. By Alabama law, he was required to pay not only $1.50 for the year he was registered to vote but also for each of the previous eleven years that he had lived in the area.

10. Jessie Parkhurst Guzman, *Crusade for Civic Democracy: The Story of the Tuskegee Civic Association, 1941–1970* (New York: Vantage Press, 1984), 19.

11. Quoted in Bernard Taper, *"Gomillion v. Lightfoot": The Tuskegee Gerrymander Case* (New York: McGraw-Hill, 1962), 62. In his 1961 opinion ordering registrars to cease such discriminatory practices, US District Judge Frank Johnson also noted how many African Americans associated with the Tuskegee Institute and possessing high school and college educations were unable to qualify as voters "while many white persons who have not even finished grammar school have been registered." See U.S. v. Alabama, 192 F.Supp. 677, 679 (1961).

12. Taper, *"Gomillion v. Lightfoot,"* 55.

13. Taper, *"Gomillion v. Lightfoot,"* 35.

14. See "An Open Letter to the Citizens of Alabama," *Montgomery (AL) Advertiser*, June 16, 1957, 12.

15. "Macon Moves Seen if Court Blocks Law," *Anniston (AL) Star*, March 22, 1960, 10.

16. "Tuskegee Negro Woman Bares Threat for Not Joining Boycott," *Montgomery (AL) Advertiser*, June 30, 1957, 2.

17. The Macon County abolishment bill was a constitutional amendment that Alabama voters approved in December 1957. It was never acted on, however, and was later repealed by a subsequent constitutional amendment (Amendment 402) in 1982.

18. "An Open Letter to the Citizens of Alabama," *Montgomery (AL) Advertiser*, June 16, 1957, 12.

19. Stuart Culpepper III, "2500 Tuskegee Negroes Urged to Boycott Stores," *Montgomery (AL) Advertiser*, June 26, 1957, 1.

20. Culpepper, "2500 Tuskegee Negroes Urged to Boycott Stores," 2.

21. Culpepper, "2500 Tuskegee Negroes Urged to Boycott Stores," 1

22. Culpepper, "2500 Tuskegee Negroes Urged to Boycott Stores."

23. Stuart Culpepper III, "2000 Ecstatic Negroes Greet King at Tuskegee," *Montgomery (AL) Advertiser*, July 3, 1957, 1.

24. Culpepper III, "2000 Ecstatic Negroes Greet King at Tuskegee."

25. The boycott ran for almost four years, during which approximately 70 percent of the downtown businesses reportedly closed down.

26. Breedlove v. Suttles, 302 U.S. 277 (1937).

27. *Breedlove*, 283.

28. United States v. Alabama, 252 F.Supp. 95, 99 (1966).
29. *United States v. Alabama*, 100.
30. *United States v. Alabama*, 100.
31. Harper v. Virginia Board of Elections, 383 U.S. 663 (1966).
32. Lassiter v. Northampton County Board of Elections, 360 U.S. 45, 52–53 (1959).
33. See Louisiana v. U.S., 380 U.S. 145 (1965).
34. Marbury v. Madison, 5 U.S. 137, 170 (1803).
35. Colegrove v. Green, 328 U.S. 549, 553–54 (1946).
36. *Colegrove*, 556.
37. Gomillion v. Lightfoot, 167 F.Supp. 405, 407 (1958).
38. *Gomillion v. Lightfoot*, 410.
39. Gomillion v. Lightfoot, 270 F.2d 594, 612 (1959).
40. *Gomillion v. Lightfoot*, 612.
41. *Gomillion v. Lightfoot*, 612.
42. *Gomillion v. Lightfoot*, 612.
43. *Gomillion v. Lightfoot*, 608.
44. "Transcript of Oral Arguments, *Gomillion v. Lightfoot*, No. 32. (1960)," in Phillip B. Kurland and Gerhard Casper, *Landmark Briefs and Arguments of the Supreme Court of the United States* (Arlington, VA: University Publications of America, 1975), 55: 289.
45. Fred D. Gray, *Bus Ride to Justice: Changing the System by the System; The Life and Works of Fred D. Gray, Preacher, Attorney, Politician* (Montgomery, AL: New South Books, 2013), 118.
46. "Transcript of Oral Arguments," Kurland and Casper, *Landmark Briefs and Arguments of the Supreme Court of the United States*, 295.
47. "Transcript of Oral Arguments," Kurland and Casper, *Landmark Briefs and Arguments of the Supreme Court of the United States*, 307.
48. "Transcript of Oral Arguments," Kurland and Casper, *Landmark Briefs and Arguments of the Supreme Court of the United States*, 328.
49. "Transcript of Oral Arguments," Kurland and Casper, *Landmark Briefs and Arguments of the Supreme Court of the United States*, 332.
50. "Transcript of Oral Arguments," Kurland and Casper, *Landmark Briefs and Arguments of the Supreme Court of the United States*, 332.
51. "Transcript of Oral Arguments," Kurland and Casper, *Landmark Briefs and Arguments of the Supreme Court of the United States*, 332.
52. "Transcript of Oral Arguments," Kurland and Casper, *Landmark Briefs and Arguments of the Supreme Court of the United States*, 337.
53. "The Tuskegee Case Is a National Case," *Montgomery (AL) Advertiser*, September 30, 1960, 4.
54. U.S. v. Alabama, 192 F.Supp. 677, 679 (1961).
55. See Baker v. Carr, 369 U.S. 186 (1962); Wesberry v. Sanders, 376 U.S. 1 (1964); and Reynolds v. Sims, 377 U.S. 533 (1964).
56. Robert J. Norrell, *Reaping the Whirlwind: The Civil Rights Movement in Tuskegee* (New York: Alfred A. Knopf, 1985), 124.

57. Davis v. Bandemer, 478 U.S. 109 (1986).

58. Vieth v. Jubelirer, 541 U.S. 267 (2004).

59. Gill v. Whitford, 138 S.Ct. 1916 (2018), and Rucho v. Common Cause, 139 S.Ct. 2484 (2019).

60. Cong. Rec. 141:191, S17927, December 4, 1995, accessed August 30, 2019, Tribute to Charles Gomillion by Senator Howell Heflin, AL, https://www.congress.gov/congressional-record/1995/12/04/senate-section/article/S17927–3.

61. Cong. Rec. 141:191, S17927.

62. Quoted in Ellwood, "An Interview with Charles G. Gomillion," 598.

Chapter 6

1. The text of the Equal Rights Amendment read: "*Section 1*: Equality of rights under the law shall not be denied or abridged by the United States or by any state on account of sex; *Section 2*: The Congress shall have the power to enforce, by appropriate legislation, the provisions of this article; *Section 3*: This amendment shall take effect two years after the date of ratification." The proposed amendment passed Congress with the constitutionally required two-thirds majority on March 22, 1972. It was then sent to the states for ratification with a seven-year deadline. By 1979, thirty-five states had ratified the amendment, but that was still three short of the thirty-eight that were necessary (three-fourths of the states as required by the Constitution). In addition, by 1979, four of the thirty-five states that had previously ratified the amendment had also voted to rescind their ratification. Congress later extended the 1979 deadline to 1982, but no additional states ratified the amendment during that time.

2. Congress authorized the BAQ in the Career Compensation Act of 1949 as an incentive for service members to reenlist. See 37 U.S.C. Sec. 401.

3. See 10 U.S.C., Sec. 1072 and 1076.

4. Frontiero v. Laird, 341 F.Supp. 201, 203 (1972).

5. *Frontiero*, 203.

6. "Army Husbands," *Time*, May 28, 1973, p. 12, accessed August 30, 2019, http://content.time.com/time/magazine/article/0,9171,910607,00.html.

7. Levin founded the Southern Poverty Law Center with Morris Dees in 1971 and the Frontieros' case became one of the organization's early landmark achievements.

8. "Brief for the Appellants, *Frontiero v. Richardson*, No. 71-1694 (1972)," in Philip B. Kurland and Gerhard Casper, *Landmark Briefs and Arguments of the Supreme Court of the United States* (Arlington, VA: University Publications of America, 1975), 76: 649.

9. "Air Force Gal Sues for Equal Dependent Housing Allowance," *Bennington (VT) Banner*, January 8, 1971, 5.

10. Bradwell v. Illinois, 83 U.S. 130, 131 (1873).

11. *Bradwell*, 139.

12. *Bradwell*, 139. In 1890, of its own accord, the Illinois Supreme Court admitted Bradwell to the Illinois bar. Two years later, she was admitted to practice before the US Supreme Court.

13. Minor v. Happersett, 88 U.S. 162, 165 and 170 (1874).

14. US Constitution, Amendment Fifteen, Section 1.

15. *Happersett*, 178.

16. Butchers' Benevolent Association of New Orleans v. The Crescent City Livestock Landing and Slaughterhouse Company, 83 U.S. 36 (1873).

17. U.S. v. Carolene Products, 304 U.S. 144 (1938).

18. *Carolene Products*, 152.

19. *Carolene Products*, 152. Footnote 4 reads as follows (internal citations omitted):

> There may be narrower scope for operation of the presumption of constitutionality when legislation appears on its face to be within a specific prohibition of the Constitution, such as those of the first ten amendments, which are deemed equally specific when held to be embraced within the Fourteenth.
>
> It is unnecessary to consider now whether legislation which restricts those political processes which can ordinarily be expected to bring about repeal of undesirable legislation, is to be subjected to more exacting judicial scrutiny under the general prohibitions of the Fourteenth Amendment than are most other types of legislation. . . .
>
> Nor need we enquire whether similar considerations enter into the review of statutes directed at particular religious, or national, or racial minorities: whether prejudice against discrete and insular minorities may be a special condition, which tends seriously to curtail the operation of those political processes ordinarily to be relied upon to protect minorities, and which may call for a correspondingly more searching judicial inquiry.

20. US Constitution, Amendment Fourteen.

21. Justice John Paul Stevens captured the frustration associated with the Court's variable Equal Protection standards in his pithy observation from *Craig v. Boren*: "There is only one Equal Protection Clause. It requires every State to govern impartially. It does not direct the courts to apply one standard of review in some cases and a different standard in other cases" (429 U.S. 190, 211–12 [1973]).

22. Reed v. Reed, 404 U.S. 71 (1971).

23. *Reed*, 73.

24. *Reed*, 76.

25. Herma Hill Kay and Martha S. West, *Sex-Based Discrimination* (Saint Paul, MN: West Publishing, 2002), 28.

26. Federal law still requires three-judge district court panels to hear reapportionment and redistricting cases.

27. Frontiero v. Laird, 341 F.Supp. 201, 205 (1972).

28. *Frontiero*, 205.

29. *Frontiero*, 206.

30. *Frontiero*, 207.

31. *Frontiero*, 207.

32. *Frontiero*, 210.

33. Quoted in Serena Mayeri, "The Story of Frontiero v. Richardson," in *Women and the Law Stories*, ed. Elizabeth M. Schneider and Stephanie M. Wildman (New York: Foundation Press, 2011), 67.

34. Mayeri, "Story of Frontiero v. Richardson," 67.

35. "Transcript of Oral Arguments, *Frontiero v. Richardson*, No. 71-1694 (1972)," in Kurland and Casper, *Landmark Briefs and Arguments of the Supreme Court of the United States*, 76: 852–53.

36. "Transcript of Oral Arguments, *Frontiero v. Richardson*, No. 71-1694 (1972)," in Kurland and Casper, *Landmark Briefs and Arguments of the Supreme Court of the United States*, 76: 855.

37. Del Dickson, ed., *The Supreme Court in Conference (1940–1985)* (New York: Oxford University Press, 2001), 764–65.

38. See "Decision Was 'Music' in the Ears of Women," *San Bernardino (CA) County Sun*, May 15, 1973, 6.

39. *New York Times*, May 22, 1973, 36.

40. Craig v. Boren, 429 U.S. 190 (1976).

41. *Craig*, 197.

42. U.S. v. Virginia, 518 U.S. 515, 524 (1996). Ginsburg was appointed to the Court by President Bill Clinton in 1993.

43. Ruth Bader Ginsburg, "Remarks for the Celebration of 75 Years of Women's Enrollment at Columbia Law School," *Columbia Law Review* 102, no. 6 (October 2002): 1444.

Chapter 7

1. Richard C. Cortner, *The Apportionment Cases* (Knoxville: University of Tennessee Press, 1970), 1.

2. Constitution of Alabama of 1901, Article IX, Section 200.

3. Constitution of Alabama of 1901, Article IX, Section 201.

4. Constitution of Alabama of 1901, Article XVIII, Section 284.

5. Sheldon Hackney, *Populism to Progressivism in Alabama* (Princeton, NJ: Princeton University Press, 1969), 10.

6. See William Warren Rogers, *The One-Gallused Rebellion: Agrarianism in Alabama, 1865–1896* (Baton Rouge: Louisiana State University Press, 1970).

7. As Alabama historian Samuel L. Webb put it, "The constitutional convention of 1901, more than any other event in Alabama's history, pointed out the cooperation between the Black Belt and the elite industrial interests." See his *Two-Party Politics in the One-Party South: Alabama's Hill Country, 1874–1920* (Tuscaloosa: University of Alabama Press, 1997), 172.

8. J. Douglas Smith, *On Democracy's Doorstep* (New York: Hill and Wang, 2014), 116.

9. Hackney, *Populism to Progressivism in Alabama*, 211–12.

10. Smith, *On Democracy's Doorstep*, 116–17.

11. Voters from Mobile and Etowah Counties later joined the suit.

12. See, for example, Waid v. Pool, 255 Ala. 441 (1951).

13. Sims v. Frink, 208 F.Supp. 431 (1962).

14. Baker v. Carr, 369 U.S. 186 (1962).

15. Thomas Paine, *Collected Writings*, ed. Eric Foner (New York: Library of America, 1995), 470.

16. The great British statesman and prime minister (1766–68) William Pitt the Elder began his forty years of service in Parliament in 1735 as a representative from Old Sarum.

17. William Carpenter, *The People's Book; Comprising Their Chartered Rights and Practical Wrongs* (London: W. Strange, 1831), 406.

18. Quoted in Smith, *On Democracy's Doorstep*, 13.

19. Thomas Jefferson, *Writings*, ed. Merrill D. Peterson (New York: Library of America, 1984), 117.

20. Jefferson, *Writings*, 243.

21. Jefferson, *Writings*, 244.

22. Jefferson, *Writings*, 244.

23. Quoted in Gordon E. Baker, *The Reapportionment Revolution: Representation, Political Power, and the Supreme Court* (New York: Random House, 1967), 21.

24. Baker, *Reapportionment Revolution*, 25.

25. Baker, *Reapportionment Revolution*, 26–27.

26. Baker, *Reapportionment Revolution*, 32.

27. The argument against the congressional model is basically that equal representation of each county and/or city in one house of a state legislature is not the same as equal representation of each state in the US Senate. Counties and cities are fundamentally political subunits of the state. In our federal system, however, states represent sovereign governments that possess separate powers within their sphere completely independent of the national government.

28. For the figures used in this paragraph, see "Appendix: State Legislative Apportionment," in Smith, *On Democracy's Doorstep*, 287–88.

29. Colegrove v. Green, 328 U.S. 549 (1946).

30. *Colegrove*, 552.

31. *Colegrove*, 554.

32. *Colegrove*, 556.

33. Gomillion v. Lightfoot, 364 U.S. 339 (1960).

34. *Baker*, 186.

35. *Baker*, 197.

36. Robert G. Dixon Jr., *Democratic Representation: Reapportionment in Law and Politics* (New York: Oxford University Press, 1968), 139.

37. Gray v. Sanders, 372 U.S. 368 (1963).

38. *Sanders*, 381.

39. *Frink*, 248

40. "Text of Gov. Patterson's Speech to Legislature on Reapportionment," *Montgomery (AL) Advertiser*, June 13, 1962, 3B.

41. "Text of Gov. Patterson's Speech to Legislature on Reapportionment," *Montgomery (AL) Advertiser*.

42. "Text of Gov. Patterson's Speech to Legislature on Reapportionment," *Montgomery (AL) Advertiser.*

43. Bob Ingram, "4 Reapportionment Bills Clear House Unit," *Montgomery (AL) Advertiser,* June 14, 1962, 2A.

44. Bob Ingram, "Reapportioning Bills Win House Approval," *Montgomery (AL) Advertiser,* July 11, 1962, 1A.

45. Ingram, "Reapportioning Bills Win House Approval."

46. Ingram, "Reapportioning Bills Win House Approval."

47. *Frink,* 437.

48. *Frink,* 440.

49. *Frink,* 440.

50. Reynolds v. Sims, 377 U.S. 533, 551 (1964).

51. *Frink,* 441.

52. WMCA, Inc. v. Lomenzo, 377 U.S. 633 (1964); Maryland Committee for Fair Representation v. Tawes, 377 U.S. 656 (1964); Davis v. Mann, 377 U.S. 678 (1964); Roman v. Sincock, 377 U.S. 695 (1964); and Lucas v. Colorado General Assembly, 377 U.S. 713 (1964).

53. Robert B. McKay, *Reapportionment: The Law and Politics of Equal Representation* (New York: Twentieth Century Fund, 1965), 99.

54. Wesberry v. Sanders, 376 U.S. 1 (1964).

55. Bob Ingram, "Floor Fight Stage Set for Reapportionment," *Montgomery (AL) Advertiser,* June 19, 1964, 1A.

56. Ingram, "Floor Fight Stage Set for Reapportionment."

57. Virginia Commission on Constitutional Government, *One Man, One Vote: A Presentation of Comments and Documentary Material Relating to the Supreme Court's Reapportionment Decision of June 15, 1964* (Richmond: Virginia Commission on Constitutional Government, 1965), 6.

58. Virginia Commission on Constitutional Government, *One Man, One Vote,* 75.

59. Virginia Commission on Constitutional Government, *One Man, One Vote,* 75.

60. Holmes Alexander, "Supreme Court Is Target of Angry Congressmen," *Indianapolis (IN) Star,* July 8, 1964, 18.

61. Although rarely invoked by members of Congress, the last part of this section reads, "In all the other cases before mentioned, the Supreme Court shall have appellate jurisdiction, both as to law and fact, with such exceptions, and under such regulations *as the Congress shall make.*" See US Constitution, Article III, Section Two (emphasis added).

62. Alexander Keyssar, *The Right to Vote: The Contested History of Democracy in the United States* (New York: Basic Books, 2000), 287.

63. Abigail M. Thernstrom, *Whose Votes Count? Affirmative Action and Minority Voting Rights* (Cambridge, MA: Harvard University Press, 1987), 67.

64. *Reynolds,* 565.

65. Wright v. Rockefeller, 376 U.S. 52 (1964).

66. See Davis v. Bandemer, 478 U.S. 109 (1986); Vieth v. Jubelirer, 541 U.S. 267 (2004); Evenwel v. Abbott, 136 S.Ct. 1120 (2016); Gill v. Whitford, 138 S.Ct 1916 (2018); and Rucho v. Common Cause, 139 S.Ct. 2484 (2019).

67. *Reynolds*, 565.

68. Quoted in Alden Whitman, "Earl Warren, 83, Who Led High Court in Time of Vast Social Change, is Dead," *New York Times*, July 10, 1974, 24.

Chapter 8

1. Thomas Jefferson, *Writings*, ed. Merrill D. Peterson (New York: Library of America, 1984), 416.

2. The Civil Rights Cases, 109 U.S. 3 (1883).

3. US Constitution, Article I, Section 8, Clause 3.

4. Hugo L. Black and Elizabeth S. Black, *Mr. Justice and Mrs. Black: The Memoirs of Hugo L. Black and Elizabeth Black* (New York: Random House, 1986), 89.

5. Greg Garrison, "50 Years Ago, the U.S. Supreme Court Ruled against Ollie's Barbecue," AL.com, December 12, 2014, accessed June 20, 2017, https://www.al.com/living/2014/12/50_years_ago_the_supreme_court.html.

6. Michael Durham, "Ollie McClung's Big Decision," *Life*, October 9, 1964, 31.

7. James Madison, *Notes of Debates in the Federal Convention of 1787* (New York: W. W. Norton, 1987), 7–8.

8. Alexander Hamilton, John Jay, and James Madison, *The Federalist*, ed. Michael Lloyd Chadwick (Springfield, VA: Global Affairs Publishing, 1987), 31.

9. Madison, *Notes of Debates*, 7.

10. Max Farrand, *The Framing of the Constitution of the United States* (New Haven, CT: Yale University Press, 1913), 7.

11. US Constitution, Article I, Section 8.

12. Gibbons v. Ogden, 22 U.S. 1, 196 (1824).

13. *Gibbons*, 196.

14. *Gibbons*, 195.

15. *Gibbons*, 195.

16. U.S. v. E.C. Knight Company, 156 U.S. 1 (1895).

17. Hammer v. Dagenhart, 247 U.S. 251 (1918).

18. Schechter Poultry Corporation v. U.S., 295 U.S. 495 (1935).

19. Swift and Company v. U.S., 196 U.S. 375 (1905).

20. Southern Railway Co. v. U.S., 222 U.S. 20 (1911).

21. Houston East & West Texas Railway Company v. U.S. (The Shreveport Rate Case), 234 U.S. 342 (1914).

22. U.S. v. Darby Lumber Co., 312 U.S. 100 (1941).

23. Wickard v. Filburn, 317 U.S. 111 (1942).

24. US District Court judges typically sit alone, but until 1976 federal law required them to sit in panels of three any time a federal statute was challenged.

25. Heart of Atlanta Motel, Inc. v. U.S., 231 F.Supp. 393, 395 (1964).

26. McClung v. Katzenbach, 233 F.Supp. 815, 823 (1964).

27. *McClung*, 825.

28. *McClung*, 825.

29. Oral argument quotes taken from audio of *Katzenbach v. McClung*, 379 U.S. 294 (1964), accessed September 13, 2018, https://www.oyez.org/cases/1964/543.

30. Oral argument quotes taken from audio of *Katzenbach v. McClung*.

31. Oral argument quotes taken from audio of *Katzenbach v. McClung*.

32. Quoted in "Negroes Receive Service at Magic City Restaurant," *Anniston (AL) Star*, December 17, 1964, A15.

33. Quoted in "Negroes Receive Service at Magic City Restaurant," *Anniston (AL) Star*.

34. U.S. v. Lopez, 514 U.S. 549 (1995).

35. *Lopez*, 557.

36. U.S. v. Morrison, 529 U.S. 598 (2000).

37. National Federation of Independent Business v. Sebelius, 567 U.S. 519 (2012).

38. Quoted in Philip B. Kurland and Ralph Lerner, eds., *The Founders Constitution* (Chicago: University of Chicago Press, 1987; reprint, Indianapolis: Liberty Fund, 2000), 521 (page references are to reprint edition).

39. Quoted in Kurland and Lerner, *Founders Constitution*, 521.

Chapter 9

1. There are two other men with close connections to Alabama and the United States Supreme Court who deserve mention. In March 1837, Andrew Jackson nominated William Smith to serve as an associate justice. Smith was a former US senator from South Carolina who had moved to Alabama the previous year. The Senate quickly confirmed his nomination but, citing an inability to stay active in Jacksonian politics if he accepted the position, Smith declined to serve. He was seventy-five years of age at the time of his nomination and died just three years later. For the rest of his life, however, Smith proudly declared that he was the first person to decline a seat on the Supreme Court after confirmation.

William Burnham Woods was an Ohio lawyer and politician whose military assignments in the Union Army brought him to Mobile. After the war, he remained in Alabama where his brother-in-law, Willard Warner, became the state's first US senator of the Reconstruction era. President Ulysses S. Grant appointed Woods to the Fifth Circuit Court of Appeals in 1869. This position required extensive travel throughout the Deep South and caused him to move to Atlanta. On December 21, 1880, Rutherford B. Hayes nominated Woods to fill a vacancy on the Supreme Court, which the Senate confirmed a week later. Residing in Georgia at the time of his appointment, Woods became the first Supreme Court justice appointed from any of the former Confederate states since John Archibald Campbell in 1853.

2. For a complete biography of McKinley, see Steven P. Brown, *John McKinley and the Antebellum Supreme Court: Circuit Riding in the Old Southwest* (Tuscaloosa: University of Alabama Press, 2012).

3. Reports of the fertility of the Creek lands spurred land sales, speculation, and settlement. One oft-quoted contemporaneous account from a North Carolina man

warned that "The *Alabama Feaver* rages here with great violence and has *carried off* vast numbers of our Citizens. I am apprehensive, if it continues to spread as it has done, it will almost depopulate the country. . . . [T]his *feaver* is contagious . . . for as soon as one neighbor visits another who has just returned from the Alabama he immediately discovers the same symptoms . . . [as]the person who has seen the allureing Alabama." Quoted in Malcom J. Rohrbough, *The Land Office Business: The Settlement and Administration of American Public Lands, 1789–1837* (New York: Oxford University Press, 1968), 91 (italics in original).

4. Anne Newport Royall, *Letters from Alabama, 1817–1822* (Tuscaloosa: University of Alabama Press, 1969), 229.

5. Quoted in Richard W. Griffin, "Athens Academy and College: An Experiment in Women's Education in Alabama, 1822–1873," *Alabama Historical Quarterly* 20 (Spring 1958): 7. See also Thomas McAdory Owen and Marie Bankhead Owen, *History of Alabama and Dictionary of Alabama Biography*, vol. 1 (Chicago: S. J. Clarke Publishing, 1921), 67.

6. *Literary Cadet and Saturday Evening Bulletin* (Providence, RI), November 18, 1826, vol. 1, no. 31, p. 2.

7. Andrew Jackson to John Coffee, February 17, 1823, *The Papers of Andrew Jackson*, ed. Harold D. Moser, David R. Hoth, and George H. Hoemann, vol. 5 (Knoxville: University of Tennessee Press, 1996), 249.

8. The others were Lucius Q. C. Lamar (appointed to the Court in 1880), George Sutherland (1922), and James F. Byrnes (1941).

9. Holmes Alexander, *American Talleyrand: The Career and Contemporaries of Martin Van Buren, Eighth President* (New York: Russell and Russell, 1968), 335.

10. See Felix Frankfurter and James M. Landis, *The Business of the Supreme Court: A Study in the Federal Judicial System* (New York: Macmillan, 1927), 44–48.

11. Christopher L. Tomlins, ed., *The United States Supreme Court: The Pursuit of Justice (*New York: Houghton Mifflin, 2005), 534–35.

12. The "expenses in attending [the circuit] courts alone will not be less than $1500 a year while other judges will not have to expend five hundred." John McKinley to James K. Polk, May 5, 1837, *Correspondence of James K. Polk*, ed. Herbert Weaver, vol. 4 (Nashville: Vanderbilt University Press, 1969), 115.

13. US Statutes at Large, vol. 5, Twenty-Fourth Congress, Second Session, Cha.3 4 1837, 176–77.

14. Gerhard Casper and Richard A. Posner, *The Workload of the Supreme Court* (Chicago: American Bar Association, 1976), 15.

15. Incidentally, when Justice Peter Daniel of Virginia was assigned to Arkansas and Mississippi after Congress redrew the circuit boundaries, he too complained vociferously about the rigors of travel in that part of the country, although he covered only half of the territory over which McKinley had previously presided. For McKinley, Daniel, and every other traveler passing through the area, it was just simply a very difficult region to traverse.

16. Martin Siegel, *The Taney Court, 1836–1864* (Millwood, NY: Associated Faculty Press, 1987), 273.

17. Hampton L. Carson, *The History of the Supreme Court of the United States* (Philadelphia: P. W. Zeigler, 1902), 301.

18. Tom Campbell, *Four Score Forgotten Men* (Little Rock, AR: Pioneer Publishing, 1950), 167.

19. First, his was a critical vote on several Supreme Court cases dealing with the power of the federal government. McKinley adopted neither the enthusiastic nationalism nor the fervent states' rights philosophy of some of his fellow justices. Rather, he held steadily to the view that the national government was supreme within its sphere of authority, which meant that some regulatory powers were enjoyed by the national government alone. See, for example, the decision he joined in *Prigg v. Pennsylvania*, 41 U.S. 539 (1842) and his seriatim opinion in *The Passenger Cases* (*Smith v. Turner* and *Norris v. City of Boston*, 48 U.S. 283 [1849]). Second, McKinley's appreciation for national governmental power extended to his own judicial branch. For whatever other faults his critics ascribed to him (see the Court's *Bank of August v. Earle*, 38 U.S 519 [1839], which overturned one of his circuit opinions), he did not avoid the opportunity to exert the authority of a federal judge in Washington or at circuit. Whether rejecting executive authority, rendering congressional laws inapplicable at circuit, making the Court's decisions final on the matter of state boundary disputes, or in joining the Court's opinion to rule that state commercial laws did not bind federal judges, McKinley knew that the federal judiciary possessed power unto itself. His majority opinion in *Lessee of Pollard v. Hagan* stated that the federal government only held title to public lands as a trustee until a state was formally recognized and admitted into the union (44 U.S. 212 [1845]). Justice Catron, the lone dissenter in the case, noted that McKinley's opinion not only overturned several Supreme Court precedents but also nullified acts of Congress that awarded land grants to people in US territories. At the time, *Pollard* was a powerful expression of judicial review between *Marbury v. Madison*, 5 U.S. 137 (1803) and *Dred Scott v. Sandford*, 60 U.S. 393 (1857) that often escapes the notice of modern legal historians. See also the opinions he joined in *Rhode Island v. Massachusetts*, 37 U.S. 657 (1838); *Kendall v. United States ex rel. Stokes*, 37 U.S. 524 (1838); and *Swift v. Tyson*, 41 U.S. 1 (1842), as well as his circuit opinion in *U.S. v. Price and Company* (unreported decision, 9th Circuit) (1838).

20. 55 U.S. iii, at v (1852).

21. The Butchers' Benevolent Association of New Orleans v. Crescent City Live-Stock Landing and Slaughterhouse Company, 83 U.S. 36 (1873).

22. For a complete biography of Campbell, see Henry G. Connor, *John Archibald Campbell* (Boston: Houghton Mifflin, 1920), and Robert Saunders Jr., *John Archibald Campbell, Southern Moderate, 1811–1889* (Tuscaloosa: University of Alabama Press, 1997).

23. Quoted in Connor, *John Archibald Campbell*, 12.

24. Goodtitle v. Kibbe, 50 U.S. 471 (1850).

25. Fillmore nominated Louisiana attorney Edward A. Bradford in August 1852; US Senator George E. Badger in January 1853; and William C. Micou, a lawyer from New Orleans, in February 1853. The inauguration of the new president, Franklin Pierce, occurred on March 4, 1853.

26. Connor, *John Archibald Campbell*, 17.

27. Charles Warren, *The Supreme Court in United States History*, vol. 2 (Boston: Little, Brown, 1937), 246.

28. Carl Brent Swisher, *Roger B. Taney* (New York: Macmillan, 1935), 446–47.

29. See his dissent in *Marshall v. Baltimore and Ohio Railroad Company*, 57 U.S. 314 (1854).

30. See his dissents in *Piqua Branch of the State Bank of Ohio v. Knoop*, 57 U.S. 369 (1854) and *Dodge v. Woolsey*, 59 U.S. 331 (1856). Further evidencing his distrust of business, Campbell wrote for a unanimous Supreme Court in upholding shareholders' right to bring suit against corporations in federal court. See *Bacon v. Robertson*, 59 U.S. 480 (1856), and *Zabriskie v. Cleveland, Columbus, and Cincinnati Railroad*, 64 U.S. 381 (1860).

31. U.S. v. Libellants of Schooner Amistad, 40 U.S. 518 (1841); Prigg v. Pennsylvania, 41 U.S. 539 (1842); Jones v. Van Zandt, 46 U.S. 215 (1847).

32. Dred Scott v. Sandford, 60 U.S. 393 (1857).

33. The Sandford party in *Dred Scott v. Sandford* was John Sanford, Mrs. Emerson's brother who later came to own Scott. Due to a clerical error at the Court, the case has forever memorialized Sanford as Sandford—perhaps the most famous misspelling in constitutional history.

34. *New Hampshire Patriot and State Gazette* (Concord), January 2, 1861, 1.

35. Quoted in Saunders, *John Archibald Campbell*, 152.

36. The law did not give the Crescent City Company the sole right to slaughter livestock, but because all other butchers had to pay the costs of transporting their cattle to the site as well as pay a fee for each animal they slaughtered there, it ended up conducting most of the slaughtering anyway.

37. US Constitution, Amendment Fourteen, Section One.

38. Plaintiffs' Brief Upon the Re-Argument, *Butchers' Benevolent Association v. Crescent City Live Stock Landing and Slaughterhouse Company*, 16 Wall. 36 (1873), p. 31, in Philip B. Kurland and Gerhard Casper, ed., *Landmark Briefs and Arguments of the Supreme Court of the United States: Constitutional Law* (Arlington, VA: University Publications of America, 1975), 2: 670.

39. Some legal scholars have argued that Campbell's motive was not so much about extending the Fourteenth Amendment's protections to white persons as it was about maneuvering the Court into a position where it could strike a blow against Reconstruction by rejecting the slaughterhouse legislation, which the Reconstruction government in Louisiana had authorized. See Warren, *Supreme Court in United States History*, 536–44, and Melvin I. Urofsky, *Supreme Decisions* (Boulder, CO: Westview Press, 2012), 121–22.

40. The Court finally repudiated the liberty of contract doctrine in *West Coast Hotel v. Parrish*, 300 U.S. 379 (1937).

41. Griswold v. Connecticut, 381 U.S. 479 (1965).

42. Washington v. Glucksburg, 521 U.S. 702, 720 (1997).

43. *Washington*, 720.

44. Quoted in Saunders, *John Archibald Campbell*, 219.

45. Quoted in Connor, *John Archibald Campbell*, 280.

46. Black has been the subject of countless studies. The following are some of the more notable book-length treatments of his life and influence: Steve Suitts, *Hugo Black of Alabama: How His Roots and Early Career Shaped the Great Champion of the Constitution* (Montgomery, AL: New South Books, 2005); Howard Ball, *Hugo L. Black: Cold Steel Warrior* (New York: Oxford University Press, 1996); Roger K. Newman, *Hugo Black* (New York: Pantheon Books, 1994); Tinsley Yarbrough, *Mr. Justice Black and His Critics* (Durham, NC: Duke University Press, 1988); Hugo L. Black and Elizabeth Black, *Mr. Justice and Mrs. Black: The Memoirs of Hugo L. Black and Elizabeth Black* (New York: Random House, 1986); Gerald T. Dunne, *Hugo Black and the Judicial Revolution* (New York: Simon Schuster, 1977); and Virginia Van der Veer Hamilton, *Hugo Black: The Alabama Years* (Baton Rouge: Louisiana State University Press, 1972).

47. For several such surveys, see Henry J. Abraham, "Hugo L. Black as a Great Justice," in *Great Justices of the Supreme Court*, ed. William D. Pederson and Norman W. Provizer (New York: Peter Lang, 1994), 258, footnote 2.

48. Virginia Van Der Veer Hamilton, *Hugo Black: The Alabama Years* (Baton Rouge: Louisiana State University Press, 1972), 18.

49. Hugo Black Jr., *My Father: A Remembrance* (New York, Random House, 1975), 16.

50. West Coast Hotel v. Parrish, 300 U.S. 379 (1937).

51. This was technically accurate, but the Klan provided critically important support for their former member in his 1926 Senate campaign. With its help, Black defeated several other prominent Alabama politicians to win the Democratic primary, which was tantamount to winning the general election in Alabama because of the utter lack of Republican support there. For more information about that election and Black's awareness of and gratitude for the KKK's role in it, see Hamilton, *Hugo Black*, 136–39.

52. Quoted in William E. Leuchtenburg, "A Klansman Joins the Court: The Appointment of Hugo L. Black," *University of Chicago Law Review* 41, no. 1 (Fall 1973): 20.

53. Black's former membership in the KKK blindsided both his supporters in the Senate and the president, something for which, according to the *Huntsville Times*, "there must ever be a cloud over him as long as he sits on the U.S. Supreme Bench, and for which he must ever be ashamed." "Wherein Black failed," *Huntsvillle (AL) Times*, October 3, 1937, 4.

54. *Montgomery Advertiser*, August 15, 1937, 4.

55. Brown v. Board of Education, 347 U.S. 483 (1954).

56. Hugo L. Black, *A Constitutional Faith* (New York: Alfred A. Knopf, 1969), 45.

57. See his opinions in Roth v. United States, 354 U.S. 476 (1957); Dennis v. United States, 341 U.S. 494 (1951); Brandenburg v. Ohio, 395 U.S. 444 (1969); New York Times v. Sullivan, 376 U.S. 254 (1964); and Barenblatt v. United States, 360 U.S. 109 (1959). Black was careful to distinguish constitutional protected speech from speech plus action or conduct that, in his view, was not protected. "The First and

Fourteenth Amendments take away from government, state and federal, all power to restrict freedom of speech, press and peaceful assembly *where people have a right to be for such purposes*. That much is clear and to me indisputable. But recently many loose words have been spoken and written about an alleged First Amendment right to picket, demonstrate, or march, usually accompanied by singing, shouting or loud praying, along the public streets, in or around government-owned buildings, or in and around other people's property. . . . I do not believe that the First Amendment grants a constitutional right to engage in the conduct of picketing or demonstrating, whether on publicly-owned streets or on privately-owned property." See Black, *Constitutional Faith*, 54 (emphasis in original).

58. Black, *Constitutional Faith*, 66.

59. Barron v. Mayor and City Council of Baltimore, 32 U.S. 243, 250 (1833).

60. Palko v. Connecticut, 302 U.S. 319, 324 (1937).

61. *Palko*, 325.

62. Adamson v. California, 332 U.S. 46 (1947).

63. Quoted in John P. Frank, *Inside Justice Hugo L. Black: The Letters* (Austin: Jamail Center for Legal Research at the University of Texas, 2000), 6.

64. California v. Adamson, 27 Cal.2d 478, 495 (1946).

65. Adamson v. California, 332 U.S. 46, 54 (1947).

66. *Adamson*, 69.

67. *Adamson*, 71–72.

68. *Adamson*, 86.

69. *Adamson*, 89.

70. In Re Oliver, 333 U.S. 257 (1948).

71. Wolf v. Colorado, 338 U.S. 25 (1949).

72. Timbs v. Indiana, 139 S.Ct. 682 (2019). The Court has still not embraced total incorporation. As of this writing, the following still only apply against the national government: the Third Amendment, the Fifth Amendment's right to indictment by grand jury, and the Seventh Amendment's right to jury trial in civil cases.

73. "Justice Black, Champion of Civil Liberties for 34 Years on Court, Dies at 85," *New York Times*, September 26, 1971, 76.

74. "Justice Black, Champion of Civil Liberties for 34 Years on Court, Dies at 85," *New York Times*.

75. Black, *Constitutional Faith*, 66.

76. Abraham, "Hugo L. Black as a Great Justice," 257.

BIBLIOGRAPHY

CASES

Adamson v. California, 332 U.S. 46 (1947).

Adler v. Board of Education, 342 U.S. 485 (1952).

Argersinger v. Hamlin, 407 U.S. 25 (1972).

Bacon v. Robertson, 59 U.S. 480 (1856).

Baker v. Carr, 369 U.S. 186 (1962).

Bank of August v. Earle, 38 U.S 519 (1839).

Barenblatt v. U.S., 360 U.S. 109 (1959).

Barron v. Mayor and City Council of Baltimore, 32 U.S. 243 (1833).

Beauharnais v. Illinois, 343 U.S. 250 (1952).

Betts v. Brady, 316 U.S. 455 (1942).

Bradwell v. Illinois, 83 U.S. 130 (1873).

Brandenburg v. Ohio, 395 U.S. 444 (1969).

Breedlove v. Suttles, 302 U.S. 277 (1937).

Brown v. Board of Education, 347 U.S. 483 (1954).

Brown v. Gilmore, 258 F.3d 265 (2001).

Butchers' Benevolent Association of New Orleans v. The Crescent City Livestock Landing and Slaughterhouse Company (the Slaughterhouse Cases), 83 U.S. 36 (1873).

California v. Adamson, 165 P.2d 3 (1946).

Chicago, Burlington & Quincy Railroad Company Co. v. Chicago, 166 U.S. 226 (1897).

Chaplinsky v. New Hampshire, 315 U.S. 568 (1942).

Civil Rights Cases, 109 U.S. 3 (1883).

Colegrove v. Green, 328 U.S. 549 (1946).

Craig v. Boren, 429 U.S. 190 (1976).

Curtis Publishing Company v. Butts, 388 U.S. 130 (1967).

Davis v. Bandemer, 478 U.S. 109 (1986).

Davis v. Mann, 377 U.S. 678 (1964).

DeJonge v. Oregon, 299 U.S. 353 (1937).

Dennis v. United States, 341 U.S. 494 (1951).

Dodge v. Woolsey, 59 U.S. 331 (1856).

Dred Scott v. Sandford, 60 U.S. 393 (1857)

Engel v. Vitale, 370 U.S. 421 (1962).

Evenwel v. Abbott, 136 S.Ct. 1120 (2016).
Everson v. Board of Education of the Township of Ewing, 330 U.S. 1 (1947).
Ex parte NAACP, 265 Ala. 349 (1956).
Ex parte NAACP, 268 Ala. 531(1959).
Ex parte NAACP, 271 Ala. 33 (1960).
Ex parte Vallandigham, 68 U.S. 243 (1864).
Fiske v. Kansas, 274 U.S. 380 (1927).
Frontiero v. Laird, 341 F.Supp. 201 (1972).
Frontiero v. Richardson, 411 U.S. 677 (1973).
Garner v. Los Angeles Board, 341 U.S. 716 (1951).
Gerende v. Election Board, 341 U.S. 56 (1951).
Gertz v. Welch, 418 U.S. 323 (1974).
Gibbons v. Ogden, 22 U.S. 1 (1824).
Gideon v. Wainwright, 372 U.S. 335 (1963).
Gill v. Whitford, 138 S.Ct. 1916 (2018).
Gitlow v. New York, 268 U.S. 652 (1925).
Gomillion v. Lightfoot, 167 F.Supp. 405 (1958).
Gomillion v. Lightfoot, 270 F.2d 594 (1959).
Gomillion v. Lightfoot, 364 U.S. 339 (1960).
Goodtitle v. Kibbe, 50 U.S. 471 (1850).
Gray v. Sanders, 372 U.S. 368 (1963).
Griswold v. Connecticut, 381 U.S. 479 (1965).
Hammer v. Dagenhart, 247 U.S. 251 (1918).
Harper v. Virginia Board of Elections, 383 U.S. 663 (1966).
Heart of Atlanta Motel, Inc. v. U.S., 231 F.Supp. 393 (1964).
Houston East & West Texas Railway Company v. U.S. (the Shreveport Rate Case), 234 U.S. 342 (1914).
In Re Oliver, 333 U.S. 257 (1948).
Jaffree v. Board of Commissioners of Mobile County, 459 U.S. 1314 (1983).
Jaffree v. Board of School Commissioners of Mobile County, 554 F.Supp. 1104 (1983).
Jaffree v. James, 544 F.Supp. 727 (1982).
Jaffree v. James, 554 F.Supp. 1130 (1983).
Jaffree v. Wallace, 705 F.2d 1526 (1983).
Jones v. Van Zandt, 46 U.S. 215 (1847).
Katzenbach v. McClung, 379 U.S. 294 (1964).
Kendall v. United States ex rel. Stokes, 37 U.S. 524 (1838).
Lassiter v. Northampton County Board of Elections, 360 U.S. 45 (1959).
Lee v. Weisman, 505 U.S. 577 (1992).
Lemon v. Kurtzman, 403 U.S. 602 (1971).
Lessee of Pollard v. Hagan, 44 U.S. 212 (1845).
Louisiana v. U.S.., 380 U.S. 145 (1965).
Lucas v. Colorado General Assembly, 377 U.S. 713 (1964).
Lynch v. Donnelly, 465 U.S. 668 (1984).
Marbury v. Madison, 5 U.S. 137 (1803).

Marshall v. Baltimore and Ohio Railroad Company, 57 U.S. 314 (1854).
Maryland Committee for Fair Representation v. Tawes, 377 U.S. 656 (1964).
McClung v. Katzenbach, 233 F.Supp. 815 (1964).
McDonald v. City of Chicago, 561 U.S. 742 (2010).
Minor v. Happersett, 88 U.S. 162 (1874).
NAACP v. Alabama, 357 U.S. 449 (1958).
NAACP v. Alabama, 360 U.S. 240 (1959).
NAACP v. Flowers, 377 U.S. 288 (1964).
NAACP v. Gaillion, 290 F.2d 337 (1961).
National Federation of Independent Business v. Sebelius, 567 U.S. 519 (2012).
Near v. Minnesota ex rel. Olson, 283 U.S. 697 (1931).
New York ex rel. Bryant v. Zimmerman, 278 U.S. 63 (1928).
New York Times v. Sullivan, 273 Ala. 656 (1962).
New York Times v. Sullivan, 376 U.S. 254 (1964).
Norris v. Alabama, 294 U.S. 587 (1935).
Palko v. Connecticut, 302 U.S. 319 (1937).
Patterson v. Alabama, 294 U.S. 600 (1935).
Permoli v. New Orleans, 44 U.S. 589 (1845).
Piqua Branch of the State Bank of Ohio v. Knoop, 57 U.S. 369 (1854).
Powell v. Alabama, 287 U.S. 45 (1932).
Powell v. State, 224 Ala. 540 (1932).
Prigg v. Pennsylvania, 41 U.S. 539 (1842).
Reed v. Reed, 404 U.S. 71 (1971).
Reynolds v. Sims, 377 U.S. 533 (1964).
Reynolds v. United States, 98 U.S. 145 (1879).
Rhode Island v. Massachusetts, 37 U.S. 657 (1838).
Roberts v. U.S. Jaycees, 468 U.S. 609 (1984).
Roman v. Sincock, 377 U.S. 695 (1964).
Roth v. United States, 354 U.S. 476 (1957).
Rucho v. Common Cause, 139 S.Ct. 2484 (2019).
Schechter Poultry Corporation v. U.S., 295 U.S. 495 (1935).
Schnell v. Davis, 336 U.S. 933 (1949).
School District of Abington Township v. Schempp, 374 U.S. 203 (1963).
Sims v. Frink, 208 F.Supp. 431 (1962).
Smith v. Turner and *Norris v. City of Boston (The Passenger Cases)*, 48 U.S. 283 (1849).
Southern Railway Co. v. U.S., 222 U.S. 20 (1911).
Stromberg v. California, 283 U.S. 359 (1931).
Sweezy v. New Hampshire, 354 U.S. 234 (1957).
Swift v. Tyson, 41 U.S. 1 (1842).
Swift and Company v. U.S., 196 U.S. 375 (1905).
Terrett v. Taylor, 13 U.S. 43 (1815).
Timbs v. Indiana, 139 S.Ct. 682 (2019).
Town of Pawlet v. Clark, 13 U.S. 292 (1815).
Twining v. New Jersey, 211 U.S. 78 (1908).

U.S. v. Alabama, 192 F.Supp. 677 (1961).
U.S. v. Alabama, 252 F.Supp. 95 (1966).
U.S. v. Carolene Products, 304 U.S. 144 (1938).
U.S. v. Darby Lumber Co., 312 U.S. 100 (1941).
U.S. v. E.C. Knight Company, 156 U.S. 1 (1895).
U.S. v. Hudson and Goodwin, 11 U.S. 32 (1812).
U.S. v. Libellants of Schooner Amistad, 40 U.S. 518 (1841).
U.S. v. Lopez, 514 U.S. 549 (1995).
U.S. v. Morrison, 529 U.S. 598 (2000).
U.S. v. Price (unreported decision, 9th Circuit) (1838).
U.S. v. Virginia, 518 U.S. 515 (1996).
Vieth v. Jubelirer, 541 U.S. 267 (2004).
Waid v. Pool, 255 Ala. 441 (1951).
Wallace v. Jaffree, 472 U.S. 38 (1985).
Washington v. Glucksburg, 521 U.S. 702(1997).
Watkins v. U.S., 354 U.S. 178 (1957).
Waugh v. Board of Trustees of the University of Mississippi, 237 U.S. 589 (1915).
Weems v. State, 224 Ala 524 (1932).
Wesberry v. Sanders, 376 U.S. 1 (1964).
West Coast Hotel v. Parrish, 300 U.S. 379 (1937).
White v. Nicholls, 44 U.S. 266 (1845).
Wickard v. Filburn, 317 U.S. 111 (1942).
WMCA, Inc. v. Lomenzo, 377 U.S. 633 (1964).
Wolf v. Colorado, 338 U.S. 25 (1949).
Wright v. Rockefeller, 376 U.S. 52 (1964).
Zabriskie v. Cleveland, Columbus, and Cincinnati Railroad, 64 U.S. 381 (1860).

NEWSPAPERS

Anniston (AL) Star
Atlanta Constitution
Bennington (VT) Banner
Chicago Daily Tribune
Christian Science Monitor (Boston, MA)
Cullman (AL) Democrat
Escanaba (MI) Daily Press
Hartford (CT) Courant
Indianapolis Star
Los Angeles Times
Literary Cadet and Saturday Evening Bulletin (Providence, RI)
Montgomery (AL) Advertiser
New Hampshire Patriot and State Gazette (Concord)
New York Age
New York Times
San Bernardino (CA) County Sun

Tampa Bay (Saint Petersburg, FL) Times
Troy (NY) Record
Tuscaloosa (AL) News
Washington (DC) Post
Weekly Town Talk (Alexandria, LA)

PRIMARY AND SECONDARY SOURCES

Abraham, Henry J. "Hugo L. Black as a Great Justice." In *Great Justices of the Supreme Court,* edited by William D. Pederson and Norman W. Provizer. New York: Peter Lang, 1994.

Alexander, Holmes. *American Talleyrand: The Career and Contemporaries of Martin Van Buren, Eighth President.* New York: Russell and Russell, 1968.

Alien and Sedition Acts, 1798, accessed August 30, 2019, https://www.ourdocuments.gov/doc.php?flash=false&doc=16.

Baker, Gordon E. *The Reapportionment Revolution: Representation, Political Power, and the Supreme Court.* New York: Random House, 1967.

"Army Husbands." *Time.* May 28, 1973, p. 12. Accessed August 30, 2019. http://content.time.com/time/magazine/article/0,9171,910607,00.html.

Ball, Howard. *Hugo L. Black: Cold Steel Warrior.* New York: Oxford University Press, 1996.

Barton, David. *Original Intent: The Courts, the Constitution, and Religion.* Aledo, TX: Wallbuilder Press, 1996.

Black, Hugo L. *A Constitutional Faith.* New York: Alfred A. Knopf, 1969.

Black, Hugo L., and Elizabeth S. Black. *Mr. Justice and Mrs. Black: The Memoirs of Hugo L. Black and Elizabeth Black.* New York: Random House, 1986.

Black, Hugo, Jr. *My Father: A Remembrance.* New York: Random House, 1975.

Brown, Steven P. *John McKinley and the Antebellum Supreme Court: Circuit Riding in the Old Southwest.* Tuscaloosa: University of Alabama Press, 2012.

——. *Trumping Religion: The New Christian Right, the Free Speech Clause, and the Courts.* Tuscaloosa: University of Alabama Press, 2002.

Bureau of Democracy, Human Rights, and Labor. "Country Reports on Human Rights Practices." 2015. Accessed March 15, 2018. https://www.state.gov/j/drl/rls/hrrpt/humanrightsreport/index.htm#wrapper.

Campbell, Tom. *Four Score Forgotten Men.* Little Rock, AR: Pioneer Publishing, 1950.

Carpenter, William. *The People's Book; Comprising Their Chartered Rights and Practical Wrongs.* London: W. Strange, 1831.

Carson, Hampton L. *The History of the Supreme Court of the United States.* Philadelphia: P. W. Zeigler, 1902.

Carter, Dan T. *Scottsboro: A Tragedy of the American South.* New York: Oxford University Press, 1971.

Carter-Ruck, Peter F. *Libel and Slander.* London: Faber and Faber, 1972.

Casper, Gerhard, and Richard A. Posner. *The Workload of the Supreme Court.* Chicago: American Bar Association, 1976.

"Civil Liberties." Gallup. Accessed April 5, 2018. http://news.gallup.com/poll/5263/civil-liberties.aspx.

Connor, Henry G. *John Archibald Campbell*. Boston: Houghton Mifflin, 1920.

Cortner, Richard C. *The Apportionment Cases*. Knoxville: University of Tennessee Press, 1970.

Crenshaw, Files, Jr., and Kenneth A. Miller. *Scottsboro: The Firebrand of Communism*. Montgomery, AL: Brown Printing, 1936.

Dickson, Del, ed. *The Supreme Court in Conference (1940–1985)*. New York, Oxford University Press, 2001.

Dixon, Robert G., Jr. *Democratic Representation: Reapportionment in Law and Politics*. New York: Oxford University Press, 1968.

Dunne, Gerald T. *Hugo Black and the Judicial Revolution*. New York: Simon Schuster, 1977.

Durham, Michael. "Ollie McClung's Big Decision." *Life*, October 9, 1964, 31.

Ellwood, William A. "An Interview with Charles G. Gomillion." *Callaloo* 40 (Summer 1989): 576–99.

Farrand, Max. *The Framing of the Constitution of the United States*. New Haven, CT: Yale University Press, 1913.

Fellman, David. *The Constitutional Right of Association*. Chicago: University of Chicago Press, 1963.

Frank, John P. *Inside Justice Hugo L. Black: The Letters*. Austin: Jamail Center for Legal Research at the University of Texas, 2000.

Frankfurter, Felix, and James M. Landis. *The Business of the Supreme Court: A Study in the Federal Judicial System*. New York: Macmillan, 1927.

Fu, Angela N., and Lucy Wang. "Faculty Vote to Include Sanctions in Handbook." March 7, 2018. Accessed April 5, 2018, http://www.thecrimson.com/article/2018/3/7/faculty-sanctions-handbook/.

Garrison, Greg. "50 Years Ago, the U.S. Supreme Court Ruled Against Ollie's Barbecue." AL.com. December 12, 2014. Accessed June 20, 2017, https://www.al.com/living/2014/12/50_years_ago_the_supreme_court.html.

Ginsburg, Ruth Bader. "Remarks for the Celebration of 75 Years of Women's Enrollment at Columbia Law School." *Columbia Law Review* 102 (October 2002): 1441–48.

Goodman, James. *Stories of Scottsboro*. New York: Vintage Books, 1995.

Gray, Fred D. *Bus Ride to Justice: Changing the System by the System; The Life and Works of Fred D. Gray, Preacher, Attorney, Politician*. Montgomery, AL: New South Books, 2013.

Griffin, Richard W. "Athens Academy and College: An Experiment in Women's Education in Alabama, 1822–1873." *Alabama Historical Quarterly* 20 (Spring 1958): 7–26.

Griffith, Rod. "A Self-Proclaimed Agnostic Who was Once a Street Preacher . . ." UPI. November 16, 1982. Accessed May 22, 2017, https://www.upi.com/Archives/1982/11/16/A-self-proclaimed-agnostic-who-was-once-a-street-preacher/7398406270800/.

Guzman, Jessie Parkhurst. *Crusade for Civic Democracy: The Story of the Tuskegee Civic Association, 1941–1970*. New York: Vantage Press, 1984.

Hackney, Sheldon. *Populism to Progressivism in Alabama*. Princeton, NJ: Princeton University Press, 1969.

Hall, Kermit L. "'Lies, Lies, Lies': The Origins of *New York Times v. Sullivan*." *Communication Law and Policy* 9 (2004): 391–421.

Hall, Kermit L., and Melvin I. Urofsky. *"New York Times v. Sullivan": Civil Rights, Libel Law, and the Free Press*. Lawrence: University Press of Kansas, 2011.

Hamilton, Alexander, John Jay, and James Madison. *The Federalist*. Edited by Michael Lloyd Chadwick. Springfield, VA: Global Affairs Publishing, 1987.

Hamilton, Virginia Van der Veer. *Hugo Black: The Alabama Years*. Baton Rouge: Louisiana State University Press, 1972.

Hays, Arthur Garfield. *Trial by Prejudice*. New York: Covici-Friede, 1933. Reprint; New York: Da Capo Press, 1970.

Heflin, Howell. "Tribute to Charles Gomillion." Congressional Record 141:191, S17927. December 4, 1995. Accessed August 30, 2019, https://www.congress.gov/congressional-record/1995/12/04/senate-section/article/S17927-3.

Hopkins, W. Wat. *Actual Malice: Twenty-Five Years after "Times v. Sullivan."* New York: Praeger, 1989.

Howard, Gene. *Patterson for Alabama: The Life and Career of John Patterson*. Tuscaloosa: University of Alabama Press, 2008.

Howard, Walter T., ed. *Black Communists Speak on Scottsboro: A Documentary History*. Philadelphia: Temple University Press, 2007.

Hutchins, Robert M. "The Future of the Wall." In *The Wall between Church and State*, edited by Dallin H. Oaks, 17–25. Chicago: University of Chicago Press, 1963.

Hylton, J. Gordon. "Virginia and the Ratification of the Bill of Rights, 1789–1791." *University of Richmond Law Review* 25 (1991): 433–39.

Irons, Peter. *The Courage of Their Convictions*. New York: Free Press, 1988.

Jackson, Andrew. *The Papers of Andrew Jackson*. Edited by Harold D. Moser, David R. Hoth, and George H. Hoemann. Vol. 5. Knoxville: University of Tennessee Press, 1996.

Jefferson, Thomas. *Writings*. Edited by Merrill D. Peterson. New York: Library of America, 1984.

Journal of the Proceedings of the Constitutional Convention of the State of Alabama. Montgomery, AL: Brown Printing, 1901.

Journal of the Senate of the State of Alabama, Regular Session of 1982. Vol. 1. Montgomery, AL: Brown Printing, 1981.

Journal of the Senate of the State of Alabama, Second Extraordinary Session of 1982. Montgomery, AL: Brown Printing, 1982.

Kay, Herma Hill, and Martha S. West. *Sex-Based Discrimination*. Saint Paul, MN: West Publishing, 2002.

Keyssar, Alexander. *The Right to Vote: The Contested History of Democracy in the United States*. New York: Basic Books, 2000.

Kinshasa, Kwando M. *The Man from Scottsboro: Clarence Norris and the Infamous 1931 Alabama Rape Trial, in His Own Words*. Jefferson, NC: McFarland, 1997.

———, ed. *The Scottsboro Boys in Their Own Words: Selected Letters, 1931–1950.* Jefferson, NC: McFarland, 2014.

Koffler, Judith S., and Bennett L. Gershman. "New Seditious Libel." *Cornell Law Review* 69 (April 1984): 816–82.

Kurland, Philip B., and Gerhard Casper. *Landmark Briefs and Arguments of the Supreme Court of the United States.* Arlington, VA: University Publications of America, 1975.

Kurland, Philip B., and Ralph Lerner, eds. *The Founders' Constitution.* Chicago: University of Chicago Press, 1987. Reprint; Indianapolis: Liberty Fund, 2000.

Leuchtenburg, William E. "A Klansman Joins the Court: The Appointment of Hugo L. Black." *University of Chicago Law Review* 41, no. 1 (Fall 1973): 1–31.

Linder, Douglas O. "The Trials of the Scottsboro Boys: An Account." Famous Trials. Accessed August 31, 2017, http://famous-trials.com/scottsboroboys/1531-home.

Madison, James. *Notes of Debates in the Federal Convention of 1787.* New York: W. W. Norton, 1987.

———. *The Writings of James Madison.* Edited by Gaillard Hunt. 9 vols. New York: G. P. Putnam's Sons, 1910.

Mayeri, Serena. "The Story of Frontiero v. Richardson." In *Women and the Law Stories,* edited by Elizabeth M. Schneider and Stephanie M. Wildman. New York: Foundation Press, 2011.

McKay, Robert B. *Reapportionment: The Law and Politics of Equal Representation.* New York: Twentieth Century Fund, 1965.

Merriam, Jesse. "Courts Not Silent on Moments of Silence." Pew Research Center: Religion and Public Life. April 24, 2008. Accessed on June 30, 2017, http://www.pewforum.org/2008/04/24/courts-not-silent-on-moments-of-silence/.

Newman, Roger K. *Hugo Black.* New York: Pantheon Books, 1994.

Norris, Clarence, and Sybil D. Washington. *The Last of the Scottsboro Boys.* New York: Putnam, 1979.

Norrell, Robert J. *Reaping the Whirlwind: The Civil Rights Movement in Tuskegee.* New York: Alfred A. Knopf, 1985.

Omang, Joanne. "Alabama Governor Tries for an End Run on Son's School Prayer." *Washington Post,* September 16, 1982. Accessed May 22, 2017, https://www.washingtonpost.com/archive/politics/1982/09/16/alabama-governor-tries-for-an-end-run-on-sons-school-prayer/5cb40e8a-71f5-4986-90c4-60cdc69de987/.

Owen, Thomas McAdory, and Marie Bankhead Owen. *History of Alabama and Dictionary of Alabama Biography.* Vol. 1. Chicago: S. J. Clarke, 1921.

Paine, Thomas. *Collected Writings.* Edited by Eric Foner. New York: Library of America, 1995.

Polk, James K. *Correspondence of James K. Polk.* Edited by Herbert Weaver. Vol. 4. Nashville, TN: Vanderbilt University Press, 1969.

Rieff, Burt. "Conflicting Rights and Religious Liberty: The School-Prayer Controversy in Alabama, 1962–1985." *Alabama Review* 54 (July 2001): 163–207.

Rogers, William Warren. *The One-Gallused Rebellion: Agrarianism in Alabama, 1865–1896.* Baton Rouge: Louisiana State University Press, 1970.

Rohrbough, Malcom J. *The Land Office Business: The Settlement and Administration of American Public Lands, 1789–1837*. New York: Oxford University Press, 1968.

Ross, Susan D., and R. Kenton Bird. "The Ad That Changed Libel Law: Judicial Realism and Social Activism in *New York Times v. Sullivan*." *Communication Law and Policy* 9 (Autumn 2004): 489–523.

Royall, Anne Newport. *Letters from Alabama, 1817–1822*. Tuscaloosa: University of Alabama Press, 1969.

Saunders, Robert, Jr. *John Archibald Campbell, Southern Moderate, 1811–1889*. Tuscaloosa: University of Alabama Press, 1997.

Siegel, Martin. *The Taney Court, 1836–1864*. Millwood, NY: Associated Faculty Press, 1987.

Smith, J. Douglas. *On Democracy's Doorstep*. New York: Hill and Wang, 2014.

Stone, Geoffrey R. "Abraham Lincoln's First Amendment." *New York University Law Review* 78 (April 2003): 1–29.

Suitts, Steve. *Hugo Black of Alabama: How His Roots and Early Career Shaped the Great Champion of the Constitution*. Montgomery, AL: New South Books, 2005.

Swisher, Carl Brent. *Roger B. Taney*. New York: Macmillan, 1935.

Taper, Bernard. *"Gomillion versus Lightfoot": The Tuskegee Gerrymander Case*. New York: McGraw-Hill, 1962.

Thernstrom, Abigail M. *Whose Votes Count? Affirmative Action and Minority Voting Rights*. Cambridge, MA: Harvard University Press, 1987.

Tocqueville, Alexis de. *Democracy in America*. Trans. George Lawrence. New York: Harper and Row, 1988.

Tomlins, Christopher L., ed. *The United States Supreme Court: The Pursuit of Justice*. New York: Houghton Mifflin, 2005.

Trest, Warren. *Nobody but the People: The Life and Times of Alabama's Youngest Governor*. Montgomery, AL: New South Books, 2008.

Urofsky, Melvin I. *Supreme Decisions*. Boulder, CO: Westview Press, 2012.

Virginia Commission on Constitutional Government. *One Man, One Vote: A Presentation of Comments and Documentary Material Relating to the Supreme Court's Reapportionment Decision of June 15, 1964*. Richmond: Virginia Commission on Constitutional Government, 1965.

Warren, Charles. *The Supreme Court in United States History*. Vol. 2. Boston: Little, Brown, 1937.

Webb, Samuel L. *Two-Party Politics in the One-Party South: Alabama's Hill Country, 1874–1920*. Tuscaloosa: University of Alabama Press, 1997.

Weiner, Mark S. *Black Trials: Citizenship from the Beginnings of Slavery to the End of Caste*. New York: Alfred A. Knopf, 2004.

Yarbrough, Tinsley. *Mr. Justice Black and His Critics*. Durham, NC: Duke University Press, 1988.

INDEX

Page numbers in italics indicate figures.